THE TAINOS

IRVING ROUSE

THE TAINOS

RISE & DECLINE OF THE

PEOPLE WHO GREETED

COLUMBUS

YALE UNIVERSITY PRESS   NEW HAVEN & LONDON

Published with assistance from the foundation established in memory of James Wesley Cooper of the Class of 1865, Yale College.

Figure 6 is reprinted from *The Physical Anthropology of the American Indian*, ed. William S. Laughlin, by permission of the Wenner-Gren Foundation for Anthropological Research, Inc., New York. Figure 7 is from *Back of History*, by William Howells. Copyright 1954, 1963 by William Howells. Used by permission of Doubleday, a division of Bantam Doubleday Dell Publishing Group, Inc. Figures 20d, f; 23b, e–g; and 24a, c, e are copyright 1964 by the American Association for the Advancement of Science (AAAS). Figure 21 is drawn from *Catálogo Arqueología de Vieques*, by Luis A. Chanlatte Baik. Used by permission of the Centro de Investigaciones Arqueológicas, University of Puerto Rico.

Designed by Jill Breitbarth and set in Sabon type by Tseng Information Systems, Inc., Durham, North Carolina. Printed in the United States of America

Library of Congress Cataloging-in-Publication Data
Rouse, Irving, 1913–
The Tainos : rise and decline of the people who greeted Columbus / Irving Rouse.
p. cm.
Includes bibliographical references and index.
ISBN 978-0-300-05181-6 (cloth)
 978-0-300-05696-9 (pbk.)
1. Taino Indians. 2. Indians of the West Indies—Antiquities.
3. West Indies—Antiquities. 4. Columbus, Christopher.
5. America—Discovery and exploration—Spanish. I. Title.
F1619.2.T3R68 1992
972.9'02—dc20   91-30512
                                                   CIP
The paper in this book meets the guidelines for permanence and durability of the Committee on Production Guidelines for Book Longevity of the Council on Library Resources.

13

To my colleagues and students,
in gratitude for their contributions
to my knowledge of the Tainos
and their ancestors

C O N T E N T S

I L L U S T R A T I O N S

P R E F A C E

This book commemorates the quincentenary of Columbus's arrival in the Americas, but it does not celebrate his achievements. Instead, it focuses on the principal ethnic group he encountered on his voyages through the West Indies—the Tainos. Who were the Tainos? Whence came their ancestors? How did they evolve and become dominant in the West Indies? Why did they decline and disappear under European rule? What innovations did they contribute to the rest of the world?

The book attempts to answer these questions. It is addressed not only to my colleagues in academia but also to the interested public. I have attempted to make the writing more accessible to the latter by using the more familiar names for peoples and cultures, locations, and periods unless they are wrong or misleading and by limiting myself to the more reasonable hypotheses. In addition, I have cited secondary references to the early literature, for they are more readily available to nonacademic readers who seek further information. Technical terms are explained in a glossary.

In each chapter I begin with a statement of the problems considered therein and an explanation of how the chapter is organized. After inferring the solutions to the problems from the pertinent lines of evidence, I summarize the results of the research and discuss its implications. General readers can skip the technical analysis of evidence without losing the train of my argument.

The methods used have been considered at length in previous books: *Introduction to Prehistory: A Systematic Approach* (New York: McGraw-Hill, 1972) and *Migrations in Prehistory: Inferring Population Movement from Cultural Remains* (New Haven: Yale University Press, 1986). Here I focus on results. Chapter 2 is adapted from a paper contributed to the *Proceedings of the Thirteenth International Congress for Caribbean Archaeology, Held in Willemstad, Curaçao, on July 24–29, 1989* (Willemstad: Archaeological-Anthropological Institute of the Netherlands Antilles, 1991). Chapter 4 is drawn from the Taino chapter in my last book, *Migrations in Prehistory,* and from an article published in a symposium volume sponsored by the Centro de Investigaciones Indígenas de Puerto

Rico, *Early Ceramic Population Lifeways and Adaptive Strategies in the Caribbean,* edited by Peter E. Siegel (Oxford: BAR International Series 506, 1989). Chapter 6 has benefited from my collaboration with José Juan Arrom on a brief discussion of its subject for the National Gallery of Art, in *Circa 1492: Art in the Age of Exploration,* edited by Jay A. Levenson (New Haven: Yale University Press, 1991).

The book is a product of fifty-five years of research on the prehistory and ethnohistory of the West Indies and the adjacent parts of North and South America. I was introduced to these subjects in the mid-1930s by Cornelius Osgood, my mentor at the Yale Graduate School, and was fortunate to be able to pursue them under the auspices of the Caribbean Anthropological Program, which he founded at the Yale Peabody Museum. I am also indebted to my fellow graduate student Froelich G. Rainey, recently retired as director of the University Museum, University of Pennsylvania, for taking me on my first field trip to the West Indies.

Whatever success the Caribbean Anthropological Program has achieved is due in large part to the Wenner-Gren Foundation for Anthropological Research, which provided a crucial series of grants during its most productive years. I have also received two grants from the National Science Foundation, and my research has been sponsored by a number of local institutions, including the Museo Antropológico Montané at the University of Havana, the Bureau d'Ethnologie de la République d'Haiti, the Museo del Hombre Dominicano and the Fundación García Arévalo in Santo Domingo, the University of Puerto Rico and the Centro de Estudios Avanzados de Puerto Rico y el Caribe in San Juan, the Antigua Archaeological Society, the Royal Victoria Museum of Trinidad, and the Museo de Ciencias Naturales and the Instituto Venezolano de Investigaciones Científicas in Caracas.

The number of individuals with whom I have collaborated is too great to list here. I can only acknowledge those who have read parts or all of the present book and commented on it: Louis Allaire, José Juan Arrom, Mary Jane Berman, Marie Boroff, Harold Conklin, Birgit Faber Morse, José R. Oliver, Miguel Rodríguez López, Peter G. Roe, David R. Watters, members of my immediate family, and especially my editors, Ellen Graham and Mary Pasti. Their advice has been most helpful. The freehand drawings were done by David O. Kiphuth, and the computerized illustrations by José R. Oliver.

IRVING ROUSE
Yale University
1990

I NTRODUCTION

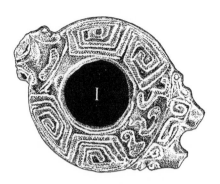

Columbus called the inhabitants of the Western Hemisphere *Indians* because he mistakenly thought he had reached the islands on the eastern side of the Indian Ocean. He could not use the term *Native American,* which is preferred by today's "Indians," because he was unaware of the continents that now bear the name America. The so-called Indians were divided into innumerable small ethnic groups, each with its own combination of linguistic, cultural, and biological traits. This book focuses upon one such group, the Tainos, who greeted Columbus when he first landed in the West Indies. Their habitat and their characteristics are discussed here, and they are differentiated from their neighbors.

The Natural Setting

The islands of the West Indies form the letter *y*, its tail stretching from Trinidad and Tobago, at the mouth of the Orinoco River in South America, and its arms reaching to the peninsulas of Yucatán in Middle America and Florida in North America. The islands are bordered on the east and northeast by the Atlantic Ocean, across which Columbus sailed, and on the northwest by the Gulf of Mexico. The Caribbean Sea separates them from the mainland of South and Middle America (fig. 1).

The Caribbean is a large body of open water, 1,500 miles long and at least 350 miles wide. Traversing it was no problem for Columbus, but so far as is known, the natives lacked ships, sails, and the ability to navigate such long distances. Hence, they are generally assumed to have traveled up and down the chain of islands, rather than across the Caribbean Sea.

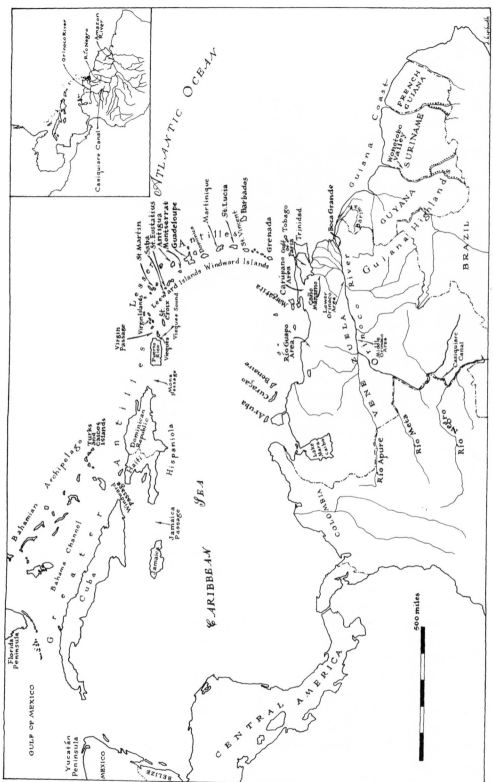

Fig. 1. The Caribbean (after Rouse 1986, fig. 2).

The island chain is divided into three parts. The Lesser Antilles form an arc extending northward from Trinidad and Tobago to the Virgin Islands, the Greater Antilles stretch westward from there to the Yucatán Peninsula, and the islands of the Bahamian Archipelago form a triangle in the Atlantic Ocean between the Greater Antilles and Florida. The islands of the Lesser Antilles are small and mostly volcanic. They consist of two groups, the Windward Islands to the south and the Leeward Islands to the north. Martinique, near the northern end of the Windwards, and Guadeloupe, at the southern end of the Leewards, are the biggest and most populous islands. Each is about half the size of Rhode Island. The Greater Antilles are composed of large, mountainous, and mostly sedimentary islands. Cuba, to the west, is almost as big as Florida; and Hispaniola, in the center, is about the size of Maine. Puerto Rico, to the east, and Jamaica, off-line to the south, are each slightly smaller than Connecticut. All four have fertile soil, capable of supporting dense populations. Two groups of tiny coral islands make up the Bahamian Archipelago. The Bahamas lie north of Cuba, and the Turks and Caicos north of Hispaniola. Both groups are rich in marine resources but lack good agricultural soil.

At present, each individual island or group of islands forms a single political unit. Hispaniola, which is shared by the Dominican Republic and Haiti, is the principal exception. In prehistoric time, the individual islands were divided among many different polities.

Natives from the mainland would have had to cross one of four water barriers to reach the West Indies. There is a distance of 65 miles between Tobago, on the continental shelf in South America, and Grenada, the southernmost of the Windward Islands. Yucatán is separated from Cuba by 124 miles of open water. The Florida Keys and Cuba are 100 miles apart, and Florida and Grand Bahama Island 80 miles apart. Strong currents flow through each of these passages, but native canoeists could have paddled across any of them in calm weather.

Most of the islands are within sight of each other, which facilitates travel. Barbados is the most isolated; it lies in the Atlantic Ocean one hundred miles east of the rest of the Windward Islands. By proceeding along the Caribbean shores of the islands, canoeists would have been sheltered from the prevailing winds, which blow from the Atlantic.

The currents favor travel from south to north and from east to west (Ricketson 1940, fig. 4). A South Equatorial current, flowing across the South Atlantic from Africa, is deflected northward along the coast of the Guianas. It carried escapees from Devil's Island, the former penal colony in French Guiana, to Venezuela and Trinidad, at the mouth of the Orinoco River. The large outpouring of fresh water from that river diverts part of the

South Equatorial current northward, especially during the summer when the river is in flood. Natural rafts of logs or sod, some carrying small plants and animals, are swept from the Guiana coast and the Orinoco Valley to the Windward Islands (Fewkes 1914: 664–65; Hostos 1941: 35–48). The remainder of the South Equatorial current continues westward along the coast of South America and northward past Central America into the Gulf of Mexico and the Florida Straits. There it meets the North Equatorial current, which has also come from the east, past the Leeward Islands and along the northern side of the Greater Antilles. The two currents join to form the Gulf Stream, which flows in a great arc past the Atlantic coasts of North America and Europe to West Africa, where it feeds back into the two Equatorial currents.

A countercurrent moves eastward along the southern side of the Greater Antilles, facilitating travel from Yucatán (Fewkes 1914: 664–65). No current links Florida with the West Indies.

The winds reinforce the westward-moving currents. Trade winds blow steadily from the northeast during most of the year. They bring heavy rainfall to the northern and eastern parts of the more mountainous islands. The southern and western parts are dryer because the winds lose their moisture before reaching them. For example, the Sierra de Luquillo in northeastern Puerto Rico is covered with a dense rain forest, whereas the southern coast is semiarid. The low islands also have relatively little rainfall; it reaches them only in squalls, as if they were in the open sea.

All the islands in the West Indies, as here defined, are oceanic, rather than continental. They have not been attached to the mainland in geologically recent time, if at all, and therefore lack land animals larger than the hutia (a small rodent) and the iguana. They resemble in this respect the islands of the Central Pacific, with which they are often compared.

The two largest islands, Cuba and Hispaniola, are exceptions, comparable to New Zealand in the Central Pacific. The two have yielded remains of ground sloths, which the first settlers may have hunted to extinction (Harrington 1921: 165, 409; Veloz Maggiolo 1976: 256). Both also offered the natives an unusually rich supply of freshwater fish.

The West Indian forests contained an abundance of wild fruits and vegetables, including palms, guava berries, and *guáyiga*, a cycad with edible roots. Saltwater fish, shellfish, and waterfowl were available along the shores, especially in estuaries, mangrove swamps, and reefs, which provided shelter from the open sea. Manatees and turtles could also be hunted there. The food resources varied from island to island, making it possible for the natives to develop extensive trading networks (Watters and Rouse 1989).

The climate and vegetation are tropical except in the northern part of the Bahamian Archipelago and at high altitudes in the mountains of the Greater Antilles, where conditions are more temperate. This difference, too, contributes to the diversity of resources and to the opportunities for trade.

The Tainos

Columbus encountered Tainos throughout most of the West Indies. They inhabited the Bahamas and all of the Greater Antilles except western Cuba, where they were separated from Middle America by a peripheral ethnic group, the Guanahatabeys. The chronicles do not clearly indicate who occupied the northern part of the Lesser Antilles, but recent archeological research has shown that its population, too, was Taino. A second peripheral group, the Island-Caribs, lived on the islands from Guadeloupe southward, separating the Tainos from South America (fig. 2).

The central group, which is our concern here, lacked an overall name in Columbus's time. Its members referred to themselves by the names of the localities in which they lived: those living in what is now Puerto Rico called themselves Borinquen, their name for the island, and those in the Bahamian Archipelago called themselves Lucayo (small islands). Ethnohistorians have grouped together the residents of various localities who shared a single language and had the same culture. The group is called Taino, meaning "good" or "noble," because several of its members spoke that word to Columbus to indicate that they were not Island-Caribs (Alegría 1981).

Daniel G. Brinton (1871) preferred to call the group Island Arawak because it shared many linguistic and cultural traits with the Arawak Indians (also known as Lokonos), whose descendants still live in northeastern South America. His followers shortened the phrase to Arawak. That was a mistake. The Indians who called themselves Arawaks lived only in the Guianas and the adjacent part of Trinidad (Boomert 1984). Columbus never met them. Moreover, they differed in both language and culture from all of the natives he did meet.

The island and mainland groups and their respective languages and cultures will here be termed Taino and Arawak, respectively. The local divisions among the Tainos will be designated binomially. For example, the inhabitants of the Bahamian Archipelago will be called Lucayan Tainos, following Keegan and Maclachlan (1989: 613).

The Ciguayan Tainos, who lived in the northeastern part of Hispaniola, are variously reported to have spoken one or two languages different from the one spoken by the rest of the Tainos (Wilson 1990a: 104). It is here

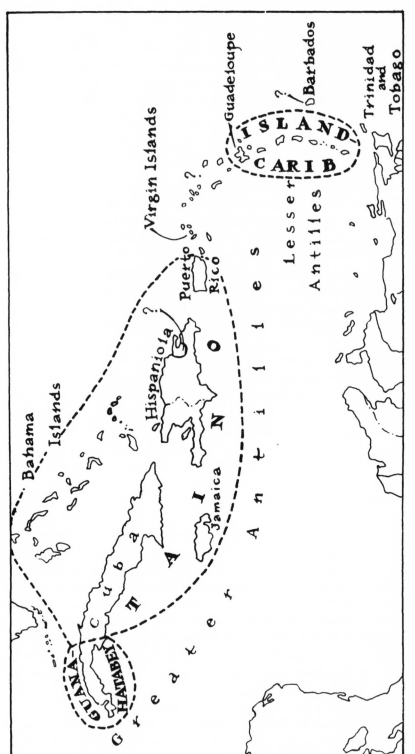

Fig. 2. The Tainos and their neighbors (after Rouse 1989a, fig. 1).

assumed that these were separate dialects. If they were different languages, the Ciguayans would have to be considered non-Taino. Unfortunately, there is not enough linguistic evidence to decide between the two possibilities.

A more widespread difference in culture is better documented. The inhabitants of Hispaniola and Puerto Rico stand apart because they were the most populous and the most advanced culturally. In a previous book I proposed calling them Classic Tainos (Rouse 1986: 114–15). With a few exceptions, discussed below, the inhabitants of the islands to their west have become known as Sub-Tainos (Lovén 1935: vi). Here I instead apply the geographical term *Western Tainos* to these Indians, who inhabited Jamaica, most of Cuba, and the Bahamian Archipelago; and I use the term *Eastern Tainos* for the inhabitants of the small eastern and southern islands, including most of the Virgins and the Leewards (fig. 3).

Early chroniclers reported from 100,000 to more than 1,000,000 Classic Tainos on the island of Hispaniola and as many as 600,000 in both Puerto Rico and Jamaica. Modern scholars doubt the higher figures; for example, Karen Anderson-Córdova (1990) estimates a maximum of 500,000 for Hispaniola. By contrast, the population of the island of Cuba, which was mostly Western Taino, is said to have been no greater than that of Puerto Rico, although its area is over ten times as large (Rouse 1948: 522, 540; Sauer 1965: 65–69).

The evidence that Jamaica, with an area only one-quarter greater than Puerto Rico's, was equally populous—indicates, as do several other points (discussed below), that the native Jamaicans were more advanced than the rest of the Western Tainos. Consequently, Ricardo E. Alegría (personal communication) has raised the question of whether they should be included in the Classic category. I prefer to consider them Western Tainos because the protohistoric archeology indicates that they were most closely affiliated with the Indians of Cuba and the Bahamas, as noted below.

The close relation between the Classic Tainos of Puerto Rico and Hispaniola is evidenced by a report that they visited each other daily (Rouse 1982a: 48). Moreover, the native Hispaniolans' term for the peninsula that led from their island to Jamaica was Guanacabibe, meaning "back of the island" (José J. Arrom, personal communication). These facts suggest that the Hispaniolans may have interacted more strongly with the Puerto Ricans than the Jamaicans and hence have resembled them more closely.

Whatever the case, we must focus on the Classic variant in Hispaniola and Puerto Rico because most of our information comes from there. The Spaniards never did colonize the Bahamian, Virgin, and Lesser Antillean islands, and by the time they settled Jamaica and Cuba, they had begun

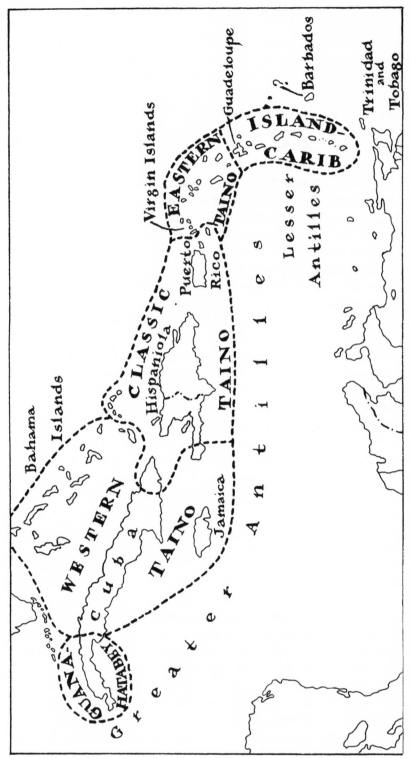

Fig. 3. Distribution of the peoples and cultures in the West Indies at the time of Columbus (after Rouse 1989a, fig. 2).

to lose interest in the native culture, which was disintegrating. Our best sources are Columbus and other observers who were in Hispaniola and Puerto Rico at the turn of the sixteenth century. Other chroniclers are less accurate; they had to depend upon hearsay, and they sometimes mixed data referring to different times and places.

CLASSIC TAINOS

Columbus encountered large, permanent villages in Hispaniola and Puerto Rico, each governed by a chief, or cacique. They contained an average of one thousand to two thousand people and ranged in size from a single building to twenty to fifty houses, all made of wood and thatch. Several related families lived together in the same house (Sauer 1966: 62–64).

The houses were irregularly arranged around a central plaza. The chief's home, larger and better made than the rest, was situated on the plaza. Round, conically roofed dwellings called *caney* predominated (fig. 4, *top*). They were accompanied, at least during colonial time, by rectangular *bohío* illustrated at the top of figure 4 (Lovén 1935: 336–49). The houses had dirt floors, and there were no partitions between families. Although some chiefs slept on wooden platforms, most people used hammocks (*hamaca*) made of cordage (fig. 4, *bottom*). Goods were stored in baskets hung from the roof and walls. The chiefs and other persons of high rank received guests while sitting on carved wooden stools, or *duho*, which reminded the Spaniards of the thrones they knew in Europe.

The villages were loosely organized into district chiefdoms, each ruled by one of the village chiefs in the district, and the district chiefdoms were in turn grouped into regional chiefdoms, each headed by the most prominent district chief. The villagers were divided into two classes (*nitaíno* and *naboria*), which the chroniclers equated with their own nobility and commoners. They searched in vain for a still lower class, comparable to their own slaves (Stevens-Arroyo 1988: 47–48).

Columbus took special notice of the Tainos' goldwork because it offered him an opportunity to repay his debt to his patrons, the king and queen of Spain. The Tainos mined nuggets of gold locally and beat them into small plates. Archeological research has shown that they were used interchangeably with cut shell to inlay wooden objects and to overlay clothing and ornaments. The Tainos could not cast the metal, but their caciques did wear *guanín*, ornaments made of a copper and gold alloy, that they obtained through trade with South America (see Sauer 1966: 25–26; Vega 1979).

The local artisans were also experienced woodworkers, potters, weavers of cotton, and carvers of wood, stone, bone, and shell. Some may have specialized in different crafts, but the Tainos do not seem to have developed

Fig. 4. Taino dwellings: *top left*, *caney*, which was in general use; *top right*, *bohío*, as used by chiefs; *bottom*, hammock set up in front of a caney (after Oviedo y Valdés 1851–55, vol. 1, pl. 1).

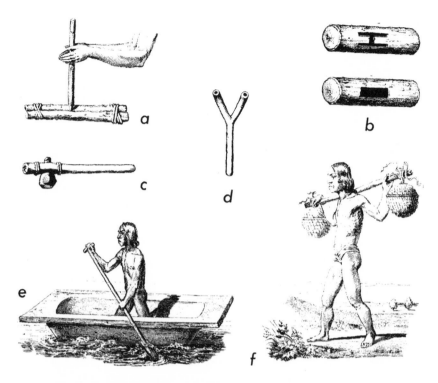

Fig. 5. Taino artifacts and activities: *a,* drill for making fire; *b,* drums, showing the variety of gonglike openings; *c,* stone celt hafted in a wooden handle; *d,* tube through which worshipers took snuff; *e,* man paddling a canoe, *f,* man carrying burdens on a balance pole (after Oviedo y Valdés 1851–55, vol. 1, pls. 1 and 2).

any craft into a full-time occupation (Sauer 1966: 59–66). They made fire with a wooden drill (fig. 5*a*).

The men went naked or covered their genitalia with cotton loincloths (fig. 5*f*). Unmarried women wore headbands; wives wore short skirts (*nagua*), the length of which indicated the wearer's rank. Both sexes painted themselves before participating in ceremonies, the men also before going to war. Red was a favorite color; this may have given rise to the misconception that Native Americans have red skins.

It was fashionable to flatten the forehead by binding a hard object against it in childhood, before the skull was fully formed. Ears and nasal septa were pierced for the insertion of feathers, plugs, and other ornaments; and waists and necks were decorated with belts and necklaces. The Spaniards reported that the chiefs were distinguished by headdresses adorned with gold and feathers. Pendants in the form of carved human masks, called *guaíza,* were also worn as a sign of rank (see Rouse 1948: 525–27; García Arévalo 1982: 26).

The Classic Tainos had a sophisticated form of agriculture. Instead of simply slashing and burning the forest to make a temporary clearing, as is common in the tropics, they heaped up mounds of earth in more permanent fields to cultivate root crops in the soft alluvial soil. The mounded fields were called *conuco.* The mounds, three feet high and some nine feet in circumference, were arranged in regular rows. They retarded erosion, improved the drainage, and thus permitted more lengthy storage of the mature tubers in the ground. They also made it easier to weed and to harvest the crops. The inhabitants of the dry southwestern part of Hispaniola are said to have constructed extensive irrigation systems (see Oviedo y Valdés 1959: 13–18; Sturtevant 1961, 1969; Sauer 1966: 51–54).

Cassava (*casabe*) was the principal root crop, followed by the sweet potato (*batata*). Cassava thrived in a broad range of local conditions, from wet to dry. It could be grown over a period of ten to twelve months and kept in the ground for up to three years. The men used digging sticks (*coa*) to plant cassava cuttings. Women grated its starchy roots and squeezed out its often-poisonous juice in a basketry tube to obtain flour, from which they baked bread on a clay griddle (*buren*). The bread, too, could be preserved for long periods of time. Sweet potato was eaten as a vegetable.

Indian corn (*maiz*) was less important, as is evidenced by the fact that it played no role in the Tainos' religion. It was grown on the forest floor by the slash-and-burn technique, and its kernels were eaten off the cob instead of being ground into flour and made into bread, as on the mainland. According to Gonzalo Fernández de Oviedo y Valdés (1959: 13–15), corn bread was inferior to cassava bread because it could not be stored in the high tropical humidity of the islands; it soon became moldy.

Other crops grown from seed included squash, beans, peppers, and peanuts. They were boiled with meat, fish, and cassava juice, a procedure that detoxified the juice. "Pepper pots" containing these ingredients were kept on the fire to provide food as needed. Alternatively, meat and fish were roasted on spits (Rouse 1948: 522–24; Sauer 1966: 54–59).

Fruits, calabashes, cotton, and tobacco were grown around the houses. The pineapple was cultivated, but not the peach palm and cacao, which were limited to the mainland and to Trinidad (Schultes 1984). Calabashes served as water containers. Tobacco was smoked in the form of cigars (*tabaco*), apparently for pleasure. Unlike the mainland ethnic groups, the Classic Tainos did not indulge in beer fermented from cassava or corn, nor did they chew coca (Sauer 1966: 51; Plowman 1984). They collected a variety of wild fruits and vegetables, such as palms nuts, guava berries, and guáyiga roots, whose remains have been found archeologically (Veloz Maggiolo, Ortega, and Caba Fuentes 1981: 169–70).

The chroniclers tell us that the Tainos caught fish in nets, speared them, and used hooks and lines. They also stupefied them with poison, trapped them in weirs, and stored both fish and turtles in weirs until they were ready to eat them. They drove hutias into corrals by burning the prairies or chasing them with dogs and torches and kept them penned there until needed. They plucked iguanas off trees and decoyed wild parrots with tame birds. In the absence of large land mammals, they augmented their supply of protein by spearing manatees in the mouths of the rivers and by eating dogs. They may also have had guinea pigs, but the evidence for this is inconclusive (Sauer 1966: 58–59).

We know more about the Classic Tainos' religion than about any other aspect of their culture, thanks to Father Ramón Pané, whom Columbus commissioned to study it. It centered on the worship of deities known as zemis. There were two supreme deities: Yúcahu, the lord of cassava and the sea, whence the Tainos obtained their sustenance; and Atabey, his mother, who was the goddess of fresh water and human fertility. Women prayed to her for a safe childbirth (Arrom 1989: 17–36). The lesser zemis included the spirits of ancestors, as well as the spirits believed to live in trees, rocks, and other features of the landscape. They are discussed in detail in chapter 5.

The term *zemi* was applied not only to the deities themselves but also to idols and fetishes representing them, which were made from the remains of ancestors or from natural objects believed to be inhabited by powerful spirits. Wood, stone, bone, shell, or pottery was used for the purpose. In historic time, at least, zemis were also made of cotton cloth. Each person had as many as ten of them, which he or she prized because of the power they were thought to confer. People boasted that theirs were the best, and they passed them on by inheritance, gift, or trade (Lovén 1935: 125–34, 650–56; Rouse 1948: 535–37).

Owners kept their zemis in niches or on tables in their homes. Some chiefs housed theirs in separate structures, presumably built like their houses, which served as temples (Roth 1887: 261–62). Zemis have also been found in caves, but they may not all have been worshiped there. Some may have been taken there to save them from destruction by the Spaniards, who considered them to be heathen idols.

When a male cacique died, one or two of his wives might be buried with him. His body was commonly flexed, bound with cotton cloth, and placed in the ground with his ornaments and other prized possessions. Alternatively, parts of the body might be preserved as zemis in temples or shrine caves. Ordinary people were interred in the ground or in caves, or else some of their bones were preserved as zemis after the flesh had decomposed (Lovén 1935: 541–59).

The Classic Tainos are said to have decorated their pottery, ornaments, and other artifacts with the figures of zemis and to have painted or tattooed them on their bodies. In addition, they carved or painted outlines of the natural spirits in places where they believed them to live, especially in caves and on rocks along streams or coasts. These so-called petroglyphs and pictographs were not necessarily objects of worship.

Before communing with their zemis, owners purified themselves by fasting or by inserting a stick in their throat to cause vomiting. They then took snuff (*cohoba*) in front of the zemi. The worshiper put the snuff, made by crushing seeds of the piptadenia tree (Arrom 1988: 19–20), on a platform surmounting the zemi or in a separate receptacle and inhaled it through a forked tube (fig. 5*d*). It caused hallucinations, through which the zemi made known his or her will (Rouse 1948: 535–37).

Owners offered food to their zemis to propitiate them. Once a year the whole village paid similar homage to the chief's zemis. The chief presided, assisted by other personages acting as priests. The ceremony began with a procession of the villagers, wearing their ornaments, carrying baskets of cassava bread, and singing songs about the zemis. The chief sat at the entrance to the temple, beating a drum (fig. 5*b*) while the priests entered and dressed the zemis. The villagers presented themselves before the temple and purified themselves by pressing a stick down their throat and vomiting. The women then brought their cassava bread to the priests, who offered it to the zemis. Dancing followed. The audience sang the praises of the zemis and of former chiefs and offered prayers for the prosperity of the village. Finally, the priests broke up the bread and distributed pieces to the heads of families. These fragments were preserved throughout the year as a protection against accidents.

The chroniclers also mention shamans (*bohuti*), who cured the sick on demand. They worked in the presence of the priests and received gifts of cassava in return for their services. They painted the figures of their zemis on their bodies and communicated with them in séances. Both the shaman and the patient fasted before the curing ritual. The shaman took snuff, presumably in front of the figure of a zemi in his own house, to learn the cause of the disease. He then proceeded to the sick person's home, where he swallowed an herb (*gioia*) to induce vomiting. He lighted a torch and sang, accompanying himself with a rattle, then approached the patient and pretended to suck an object from the latter's body. This object was considered to be the cause of the disease; often the shaman would give it to the patient after recovery to keep as a zemi (Rouse 1948: 537–38).

The cacique's house—and presumably also his or her temple—faced on the central plaza, where dances and ceremonies were held. The areas in which these activities took place may be termed dance grounds, for the chroniclers do not state that the areas were bounded by walls or other structures. Archeologists, however, have identified enclosures that Classic Tainos built to take the place of dance grounds. These structures, which consist of embankments of earth and/or stone slabs, often decorated with engravings of zemis (fig. 28, *top*), are oval, rectangular, or long and narrow, like roads. They occasionally contain monumental carvings of zemis. They may be termed dance courts.

The annual homages to the chief's zemis took place on the central dance ground or court. Other rituals were performed there before and after battles and upon the marriage or death of a chief, and so were ceremonies (*areito*) celebrating the deeds of ancestors. The dancers were accompanied by singing, drumming, and rattling (Lovén 1935: 492–97).

The Classic Tainos also played ball on the central plaza and elsewhere. Their ancestors appear to have used nonstructured areas, which may be termed ball grounds. They themselves often constructed specially designed ball courts, applying the term *batey* to both the game and the court where it was played. The court is said to have been rectangular. Ordinary spectators sat on its stones or embankments, the caciques and nobles on their stools. The courts within the villages were for intramural games; other courts, in the countryside, were for games between villages. Gary S. Vescelius (personal communication) has noticed that the most elaborate courts in Puerto Rico were on the putative boundaries of chiefdoms and has suggested that they were used for games between polities.

Both men and women participated, always separately. The teams, each with ten to thirty players, occupied opposite ends of the court, as in tennis, and alternated in serving the ball. Players attempted to keep it in motion by bouncing it back and forth from their bodies to the ground inside the limits of the court. They were not allowed to touch it with their hands or feet. Its elasticity amazed the Spaniards, who had never seen rubber, the substance of which it was made (Stern 1949: 29–32).

Courts are said to have been in constant use. Wagers were made by the players and, in the case of intervillage games, by their caciques, who also offered small prizes—food, for example. The game was occasionally played before public decisions were made (Lovén 1935: 524–26; Alegría 1983: 4).

Archeological research has confirmed the foregoing ethnohistorical information. Earth- and stone-lined courts in which the ball game could have been played have been found throughout Hispaniola and Puerto Rico. The distribution of these structures extends to the eastern tip of Cuba and to St. Croix, in the Virgin Islands. There is reason to believe that the Classic Tainos established outposts in both places, possibly in order to trade with the Western and Eastern Tainos.

Unlike the present inhabitants of the West Indies, the natives traveled by sea whenever possible. They used canoes (*canoa*), which they hollowed out of logs by alternately charring and chopping them with petaloid stone axes, known as celts (fig. 5c). Spade-shaped paddles were the only means of propulsion until the Spaniards introduced sails (fig. 5e). The largest canoes belonged to the chiefs. They were carved, painted, and kept in special boathouses reminiscent of those in Polynesia. Columbus reported that they could hold up to 150 people. On land, the chiefs traveled in litters, and the ordinary people by foot. The latter carried burdens suspended from balance poles (fig. 5f; see also Lovén 1935: 414–20; McKusick 1970; Glazier 1991).

Both men and women were eligible to serve as chiefs and, as such, to live in specially built houses, sit on thronelike stools, have special forms of transportation, and wear insignia of their rank. Each cacique presided over the village in which he or she lived. They organized the daily activities and were responsible for the storage of surplus commodities, which they kept in buildings constructed for the purpose and redistributed among the villagers as needed. They acted as hosts when the villages received visitors, and had charge of the political relations with other villages. The caciques owned the most powerful zemis and supervised their worship. They organized the public feasts and dances and, having learned the songs by heart, directed the singing. Because their canoes were the largest in the village, they were responsible for public forms of transportation (Lovén 1935: 498–540; Rouse 1948: 528–30; Wilson 1990a: 119–25).

Village chiefs reportedly had the power of life or death over their subjects. The district and regional chiefs did not exercise this kind of control but could requisition food and military service. Their ability to do so depended upon their personalities and political relations (Wilson 1990b).

The Classic Tainos believed that they had originally come from caves in a sacred mountain on the island of Hispaniola (Alegría 1978: 57–94; Rouse and Arrom 1991). Individuals traced their descent through their mothers rather than their fathers. Goods, class status, and the office of chief were also inherited matrilineally. A man resided in the village of his mother's lineage. If he chose a wife from another village, he brought her to his own (Keegan and Maclachlan 1989: 617–18).

Polygyny was prevalent. Most men probably obtained wives in or near their own villages, but chiefs sometimes arranged long-distance marriages for political purposes (Wilson 1990a: 111–19). A commoner had to temporarily serve his prospective bride's family to compensate it for her loss; a chief could instead make a payment of goods. Only a chief could afford to have many wives.

Trade was widespread. Parties or single persons undertook long sea voyages for the purpose. Some districts excelled in making particular products; for example, Gonâve Island off the western coast of Haiti was known for its wooden bowls (Lovén 1935: 60–61). Residents of eastern Hispaniola and western Puerto Rico are said to have exchanged daily visits across the Mona Passage (Rouse 1982a: 48). Such interaction was facilitated by a common language.

The Classic Tainos fought among themselves to avenge murders, to resolve disputes over hunting and fishing rights, or to force a chief who had received a bride price to deliver the woman purchased. They did not themselves obtain additional wives by raiding other communities and had difficulty fending off the Island-Caribs, who did (Rouse 1948: 532–33).

Only the chiefs and nobles attended meetings at which war was declared. A chief was elected to lead the attack; the nobles served as his or her bodyguard. Before going into battle they painted their bodies red, hung small images of zemis on their foreheads, and danced. They fought with clubs (*macana*), with spears propelled by throwing sticks, and, in the eastern part of their territory, with bows and arrows. The Ciguayan and Borinquen Tainos, of northeastern Hispaniola and Puerto Rico, respectively, are said to have been the most warlike, probably because they were forced to defend themselves against Island-Carib raids.

WESTERN AND EASTERN TAINOS

Because of the scarcity of documentary evidence about the people who lived immediately to the west and to the east of the Classic Tainos, ethnohistorians have had to use the results of archeological research to fill out their knowledge. That research has confirmed the presence of the Western Tainos in Jamaica, central Cuba, and the Bahama Islands and has shown that the Classic Tainos established outposts in eastern Cuba and the Turks and Caicos Islands. It also indicates that the Classic Tainos had an eastern outpost on St. Croix Island and that the rest of the Virgin Islands and all except the southernmost Leeward Islands were populated by Eastern Tainos (Allaire 1985a, 1985b).

The Western Taino villages appear to have been large except in the Bahamian Archipelago, where they contained only an estimated 120–225 people, divided among twelve to fifteen houses (Sauer 1966: 62–64). The Eastern Taino settlements probably had a similar range; some islands may have become completely depopulated because their villages were too small to defend themselves against Island-Carib raids.

The density of Jamaica's population suggests that its inhabitants practiced the same advanced form of agriculture as the Classic Tainos. In the absence of information to the contrary, the other Western Tainos and all of the Eastern Tainos are presumed to have used only the slash-and-burn technique. Carl O. Sauer (1966: 183) has theorized that the clay soil of the Cuban plains was too heavy to be mounded up with digging sticks, in addition to which it would not have drained as well as the granular soil heaped up in the conucos of the more central islands.

There is archeological evidence that some Bahamian villages were divided into halves. William F. Keegan and Morgan D. Maclachlan (1989: 615–16) conclude that if and when these moeities split and became separate villages, they may have continued their affiliation and that the affiliated villages may have evolved into district chiefdoms. They note that the Spaniards encountered such a chiefdom on Aklin Island in the Bahamas. No regional chiefdoms, like those also present among the Classic Tainos, are reported. Independent villages must have been the rule in less developed areas.

The chronicles indicate that the native Jamaicans had the greatest variety of ornaments among the Western Tainos, many showing rank. The class system of the Classic Tainos may therefore have extended into Jamaica (Rouse 1948: 543–44).

By combining documentary and archeological evidence ethnohistorians have been able to demonstrate that zemis were worshiped in homes and in caves throughout Western and Eastern Taino territory, especially in Jamaica. The sources do not mention the construction of specialized structures for the worship of zemis, nor have archeologists encountered the remains of central courts that could have been used for that purpose (Rouse 1948: 542–45). However, the ball game is recorded for the Western and probably also the Eastern Tainos (Alegría 1983: 7). It must have been played on unstructured grounds; no traces of ball courts have been found.

The Western Tainos are said to have been more peaceful than the Classic and Eastern Tainos (Lovén 1935: 69). This was to be expected, for they lived in isolation, bordered only by the Classic Tainos and the Guanahatabeys, who do not seem to have been aggressive toward their neighbors. The Western Tainos' attitude worked to Columbus's advantage after landfall and during his subsequent voyage through the Bahamas to central Cuba.

The inhabitants of both places received him and his men hospitably and assisted them in recuperating from their long voyage.

The Eastern Tainos were more hostile because they had to contend with Island-Carib raids from the south. It was only natural, therefore, for them to react against Columbus when he encountered them during his second voyage (Sauer 1966: 72). Their hostility has created the false impression that they were Island-Caribs, an error that has only recently been corrected by archeological and historical research (chaps. 5 and 6).

We do not know whether the Eastern Tainos used the bow and arrow. They probably did, for this weapon is present among the Island-Caribs to their south and among the Classic Tainos of St. Croix, Puerto Rico, and the eastern tip of Hispaniola to their north and west. The bow and arrow are not exclusively an Island-Carib weapon, as some authorities have assumed.

LEVELS OF DEVELOPMENT

Columbus was disappointed that the Tainos were less civilized than the East Asians he had expected to find. Nevertheless, Classic Taino culture appears to have been evolving toward full civilization. Its bearers possessed a good agricultural base and were organized into complex chiefdoms. If they had been allowed a few centuries of reprieve from Spanish rule they might well have bridged the gap across Guanahatabey territory in western Cuba and developed the kind of commercial linkage with the civilized peoples of Middle America that they had already established with the inhabitants of northern South America. This would have made it possible for them to acquire writing, statehood, and other elements of the mainland civilizations, as their fellow islanders, the British and the Japanese, had already done in Europe and Asia.

Classic Taino culture has been termed Formative because it was on the verge of civilization (Rouse 1986: 148). By contrast, the Eastern and Western Tainos were on a somewhat lower level of cultural development, which Julian H. Steward (1947) has called Tropical Forest.

Neighboring Ethnic Groups

The Tainos cannot be understood in isolation. They must also be viewed in terms of their immediate neighbors, the Guanahatabeys and Island-Caribs, with whom they interacted and exchanged cultural, linguistic, and biological traits. There is no evidence that they were in direct contact with the ethnic groups beyond these two, in either Middle or South America, and hence the mainland will not be considered here.

GUANAHATABEYS

Scholars have mistakenly called the western neighbors of the Tainos by another name, Ciboney. That term actually applies to a local group of Western Tainos in central Cuba (Alegría 1981: 4–9). The Guanahatabeys lived at the far end of Cuba, separating the Western Tainos from the fully civilized peoples of Middle America. They must have spoken a language different from their neighbors', for Columbus's Taino interpreter was unable to converse with them. Unfortunately, they became extinct before their language could be studied. We know it only from local place names, which are not sufficient to determine its affiliation (Granberry 1980, 1987).

None of the chroniclers had an opportunity to study the local culture before it, too, became extinct. The Tainos told them that the Guanahatabeys were "savages having neither houses nor farms, subsisting on game captured in the mountains, or on turtles and fish" (Cosculluela 1946: 11; Alegría 1981: 7–8). Keegan (1989) has questioned the validity of this evidence because it is hearsay. He argues that the chroniclers were reporting legend rather than historical reality. It is possible that the Guanahatabeys were a local group of Tainos. However, no sites inhabited by Tainos have been found in their territory, even though it is one of the more intensively investigated parts of the West Indies. The fact that the Guanahatabeys spoke a different language also indicates that they formed a separate ethnic group.

Archeological research in Guanahatabey territory has shown only the remains of prehistoric peoples who lived in the open as well as in caves and relied heavily on shellfish, as well as on fish and game. They used the techniques of chipping and grinding to make tools of stone, bone, and shell. Apparently they were organized into small bands rather than villages. No demonstrably prehistoric pottery has been found in their territory (Sauer 1966: 184–85).

Given the similarity between these remains and the ethnohistorical accounts, it is reasonable to assume that the peoples who deposited them were ancestral to the Guanahatabeys. Both groups are generally thought to be relics of the original population of the islands, pushed back by the Tainos into the peripheral position they occupied in Columbus's time. Archeologists apply the term *Archaic* to cultures such as theirs, which lacked pottery, agriculture, and sedentary life (Alegría 1981: 4–6).

Little is known about the relations between the Guanahatabeys and the natives of southern Florida. Both populations were on the Archaic level of cultural and social development in the time of Columbus; and their archeological remains show some resemblances, especially in shellwork and woodwork. To what extent these resemblances are the result of interaction or of parallel adaptation to similar ecological conditions remains to be determined.

ISLAND-CARIBS

The members of the second peripheral group called themselves Carib or Kalina. Ethnohistorians have added the prefix *Island* to distinguish them from the Caribs proper, who lived on the mainland. In the time of Columbus the Island-Caribs occupied the Windward Islands, Guadeloupe, and possibly also neighboring islands at the southern end of the Leewards (Dreyfus 1983–84: 47). They were situated between the Eastern Tainos and the Arawaks and Caribs proper, who lived side by side on the mainland to their south.

Their overall population was small compared to that of the Tainos. They were concentrated on the larger islands, such as Guadeloupe and Martinique. Some smaller islands, such as Barbados, were apparently depopulated in the time of Columbus.

Unlike the Tainos and Guanahatabeys, they had arrived in the West Indies recently enough to have retained traditions of their mainland origin. They told the Europeans that they had come from the south and had conquered an ethnic group named Igneri or Eyeri (Allaire 1977). They are thought to have been mainland Caribs who imposed their name on the Igneris.

We are here concerned with conditions among the Island-Caribs in the time of Columbus. Unfortunately, our information about them comes mostly from the French, who colonized Guadeloupe and Martinique more than a century later. By that time an influx of Taino people, fleeing from repression by the Spaniards in Hispaniola and Puerto Rico, had modified the Island-Caribs' language and culture. We must attempt to take these influences into consideration.

Because of the change in name from Igneri to Island-Carib, linguists originally thought that the new ethnic group spoke a Cariban language (Steward 1946–59, vol. 6, map 18). They found, however, that the Island-Caribs had an Arawakan language, as distinct from that of the Tainos to their north as from that of the Arawaks on the mainland to their south (Goeje 1939: 2–4). To account for this unexpected relation, they have hypothesized that the mainland-Carib conquerors of the Igneris settled among them without displacing them, and eventually adopted their language. Indeed, many linguists prefer to call the Island-Caribs' language Igneri (alternatively spelled Eyeri or Ieri; Loukotka 1968: 125; Granberry 1987).

In French colonial times, if not earlier, the Island-Carib men also spoke a pidgin language among themselves, which was basically Cariban (Taylor 1977a: 26–27). The Caribs and Arawaks, who still live side by side in the Guianas, use this pidgin to communicate with each other. Douglas Taylor and Berend J. Hoff (1980) theorize that the Carib warriors who conquered the Igneris retained the mainland pidgin as a symbol of their origin. They probably also used it to trade with their neighbors on the mainland, as noted below.

According to French observers, the seventeenth-century Island-Caribs made only undecorated pottery, reminiscent of that among their contemporary namesakes on the mainland (Allaire 1984). Whether the pottery was produced by the men or by the women is unclear. Archeologists have been unable to locate sites containing this kind of pottery or to determine whether it was already in existence when Columbus arrived more than a century earlier. Repeated attempts to locate native villages mentioned in the historic sources have also failed, and so have efforts to find native sites containing European trade objects. Consequently, the results of archeological research cannot yet be used to expand our knowledge of Island-Carib culture.

The invading warriors appear to have imposed the masculine aspects of their ancestral Carib culture on the domestic life of the preceding Igneri culture. In French colonial times and presumably earlier, the male inhabitants of each village lived together in a men's house, from which they visited their wives in surrounding family homes.

The villages are not reported to have contained plazas, ball courts, temples, or other public structures, but there is unconfirmed evidence that the seventeenth-century Island-Caribs played ball (Meyer 1987). They could have inherited this practice from their Igneri predecessors, or they could have acquired it from the Tainos who took refuge among them during the sixteenth century.

The Island-Carib men of the fifteenth century emphasized warfare, raiding Taino villages to obtain additional wives. Columbus rescued several Taino women when he visited Island-Carib villages on Guadeloupe during his second voyage, and returned them to their homes in the Greater Antilles. We do not know how the Island-Carib men of his time obtained wives from within their own group.

The Island-Carib men of the sixteenth and seventeenth centuries, if not earlier, lacked permanent chiefs. They elected temporary war chiefs to lead their raids. More skilled in the use of bows and arrows than the Tainos, they ate bits of the flesh of opposing warriors in order to acquire the latter's prowess. Our term *cannibal* is derived from this practice; it is a corruption of the Spanish word *caribal*. The men also undertook long-distance trading expeditions to South America. These, too, were led by temporary chiefs elected for the purpose (Dreyfus 1983–84: 47–48). The men presumably used their pidgin language on these trips. They built excellent dugout canoes, which they employed for hunting and fishing as well as for warfare and trade.

The women continued to practice the Igneri form of agriculture, which appears to have been similar to that of the Eastern Tainos, and to gather wild fruits and vegetables. Like the Igneri before them, they seem to have worshiped zemis in their houses, if not in shrine caves (Lovén 1935: 578–94).

Island-Carib culture may be classed with Western and Eastern Taino, Igneri, and Arawak cultures on the Tropical Forest level of development. All five lagged behind Classic Taino culture. Nevertheless, the Island-Caribs were not savages, as has sometimes been assumed because of their ritualistic cannibalism (Pinchon 1952: 305).

Conclusions

A ship's captain interested in Caribbean ethnohistory once expressed surprise to me that he had been unable to find the names Taino or Arawak on any of his charts (Rouse 1987: 83). Why, he wondered, is the region named after the Island-Caribs, who were peripherally located, occupied much less territory than the Tainos, had a much smaller population, and lagged in cultural development? The captain was perceptive. The Tainos have not received the recognition they deserve for their role in the events relating to the conquest of the Americas. Not only has their identity suffered because they had no overall name for themselves but the Island-Caribs attracted more attention because of their warlike nature and their practice of cannibalism, which the Spanish colonists greatly exaggerated in order to justify enslaving them (Sued Badillo 1978; Arens 1979).

The two groups had many other differences. Taino homes were clustered around a central plaza, where both men and women participated in ceremonies, dances, and ball games. Island-Carib homes were instead grouped around a house where the men lived and carried out a gender-oriented range of activities. The Tainos spoke a single language; the Island-Caribs supplemented theirs with a pidgin, which was used only in the men's house and on expeditions to the mainland. The Tainos emphasized religion and burial, the Island-Caribs warfare and trade. The Tainos had hereditary chiefs, the Island-Caribs only temporary chiefs elected to lead their expeditions. The Tainos did service or made payments to obtain their brides; the Island-Caribs raided for theirs. The Tainos had a homogeneous society, and the Island-Caribs a dual one, in which the men dominated the women.

The third ethnic group, the Guanahatabeys, lived in mobile bands rather than sedentary villages. They lacked the pottery and agriculture shared by the Tainos and the Caribs.

Because the Tainos were the first inhabitants of the Western Hemisphere to come into contact with Europeans, they played a major role in the so-called Columbian exchange, whereby the Spaniards and the natives traded diseases, crops, artifacts, customs, and ideas (Crosby 1972). The contributions of the Tainos to that exchange are discussed in the Epilogue.

The ethnohistorians' division of Taino culture into Western, Classic, and (thanks to recent archeological research) Eastern variants foreshadows another theme that will recur in subsequent chapters: the contrast between conditions in the center of the distribution of a population group and on its frontiers. The central conditions, in this case among the Classic Tainos, are typical of a group's culture and language. Those who live on the frontiers, as the Western and Eastern Tainos did, tend to be more conservative and to lag in cultural and linguistic development. At the same time, because of their peripheral position, they are able to interact more closely with the neighboring ethnic groups and hence become transitional to them.

A third recurring subject is the duality of culture among the Island-Caribs. We shall find that the prehistoric peoples in the West Indies had other dualities, probably not based upon gender, and shall examine the effect of these dualities on the development of new peoples and cultures.

Ethnohistorians have inferred conclusions about the origins of the Tainos and their neighbors from the documentary evidence. The Guanahatabeys' peripheral position and low level of development has led to the belief that they were a relict of the original peopling of the Antilles. Their ancestors could have come from Middle America, taking advantage of the counter-current that flows along the south side of Cuba, or from South America, following the main thrust of currents into the West Indies.

The ancestors of the Tainos were the next people to invade the West Indies. By alternatively calling them Arawaks, ethnohistorians have implied that they were an offshoot of the ethnic group of that name which inhabited parts of the Guianas and Trinidad in the time of Columbus. In fact, the two groups were descended from a common ancestor. It is generally agreed that the progenitors of the Tainos rode the South Equatorial current and the outpouring of water from the Orinoco River into the Windward Islands, whence they continued through the Leeward Islands and the Greater Antilles into the Bahamian Archipelago, leaving only an isolated pocket of Guanahatabeys at the western end of Cuba. These events must have happened some time ago, for the Tainos did not recollect having come from the mainland; they believed that they had emerged from caves in Hispaniola.

The traditions of the Island-Carib warriors indicate that their ancestors followed in the footsteps of the ancestors of the Tainos. They, too, came from the Guianas and Trinidad, where they had lived side by side with the Arawaks. By the time of Columbus they had penetrated the Lesser Antilles, but only as far as the southern end of the Leeward Islands. If my inferences from their traditions are correct, they arrived in war parties, which conquered the Igneri population, subjugated or drove out its men, and took its women as wives. The warriors were apparently too few in number to have substantially changed the biological composition of the previous population or to have replaced its language and the domestic aspects of its culture. The invaders were only able to impose their own name, their pidgin language, and masculine aspects of their ancestral culture. In other words, they were eventually assimilated into the local population, like the Normans who invaded England and the Moors who conquered southern Spain (Rouse 1990).

These working hypotheses have been inferred from the geographical and ethnohistorical data presented in this chapter and are subject to testing against other lines of evidence. The work done to test them is discussed in the next chapter.

THE ANCESTRIES

OF THE TAINOS

The region known as the West Indies offers an unusual opportunity to study problems of origin because its islands extend like a series of stepping stones between South, Middle, and North America. Its natives could have come from, and later acquired traits from, any or all parts of the mainland.

The study of human origins falls within the academic discipline of anthropology. It is done not only by ethnohistorians, whose results have just been summarized, but also by physical anthropologists, archeologists, and linguists. These four groups of specialists have become organized into separate subdisciplines because they base their conclusions on different kinds of evidence, ethnohistorians on the chroniclers' descriptions, physical anthropologists on the Tainos' biological remains, archeologists on their cultural remains, and linguists on their language. Ethnologists, who study contemporary cultures and societies, cannot also participate because the Tainos are extinct.

In the previous chapter we saw how ethnohistorians have used the documentary evidence to distinguish ethnic groups and draw conclusions about their origins. In this chapter we shall consider the classifications made by physical anthropologists to form races and investigate their biological heritages, by archeologists to form peoples and study their cultural heritages, and by linguists to form speech-communities and examine their linguistic heritages. The names for the three kinds of heritages will here be shortened to biologies, cultures, and languages, respectively; and their characteristics will be termed traits.

Ethnic classification mixes cultural and linguistic, if not also biological, traits. These kinds of criteria are treated separately in the other three kinds of classification. Physical anthropologists use the Linnaean system; archeologists and linguists have had to develop parallel taxonomic systems tailored to their own subject matter (Rouse 1986: 158–63). Biological, cultural, and linguistic criteria can be mixed in ethnic classification because it is limited to the contemporary scene. They must be kept separate in biological, archeological, and linguistic classifications because the ancestors of contemporary groups are also included. Experience has shown that biologies, cultures, and languages are discrete phenomena that can, and often do, develop independently through different lines of descent.

The anthropologists who pioneered research on the origins of the Tainos during the late nineteenth and early twentieth centuries had not yet learned to make the foregoing distinctions. They worked indiscriminately with biological, cultural, and linguistic traits, studying their spread from the mainland to the islands (for example, Brinton 1871; Gower 1927; Lovén 1935) and failing to distinguish individual traits from whole biologies, cultures, and languages. In the absence of chronological evidence, which would have enabled them to proceed period by period, they drew their conclusions solely from the geographical distributions of the traits.

Because most of the traits appeared to have originated in South America, they concluded that the Tainos must have come from there (Lovén 1935: 2). They assumed that the migrants had reached the islands too recently to develop new biologies, cultures, or languages after their arrival. If the migrants had reached the West Indies early enough to have evolved in any of these ways, they would have been ancestors of the Tainos rather than the Tainos themselves.

Only the emerging specialists in linguistic and physical anthropology went beyond the study of traits to investigate ancestries. As we saw, linguists classified the Tainos' language within the Arawakan family, named after the Arawak language of Trinidad and the Guianas (Goeje 1939). They inferred from the distribution of this family that it had originated in the Amazon Basin, in the heart of lowland South America (Noble 1965: 105–06). Physical anthropologists reached a similar conclusion. José Imbelloni (1938) assigned the native West Indians to an Amazonid race, which he contrasted with an Isthmid race in the western half of the Caribbean area (fig. 6). In effect, Imbelloni traced the biological ancestry of the Tainos back through the Guianas and the Orinoco Valley into Amazonia.

The pioneer research on the distribution of cultural traits was summarized in the *Handbook of South American Indians*, edited by Julian H. Steward (1946–59). Impressed by evidence that the Andean and Circum-Caribbean Indians had shared many such traits and that many of the traits had spread from the Peruvian Andes to the coast, Steward (1947) postu-

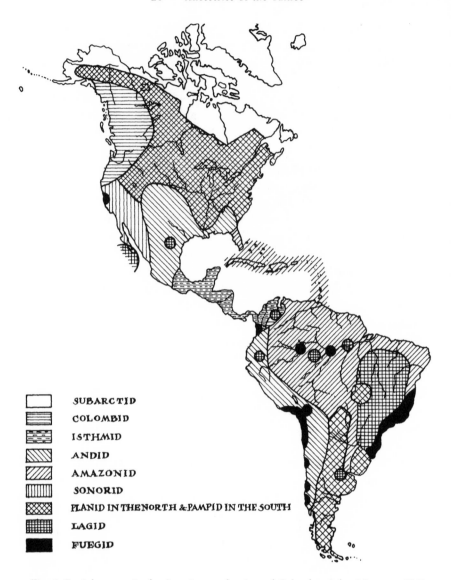

Fig. 6. Racial groups in the Americas at the time of Columbus (after Newman 1951, pl. 9).

lated a parallel diffusion from the Colombian Andes to the Caribbean coast and a radiation along that coast: westward into Central America; eastward into Venezuela, the Guianas, and Amazonia; and northward through Trinidad and Tobago into the West Indies. Subsequent authors extended the diffusion farther northward, through Mexico into the southwestern

Fig. 7. Steward's Circum-Caribbean theory of cultural diffusion (after Howells 1954: 298).

United States and through the West Indies into the southeastern United States (fig. 7).

Steward's postulate has come to be known as the Circum-Caribbean theory (Rouse 1953a). He did not attempt to reconcile it with the linguists' and physical anthropologists' theory that the ancestors of the Tainos had migrated from Amazonia through the Orinoco Valley into the West Indies. Instead, he explicitly limited himself to cultural evidence and examined it solely in terms of traits. It did not occur to him to trace the ancestry of the Tainos and their neighbors in terms of whole cultures, comparable to the languages and biologies being studied by linguists and physical anthropologists.

Followers of Steward have deleted the spread into Amazonia from his Circum-Caribbean theory and added diffusion from the Andes into both the Amazon and Orinoco valleys (Meggers and Evans 1957, fig. 206; Sanoja and Vargas 1983: 237–38). They have continued to focus on individual traits (Ford 1969) but, in belated reaction to the conclusions of the linguists and physical anthropologists, have also begun to draw inferences about the ancestries of whole cultures. Tracing the Tainos' cultural ancestry back to the Andes via the Circum-Caribbean route has brought them directly into conflict with the linguists and the physical anthropologists. In the next section I seek to determine whether the ancestral cultures came from Amazonia, as the ancestral languages and biologies apparently did, or whether they originated in the Andes, as some of their constituent cultural traits obviously did. I examine the Tainos' linguistic and biological ancestries in the subsequent sections.

Cultural Ancestry

In the absence of Taino survivors, who could be studied ethnologically, archeologists have had to assume sole responsibility for investigating the cultural ancestry of the Tainos. They have split into two schools. One has argued that the ancestral cultures spread along Steward's Circum-Caribbean route (for example, Meggers and Evans 1983). The other, impressed by the linguists' success in tracing the Tainos' linguistic ancestry back through the Orinoco Valley into Amazonia, has attempted to show that the ancestral cultures also came from there (for example, Lathrap 1970).

In effect, the two schools have used the Circum-Caribbean theory and the linguists' conclusions as competing models. Following Steward's example, they have focused on traits, clusters of traits, and the sequences of the two that archeologists call traditions, instead of focusing on whole cultures. Each school has attempted to show that the geographical distribution of key traits, clusters, and traditions better fits its model.

They have supported their positions with ecological arguments. The Circum-Caribbeanists claim that the ancestors of the Tainos must have come from the Andes because the environment there is more conducive to cultural development. The Amazonists contend that equally favorable conditions are available in the tropical lowlands. With the advent of radiocarbon dating, each school has also sought to demonstrate that key trait-units appeared earlier along the chosen route. The results of this research have also been inconclusive. For example, the Amazonists have obtained relatively early dates for trait-units in the Orinoco Valley, whereas the Circum-Caribbeanists have found reasons to reject those dates in favor of later ones more consistent with their model (compare Rouse 1978 with Sanoja and Vargas 1983).

In my opinion, the study of cultural ancestries should not be conducted on the level of trait-units, as in these cases, but on the level of whole cultures and the peoples who possessed them. Archeologists interested in the cultural ancestry of the Tainos ought to be studying the ancestral peoples and their cultures, just as linguists study the ancestral speech-communities and their languages, and physical anthropologists the ancestral races and their biologies. Research on individual trait-units is irrelevant; it informs us about the origins of these units, not about the ancestries of the populations that possessed them.

The distinction between peoples and cultures, on the one hand, and the peoples' cultural traits, on the other hand, is fundamental to research on origins. The archeologists Willey, DiPeso, Ritchie, Rouse, Rowe, and Lathrap (1956) have named the former category site-unit to distinguish it from trait-unit.

Both the Circum-Caribbeanists and the Amazonists trace the Tainos' cultural ancestry in terms of ceramic traditions, each consisting of a single trait-unit that has passed from one site-unit to another. They ought instead to be focusing on the manner in which the ancestral site-units developed from other ones. They should distinguish peoples and cultures by constructing chronological charts, which delimit the peoples' boundaries in space and time, and by reconstructing the cultures within those boundaries. Then they should classify the resultant site-units into series, that is, lines of development. Finally, they should return to their chronological charts and trace the development of the series from one people and culture to another, thereby determining their ancestries (Rouse 1986: 159–61).

Since World War II, I have been constructing detailed charts for the Caribbean area, modeled after those for Mexico, Peru, and other parts of the world (for example, Lumbreras 1974, fig. 11*a–e*). I revise the charts as new evidence comes in and use them to delimit peoples and cultures and to delineate their ancestries. The latest version of my West Indian chart is summarized in figure 8. The areas across the top are named after the passages between islands, because the archeological remains on either side of each passage resemble each other more than they do the remains elsewhere on the same islands (Rouse 1982a, fig. 2). This distribution reflects the canoeing expertise of the Tainos, who interacted more closely across the waterways than overland, contrary to the practice of the present inhabitants of the islands.

The vertical dimension of the chart shows the passage of time, from bottom to top. The temporal positions of the peoples and cultures were determined by studying the stratigraphy of the remains and arranging the resultant stratigraphic units in the order of the changes from one unit to

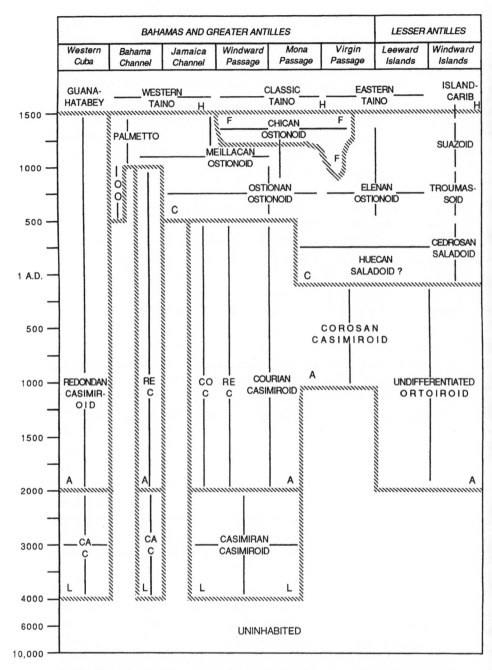

Fig. 8. Chronology of the series and subseries of cultures in the West Indies. Ages:
A, Archaic; C, Ceramic; F, Formative; H, Historic; L, Lithic. The Bahama Channel
area includes the Bahama Islands, the Turks and Caicos islands, and central Cuba; the
Jamaica Channel area, Jamaica and southwestern Haiti; the Windward Passage area,
eastern Cuba and the adjacent parts of Haiti; the Mona Passage area, the Dominican
Republic and western Puerto Rico; and the Virgin Passage area, eastern Puerto Rico and
the Virgin Islands.

the next. The calendric dates along the side of the chart were obtained through radiometric analysis (Rouse 1972: 122–29, 131–36). The striped lines within the body of the chart indicate the boundaries of successive ages, each defined by the appearance of new cultural traits. The Lithic age is marked by stone chipping and food gathering, the Archaic age by the addition of stone grinding, the Ceramic age by the arrival of pottery and agriculture, and the Formative age by the first public monuments, like those of the Classic Tainos. A parallel social development from bands in the Lithic and Archaic ages through villages in the Ceramic age to chiefdoms in the Formative age is also inferred from the remains.

The historical part of figure 8 shows the three cultural variants discussed in chapter 1 and mapped in figure 3: the Classic Tainos, who centered in Hispaniola and Puerto Rico; the Western Tainos, who lived in Jamaica, much of Cuba, and most of the Bahamas; and the Eastern Tainos, who occupied almost all of the Virgin and Leeward islands. The immediate neighbors of the Tainos are also included: the Guanahatabeys in western Cuba and the Island-Caribs in the southern part of the Lesser Antilles. The name of each ethnic unit is placed in the center of its distribution, where its culture was most typical. The lines extending horizontally from each name show the maximum geographical distributions of the unit, and the line extending vertically, its maximum temporal distributions.

The prehistoric peoples and cultures of the West Indies are depicted beneath the historic ones. In tracing the ancestors of the Tainos back through these peoples and cultures, Caribbean archeologists rely primarily on their pottery, for it makes up the bulk of their remains. They group all of the pottery found within each people's spatial and temporal limits into a unit called a ceramic style, complex, or phase and flesh out this skeleton by reconstructing the rest of the people's culture. Then they classify the peoples and cultures by comparing their ceramic styles and associated traits and grouping together peoples that resemble each other most closely in their styles and in other diagnostic traits.

Recently, they have begun to make the classification hierarchical in order to express the degree of difference between individual cultures and to facilitate comparison with languages and biologies, which are also organized hierarchically (Rouse 1986: 126–51; Oliver 1989: 319–22). The ceramic styles and the peoples and cultures that they define are grouped into series, whose names end in -oid, and divided into subseries, whose names end in -an. (This taxonomy was introduced into Caribbean archeology by Gary S. Vescelius in 1980.)

All the Historic-age Tainos made pottery belonging to a single Ostionoid series of local styles. The ancestry of the Classic Tainos can be traced back into prehistory through a Chican Ostionoid subseries, the ancestry of the Western Tainos through a Meillacan Ostionoid subseries, and the ancestry of the Eastern Tainos through an Elenan Ostionoid subseries. The three ancestries converge in the Cedrosan Saladoid subseries of Puerto Rico and the Lesser Antilles. From there the trail leads back to similar deposits on the Guianan and Venezuelan coasts (fig. 9).

The progress of the ancestors of the Tainos as they moved along this trail can be seen in figures 9 and 8 by following the striped line that marks the start of the Ceramic age. The jogs in the line indicate successive frontiers, where first the Saladoid and then the Ostionoid peoples halted long enough to develop new subseries or series. The final jog marks the frontier where the Tainos confronted the Guanahatabeys in the time of Columbus. The frontiers are mapped and numbered in figure 10.

If we knew only pottery, we could not be sure whether the Saladoid peoples actually entered the West Indies or merely passed their ceramics on to its Archaic-age inhabitants. There is good evidence, however, that Cedrosan Saladoid pottery was accompanied into the West Indies by the first sedentary villages, by greater dependence on riverine resources than in the preceding Ortoiroid cultures, and by the introduction of agriculture and the worship of zemis. The practice of dancing and playing ball on unstructured grounds may also have been introduced at this time.

Less progress has been made in tracing the Tainos' cultural ancestry further back, from the coast to the interior of South America, because chronological research has lagged there. At present we can only move from the Cedrosan Saladoid subseries on the coast, through Frontier 1 in figure 10, to the Ronquinan Saladoid subseries in the lower and middle Orinoco areas. According to current knowledge, the Ronquinan Saladoid subseries extended from the Orinoco Delta to the head of navigation on the Orinoco River, just above its juncture with the Río Apure.

The precursors of the Ronquinan Saladoid subseries could have come either from Amazonia via the Río Negro and the Casiquiare Canal or from western South America via the Ríos Meta or Apure. Donald W. Lathrap (1970) advocates the former route, whereas Betty J. Meggers and Clifford Evans (1983, fig. 7.11) favor the latter. Archeologists should eventually be able to decide between the two by searching for a previous ceramic horizon along the upper Orinoco, Meta, or Apure river and by seeking a frontier at the end of that horizon, behind which the original Ronquinan Saladoid pottery could have developed prior to its spread downstream to the Orinoco Delta.

A recent discovery by Anna C. Roosevelt (1989: 82; personal communication) favors the Amazonian route. She has obtained the earliest

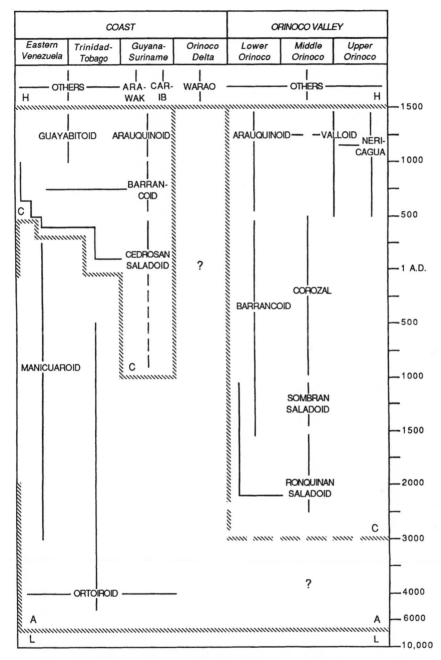

Fig. 9. Chronology of the series and subseries of cultures in northeastern South America. Ages: *A*, Archaic; C, Ceramic; *H*, Historic; *L*, Lithic.

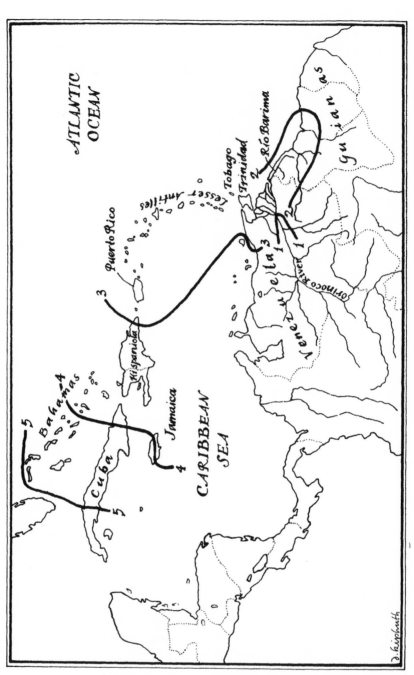

Fig. 10. Advance of the Ceramic/Archaic-age frontier through the Caribbean. Frontier 1 was in existence from 2000 to 1000 B.C.; Frontier 2, from 1000 to 200 B.C.; Frontier 3, from 200 B.C. to 600 A.D.; Frontier 4, from 600 to 1000 A.D.; and Frontier 5, from 1000 to 1500 A.D. (Rouse 1986,

dates for pottery in the Americas—thirteen of them ranging from 5140 to 4250 B.C.—at the bottom of a deep shell mound at Tapariña, near Santarem, in the middle of the Amazon Basin. She notes, however, that this pottery does not closely resemble the Ronquinan Saladoid pottery on the Orinoco River; it is more like the earliest pottery obtained by Gerardo Reichel-Dolmatoff (1985: 175) at Monsú, in northern Colombia. Consequently, the possibility of a western origin cannot be ruled out.

The ancestry of a subseries or series cannot be adequately determined by pottery alone. The ancestors of the Ronquinan Saladoid peoples may have brought agriculture and other basic elements of their culture from the south and synthesized them with pottery from the west, forming a dual culture. If so, the Ronquinan Saladoid peoples' cultural ancestry could be traced back into Amazonia, for southern elements would be dominant in the duality. If no dominant elements could be distinguished, our taxonomic research would have to end in the middle of the Orinoco Valley.

At present, we can only trace the cultural ancestry of the Tainos back to the Ronquinan Saladoid peoples along the Orinoco River. They eventually broke through its delta to the Guianan and east Venezuelan coasts and there developed a Cedrosan Saladoid subseries. Members of the new subseries invaded the West Indies and conquered its Archaic-age inhabitants as far north as Puerto Rico, where they established a frontier with the Archaic-age peoples in the rest of the Greater Antilles. On and behind the new frontier, the Cedrosan Saladoid cultures evolved into an Ostionoid series. This culture spread throughout the rest of the West Indies, excepting only the far end of Cuba, where the previous Archaic-age cultures appear to have survived until historic times. The Ostionoid cultures developed through Elenan, Ostionan, Meillacan, and Chican subseries into the Taino culture encountered by Columbus.

Linguistic Ancestry

The Island-Carib language was originally assigned to the Cariban family, but linguists have found that it, like Taino, is a member of the Arawakan family. (See chapter 1 for the pertinent references.) The ancestries of both languages must be traced within the Arawakan family, along with the Arawak language itself, which was spoken on the mainland just south of where the Island-Carib language was spoken.

In studying the ancestry of the Taino language, linguists have been handicapped by the lack of a detailed vocabulary; the Tainos became extinct before one could be recorded. Many Taino terms are known, but they refer mostly to localities, artifacts, activities, and beliefs, all of which are considered unreliable for tracing ancestries because they could easily have been borrowed from neighboring languages. Linguists prefer to use basic vocabularies, that is, words expressing ideas that are common to all human beings and hence are not so susceptible to foreign influence, such as the names for parts of the human body and for kinds of geographical features (Hock 1986: 214–16). Unfortunately, the chroniclers tended to overlook words like these. By contrast, Father R. P. Raymond Breton (1892), a seventeenth-century French missionary, has left us a reasonably complete dictionary of the Island-Carib language, and an offshoot of that language still survives among the so-called Black-Caribs of Central America, whom the British moved there in the eighteenth century. The Arawak language, now called Lokono, is likewise available for study in the Guianas (Taylor 1951, 1977a). The scarcity of information about the Taino language, relative to knowledge of Island-Carib and Arawak, is the reason why I discuss the cultural ancestry of the Tainos first, then their linguistic ancestry, contrary to the practice of those archeologists who model their research after the linguists' conclusions.

Linguists who study the ancestries of contemporary and well-documented historic languages are able to work back, comparing each language with its predecessors, as I have done in linking the three variants on Taino culture with the archeologically defined cultures that preceded them. Limiting themselves to basic vocabularies in order to eliminate as many foreign influences as possible, they search for words that have the same meaning and are composed of sounds that have evolved one from another in a regular manner, for example, from *pater* in Latin to *father* in English, use such cognates to trace the languages back to the common ancestors, and corroborate their results by looking for parallel sound shifts along different lines of descent (Lehmann 1962: 63–106).

Continuing backward along the lines, they eventually arrive at a proto-language, from which all the subsequent languages evolved. They arrange the lines in a family tree, or phylogeny, which shows how the languages successively diverged from the proto-language, and check this tree against other kinds of linguistic evidence, such as grammar. The languages within the tree are collectively known as a family. Families are named by adding the suffix -*an* to the term for a member language.

The number of cognates shared by a pair of languages indicates how long ago the two diverged from their common ancestor; the smaller the number, the earlier the time of divergence. Linguists use the numbers as a basis for dividing each family tree into branches, corresponding to subseries in archeology. These branches, or subfamilies, are named the way language families are, by adding the suffix -*an* to the term for a member language (Hock 1986: 567–80).

When linguists extend their studies of ancestries further back into prehistory, as they do in the Caribbean area, they must add another step to the procedure: they have to reconstruct the prehistoric languages from the documented ones before putting them in the family tree. To do this, they project the changes in documented cognates backward in time and infer undocumented cognates from them, marking the undocumented ones with asterisks to indicate that they are conjectural. At each step in the procedure they establish a cluster of cognates that defines a prehistoric language, and name it by prefixing *proto-* to the term for a documented language in its line of descent.

Linguists caution that family trees containing prehistoric languages only approximate the truth. They are most reliable in dealing with speech-communities that became separated by strong geographical or social barriers, which prevented them from interacting. When studying speech-communities that remained in close contact, researchers' success depends on their ability to discriminate between the changes in cognates due to inheritance from a common ancestor and those due to mutual influence (Bloomfield 1933: 311–19).

Fortunately, the situation among the ancestors of the Tainos is favorable to the establishment of family trees. The ancestral speakers expanded linearly, first along the major rivers of northeastern South America and then along the chain of islands that constitutes the West Indies. As a result, each successive speech-community became more and more isolated from those that preceded it, with less and less opportunity for strong interaction with them.

Linguists contrast the family-tree model, which depicts ancestries, with a wave model, which applies to the spread of loan words (Lehmann 1962: 137–42). The two models are sometimes assumed to be alternatives. In my opinion, they should instead be considered complementary. Like the Amazonian and Circum-Caribbean models in archeology, each should be used only for the purpose for which it is best suited, to study either the inheritance or the diffusion of linguistic traits.

The position of the Taino language within the Arawakan family was originally worked out by G. Kingsley Noble (1965: 108). He limited himself largely to basic vocabulary. Finding that the Taino language shared few cognates with its nearest neighbors, Island-Carib and Arawak, he concluded that its line of development had branched off the trunk of the family tree earlier than had the lines leading to Island-Carib and Arawak. He assigned the Taino branch to the original, Proto-Arawakan subfamily and the Island-Carib and Arawak branches to a later Maipuran subfamily.

Other linguists have criticized Noble for assuming that the Tainos lacked all the Island-Carib and Arawak cognates not recorded by the conquistadors, when in fact the conquistadors may have overlooked some of them. Furthermore, Douglas Taylor (1977b: 60) has discovered additional cognates in the Black-Carib and Arawak languages that lead back to the common ancestor they share with Taino, and José J. Arrom (personal communication) has called attention to additional Taino cognates incorporated into medieval and modern Spanish that also lead back to the common ancestor. These discoveries indicate a closer relation among Taino, Island-Carib, and Arawak than Noble had thought. Linguists now believe that the Taino, Island-Carib, and Arawak languages diverged from the main line of Arawakan development at the same late date and that all three belong in the Maipuran subfamily (Rouse 1986: 120–23; Oliver 1989: 105).

The family tree in figure 11 incorporates these changes. It indicates that the Proto-Arawakan language arose in the middle of the Amazon Basin. Proto-Arawakan speakers moved up the Río Negro, passed through the Casiquiare Canal, and descended the Orinoco River. Along the way, they produced a new, Proto-Maipuran language, thereby giving rise to the Maipuran subfamily.

Within the Orinoco Valley the Proto-Maipuran language evolved into Proto-Northern. Its speakers expanded into the Guianas and the West Indies. The Proto-Northerners who settled in the Guianas developed the Arawak language, also known as Lokono. Those who colonized the Lesser Antilles developed the Igneri language, which later became Island-Carib. Some Proto-Northerners continued into the Greater Antilles. In that remote and isolated locale, they gave rise to the Taino language (fig. 12). They presumably pushed the previous speech-communities of the Greater Antilles back into western Cuba, where they survived as the Guanahatabeys of Columbus's time. They also colonized the Bahamian Archipelago, which, to judge by the absence of place names in another language, had previously been uninhabited.

The dates in figure 11 have been obtained by glottochronological research, that is, by estimating the amount of time it would have taken for each pair of languages to diverge from their common ancestor (Rouse 1986: 121). This research indicates that the Proto-Northern language developed circa 1000 B.C. and the Arawak/Lokono, Igneri/Island-Carib, and Taino languages around the time of Christ. The first conclusion agrees with the archeologists' radiocarbon dates for the Ronquinan Saladoid peoples' movement from the Orinoco Valley to the coast, and the second with their

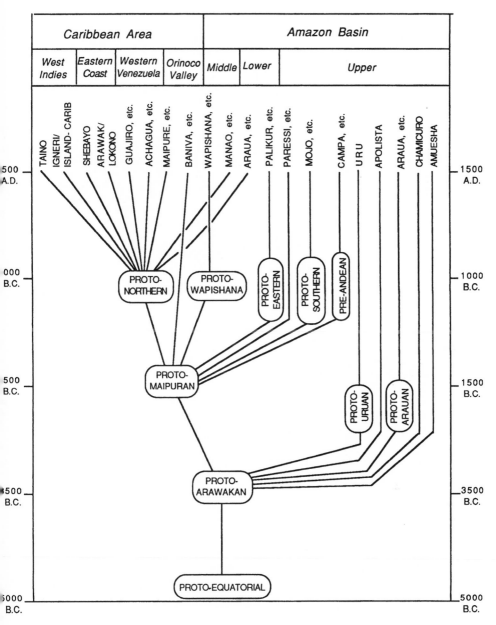

Fig. 11. Family tree of the Arawakan languages (after Rouse 1986, fig. 22).

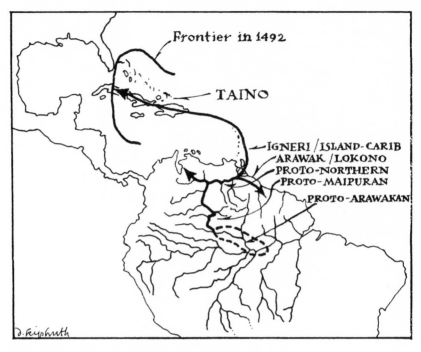

Fig. 12. Advance of the Arawakan-speech-communities from Amazonia into the West Indies (after Rouse 1989b, fig. 6).

dates for the Cedrosan Saladoid invasion of the West Indies. Linguistic research, therefore, has independently confirmed the archeologists' conclusions about the migration of the Tainos' ancestors into the West Indies.

Biological Ancestry

Stanley M. Garn (1965: 12–22), a physical anthropologist interested in problems of taxonomy, makes a distinction between local races, which are the biological equivalent of peoples and speech-communities, and geographical races, which correspond to series of peoples and families of speech-communities. Caribbean physical anthropologists have implicitly used his distinction as follows.

1. In comparing the skeletons associated with Saladoid and Ostionoid pottery at the Maisabel site in Puerto Rico, Linda C. Budinoff (1991) has found them similar enough to be assignable to a single local race. She notes that this racial continuity is consistent with the

archeologists' hypothesis of local development from the Saladoid to the Ostionoid series of cultures.

2. Some skeletons excavated from Antillean graves have been identified as Indian, and others as Black African (Goodwin 1978: 491–92). In Garn's terminology, the former belong to the American geographical race and the latter to the African geographical race, whose members were brought in by Europeans to replace the Tainos as they became extinct.

Imbelloni's prewar classification divided the American geographical race into units corresponding to subseries of cultures and subfamilies of languages. These units may be called lineages. Marshall T. Newman (1951: 73–78) considered them "unproven" because Imbelloni did not fully exclude cultural criteria, failed to take local races into consideration, and was unable to proceed period by period because the time perspective was too short.

The assemblages of human skeletal material excavated and dated by archeologists since Imbelloni's time provide a means of testing his classification. I would suggest that they be grouped into local races, each occupying its own spatial and temporal niche, as in the case of a culture or a language. The local races could then be classified into lineages. The units of the Imbelloni classification that corresponded to the new lineages would be validated by this procedure; the remaining units would have to be changed.

Pending such taxonomic research, some idea of the validity of the Amazonid-Isthmid dichotomy, which is our concern here, may be gained by generating hypotheses from the results of the archeological and linguistic research and testing them against the skeletal record as follows.

1. Archeologists trace the cultural ancestry of the Guanahatabey Indians, who appear to have been Archaic-age survivors in western Cuba, back through the earlier Archaic-age peoples of Hispaniola and Cuba to those of Middle America. If they are right and if Imbelloni's classification is valid, the Guanahatabeys and their ancestors should belong to his Isthmid lineage (fig. 13). This hypothesis could be tested by comparing the Archaic-age skeletal assemblages from Hispaniola and Cuba with the corresponding Middle American assemblages and determining whether they resemble each other more than they do the Ceramic-age and Formative-age assemblages in the islands.

2. The Warao Indians of the Orinoco Delta are also a relict of the Archaic age. Unlike the Guanahatabeys, they retain their cultural, lin-

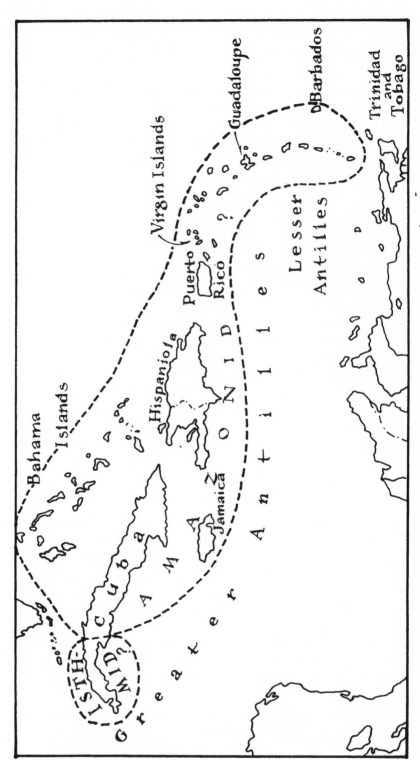

Fig. 13. Hypothesized distribution of racial lineages in the West Indies at the time of Columbus (after Rouse 1989b, fig. 17)

guistic, and biological heritages. Joseph H. Greenberg (1960: 793, 1987: 382) has classified their language in the macro-Chibchan family of Colombia and Central America. It is more likely to be derived from the lowland than the highland branch of this family (Granberry 1980: 55; Wilbert and Layrisse 1980: 5–6). The ancestral speakers may have moved eastward along the northern coast of South America, colonizing the islands of Aruba, Curaçao, and Bonaire on the way. They would have arrived on those islands prior to the Arawakan speakers who introduced the Ceramic age around 450–500 A.D. (Haviser 1987: 148). If, therefore, Imbelloni's Isthmid-Amazonid dichotomy is correct, the Warao Indians and the Archaic-age inhabitants of Aruba, Curaçao, and Bonaire should belong to his Isthmid race, and the subsequent Ceramic-age peoples to his Amazonid race.

Jouke Tacoma (1991) and Aad H. Versteeg (1991) report that the Archaic-age and Ceramic-age assemblages excavated from cemeteries on Aruba and Curaçao do indeed differ cranially. The Archaic-age skulls are long, narrow, and high, and the Ceramic-age skulls broad and low. I would suggest that this comparison be extended to the Warao Indians and be expanded to include the study of other parts of the human body to determine whether the Isthmid-Amazonid dichotomy hypothesized for the West Indies is also applicable to northern South America.

In undertaking both (1) and (2) above, special attention might be paid to dental morphology, for teeth have a high survival rate (particularly among the Tainos and their ancestors, who preserved them as fetishes) and are complex enough to exhibit genetically significant differences. Dental morphology has been successfully used to trace biological ancestries in other parts of the world (see Turner 1976, 1983).

It would also be desirable to test the results of the proposed research on the Guanahatabeys' biological ancestry (1) against information about that ethnic group's linguistic ancestry and to compare the results of the research on the Waraos' biological ancestry (2) with conclusions about their cultural ancestry. Unfortunately, we know too little about either subject to be able to do so at the present time.

Conclusions

The late Herbert J. Spinden, curator of anthropology at the Brooklyn Museum, remarked in a lecture given at Yale University in the 1940s that the Tainos had traveled farther than Columbus to reach their rendezvous with him. He thought that they had come from the most remote head-waters of the Amazon River, in Bolivia and Peru, because the linguists of his time had traced the ancestry of their language to that area. Now we know better.

It was only natural for Spinden to assume that the Tainos were foreigners like Columbus because all of the ethnic groups that followed them had come from abroad—from South America in the case of the Island-Caribs and from Europe, Africa, or Asia in the case of the present population. But the Tainos themselves believed that they had arisen locally, and their belief seems reasonable, even though they expressed it mythologically.

Spinden's generation further assumed that the West Indies had been peopled too recently to allow time for local development. With the advent of radiocarbon dating, however, it has become evident that the settlement of the West Indies is to be measured in millennia rather than centuries. The longer time span has increased the likelihood that the Tainos developed their culture and their language, if not also their biology, within the archipelago.

The research summarized here shows that it was indeed the Tainos' ancestors who came from South America. The Tainos themselves originated within the territory in which Columbus found them and did not need to migrate to reach their rendezvous with him, as Spinden supposed. The four lines of research considered here—ethnohistorical in the first chapter and archeological, linguistic, and biological in this one—all support the new hypothesis. The ancestral cultures have been traced back as far as the Orinoco Valley, and the ancestral languages, to the center of the Amazon Basin. An Amazonian origin has also been hypothesized for the Tainos' biological ancestry, but further tests are needed.

It does not follow that the alternative model, which the Circum-Caribbeanists employed to trace the cultural ancestry of the Tainos, must be abandoned. Because that model refers to elements of culture rather than whole cultures, it continues to be useful in identifying the traits, clusters of traits, and traditions that the ancestors of the Tainos borrowed from the neighboring peoples with whom they came into contact. Such foreign trait-units are comparable to loan words in the study of languages and gene flow in the study of biologies.

Some foreign trait-units, such as urn burial, do seem to have diffused along the Circum-Caribbean route (Meggers and Evans 1983: 328). Others appear to have originated in the Caribbean parts of the route. For example, three-pointed zemis have been found only in the Malambo culture of northern Colombia (Veloz Maggiolo and Angulo Valdés 1981), in the Valencia culture of north-central Venezuela (Kidder 1944: 166, pl. XI-6,7), and in undetermined contexts on Curaçao and in northwestern Venezuela (Josselin de Jong 1924). Still other trait-units, like the tradition of decorating pottery with zoned, incised crosshatched designs, may have spread from Amazonia by way of the Guianas (Durand and Petitjean Roget 1991).

Two lessons can be drawn from the debate between the Amazonists and Circum-Caribbeanists about the cultural ancestry of the Tainos. The first is that archeologists need to distinguish more clearly between cultures and the traits of which they are composed. A culture is more than the sum of its parts. It is an overall system, open rather than closed because it is subject to outside influences, but a system nonetheless. Simply to trace the diffusion of a trait-unit from one culture to another is not sufficient; how and why it became integrated in the new culture must also be examined (Rouse 1972: 140–242).

The second lesson is that archeologists need to make a distinction between two kinds of trait-units, inherited and foreign. Inherited trait-units, like cognates in linguistics and diagnostic features in biology, are passed down from ancestors. Foreign trait-units, like loan words in linguistics and genes that flow from one race to another, are obtained from neighboring populations. Both kinds of trait-units must be taken into consideration in studying cultural ancestries.

In the following chapters I review the changes that took place as the peoples ancestral to the Tainos moved from South America into the West Indies, concentrating on the cultures and the foreign traits incorporated into them. The languages and loan words of the ancestral speech-communities and the the biologies and gene flows of the ancestral races are beyond the scope of this book.

The ancestral peoples themselves can play only a secondary role in studies of cultural ancestries. They cannot be the major players because they are defined by their cultures. Each people becomes a new one every time its culture changes, whether or not there is a corresponding change in its membership. Nevertheless, peoples must be taken into account because they are the agents of change in their cultures, just as speech-communities are the agents of change in languages, and races in biologies.

Every people is organized into a number of social groups or societies. The two kinds of units should not be confused. A people consists simply of the population of a culturally homogeneous period and area. Its societies are composed of members of that population who have joined together to carry out specific activities, such as the production of food or the practice of politics. It is the societies, rather than the people to whom they belong, that initiate changes in cultures, and hence they, too, must be taken into consideration.

Each society is organized in terms of social norms and uses cultural norms to achieve its goals. Its norms are collectively known as its subculture. They are primarily functional, because societies exist to perform particular activities. By contrast, the norms diagnostic of a people's culture are basically stylistic, because they reflect the times and places occupied by the people and their culture (Rouse 1989a: 384–86).

Since the 1960s, archeologists have been debating whether they ought to be studying peoples and the development of their cultures, or societies and their adaptation to the conditions under which they lived (see, for example, Binford 1973). It is here assumed that the two approaches are complementary. I concentrate on cultural development because, as my subtitle indicates, I am writing about the rise and decline of the Taino people. I would be remiss, however, if I did not also call attention to the research that is currently being done on societal adaptation in the West Indies (see, for example, Veloz Maggiolo and Vega 1982). To put this another way, my book is addressed to readers who are interested in the Tainos' cultural history. At the same time, it is intended to provide a frame of reference within which others may study the Tainos' cultural ecology.

Delineation of the Tainos' ancestries is but the first step in studying their cultural history. We must now examine the developments that took place among the ancestral peoples as they expanded into the West Indies, and seek to identify the traits that they borrowed from their neighbors. In addition, we need to consider the roles played by the peoples themselves in these processes—the extent to which foreign intruders replaced the native populations or were absorbed by them.

THE PEOPLING OF
THE WEST INDIES

The ancestors of the Tainos did not reach the West Indies until long after the first settlers had arrived. Why, then, discuss the peopling of the West Indies in a book on the rise of the Tainos? There are three reasons. We need to know how the original settlers modified the pristine environment in order to take into consideration the conditions faced by the ancestors of the Tainos when they arrived. We need to learn about their contrasting ways of life in order to understand how the ancestors were able to replace the previous population. Finally, because the ancestral peoples came to a temporary halt at a frontier in Puerto Rico and on the eastern tip of the Dominican Republic (fig. 10), we need to become acquainted with the peoples on the far side of the frontier in order to study the invaders' interaction with them. Did the two populations interchange traits, as in the case of the Columbian exchange?

The time before the arrival of the Tainos' ancestors is divided into two ages: Lithic, or Paleo-Indian, and Archaic, or Meso-Indian. The Lithic age began around 4000 B.C., and the Archaic around 2000 B.C. (fig. 8). Each is defined by the first appearance of a technological innovation: stone flaking in the Lithic age and the grinding of stone, bone, and/or shell artifacts in the Archaic age.

Because innovations normally survive into subsequent ages, the one that defines an earlier age cannot also be used to identify a later one. In Europe, for example, the presence of bronze artifacts in Iron-age deposits is not taken to mean that these deposits date from the Bronze age. One must always proceed in terms of the most recent innovation. Consequently, single artifacts cannot be assigned to ages; the method can only be applied to assemblages of artifacts deposited at the same time, and then only if the assemblages are large enough to contain the total range of innovations.

The artifacts produced by the innovation diagnostic of an age are used to define the local cultures of that age and to identify the peoples who possessed them. In Europe, for example, the cultures of the Middle Paleolithic age are defined, and their peoples are identified, by analyzing their flaked stone tools. The definitions and identifications are then checked and, when advisable, modified by studying the rest of the cultural and social information inferrable from the assemblages.

The criteria used to assign peoples and cultures to ages cannot also be used to place them in series and subseries, for even subseries often extend from age to age (fig. 8). It is necessary to employ criteria that span the ages, such as cultural traditions, which indicate lines of development.

My colleagues and I have systematically applied these procedures to the Ceramic and Formative ages, as the earlier discussion of the cultural ancestry of the Tainos illustrated, but we have been inconsistent in selecting criteria to define the Lithic and Archaic ages, to distinguish their cultures and identify their peoples, and to classify the cultures and the peoples into series and subseries. As a result, conflicting taxonomies for the two preceramic ages have been produced (compare Rouse 1960, Veloz Maggiolo and Ortega 1976, and Kozłowski 1974).

In this chapter I try to be more systematic. I assign all purely flaked-stone assemblages to the Lithic age and all assemblages with ground stone, bone, and/or shell artifacts to the Archaic age—disregarding utensils ground solely from use—and employ the traits of flaked-stone work to differentiate cultures within the Lithic age and the traits produced by grinding to define the cultures of the Archaic age. When assigning the cultures of an age and the peoples who possessed them to series and subseries, I turn to artifactual criteria that cut across the ages, and check my results against the information about other kinds of cultural and societal traits that have been inferred from the assemblages. My aim is to delineate cultural and social developments, first within the Lithic age and then within the Archaic age.

The units I have formulated through these procedures are diagrammed in figures 14 and 15. For the sake of simplicity, the Lithic and Archaic ages are lumped together here, and so are the Ceramic and Formative ages. The division between each pair of ages is demarcated by a heavy black line. The names of local cultures are enclosed within light lines. The series and, if possible, the subseries to which each local culture belongs are shown by the shadings in the area and period in which it occurred.

As the keys to the charts indicate, two series of peoples and cultures,

Casimiroid and Ortoiroid, can be distinguished within the West Indies prior to the arrival of the ancestors of the Tainos. The Casimiroid peoples were the first settlers, apparently moving from Middle America into Cuba and Hispaniola around 4000 B.C., while still in the Lithic age, and advancing into the Archaic age several millennia later. The Ortoiroid peoples are more poorly known. According to present evidence, they migrated from South America into the Lesser Antilles and Puerto Rico around 2000 B.C., bringing with them their own Archaic-age way of life.

The Casimiroid Peoples, 4000–400 B.C.

This series, also known as Barreroid or Mordanoid, has been found only on the two largest islands, Cuba and Hispaniola. It may be divided into three subseries: Casimiran, which occurred in both islands during the Lithic age; Courian, which succeeded it in Hispaniola during the Archaic age; and Redondan, which replaced it in Cuba.

CASIMIRAN SUBSERIES

Until recently, flaked-stone artifacts were known only as isolated finds, which could have dated from any of the ages (Hatt 1932: 1; Roumain 1943). The first assemblages of artifacts large enough to indicate the absence of both grinding and pottery and hence the presence of a Lithic age were obtained in the 1960s by José M. Cruxent, a Venezuelan expert (Cruxent and Rouse 1969). Working with local colleagues, he excavated at the sites of Casimira and Barrera-Mordán, in the southwestern part of the Dominican Republic.

These two sites appear to have been workshops, where artisans dug up pieces of flint or other fine-grained rock and made them into tools. The excavators were unable to find structures such as hearths nor to obtain appreciable amounts of food remains, but their absence does not necessarily mean that nobody lived there. Because all the sites are in the open and on the surface, any remains of habitation may have been destroyed. Some archeologists have dismissed the finds as workshops where peoples of later ages came periodically to make flaked-stone tools without leaving behind their diagnostic artifacts. We cannot, however, rule out the possibility that the sites were also exploited, and perhaps inhabited, by Lithic-age peoples.

In 1974, A. Gus Pantel, a North American archeologist based in Puerto Rico, encountered similar conditions in excavations at Cerrillo, just across the Mona Passage from the Dominican Republic. In 1975 he dug again at Barrera-Mordán, in the Dominican Republic, but was able to add only a

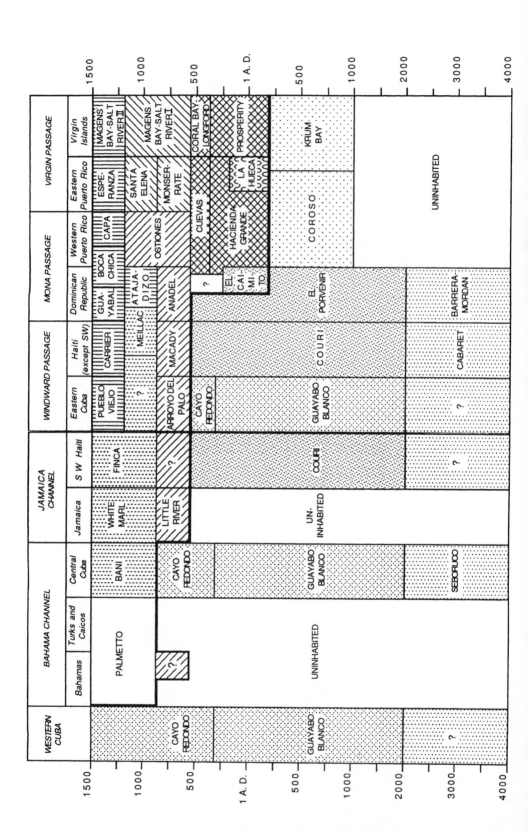

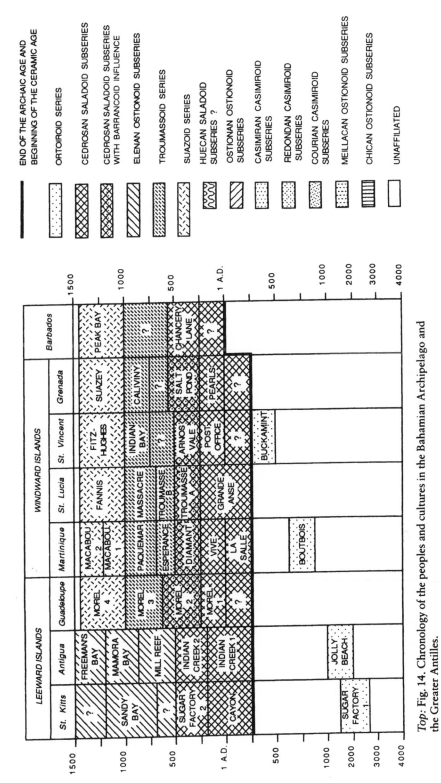

Legend (right side):

END OF THE ARCHAIC AGE AND BEGINNING OF THE CERAMIC AGE

- ORTOIROID SERIES
- CEDROSAN SALADOID SUBSERIES
- CEDROSAN SALADOID SUBSERIES WITH BARRANCOID INFLUENCE
- ELENAN OSTIONOID SUBSERIES
- TROUMASSOID SERIES
- SUAZOID SERIES
- HUECAN SALADOID SUBSERIES ?
- OSTIONAN OSTIONOID SUBSERIES
- CASIMIRAN CASIMIROID SUBSERIES
- REDONDAN CASIMIROID SUBSERIES
- COURIAN CASIMIROID SUBSERIES
- MEILLACAN OSTIONOID SUBSERIES
- CHICAN OSTIONOID SUBSERIES
- UNAFFILIATED

Top: Fig. 14. Chronology of the peoples and cultures in the Bahamian Archipelago and the Greater Antilles.

Bottom: Fig. 15. Chronology of the peoples and cultures in the Lesser Antilles (where known).

few shell fragments to the inventory of cultural traits previously obtained (Pantel 1988: 70–75). Clark Moore (1991) is currently surveying like deposits in central and northern Haiti.

Meanwhile, Janusz Kozłowski, a Polish archeologist, excavated several rock shelters along the Seboruco and Levisa rivers, in central Cuba, in 1972 and 1973, which did yield identifiable traces of habitation. In the basal parts of several deep, undisturbed deposits, Kozłowski (1974: 58–59) found not only assemblages of tools like those in the Hispaniolan and Puerto Rican workshop sites but also food remains, such as mussel shells and the bones of hutias, lizards, and snakes. He obtained evidence that this Lithic-age culture gradually developed during the period in which the rock shelters were occupied into a full-fledged Archaic-age culture, with the addition of ground-stone tools and a broader range of food remains.

Dominican archeologists have encountered a comparable stratigraphic sequence at the rock shelter of Honduras del Oeste and the open site of Tavera, in the center of their country (Veloz Maggiolo and Ortega 1976: 155–57). Even though the bottom of the Honduras del Oeste site did contain stone implements ground in processing vegetable foods, artifacts intentionally shaped by grinding were limited to the upper part of the deposit. Hence the lower layers of both sites can be assigned to the Lithic age, and the upper layers to the Archaic age.

All these finds clearly indicate that Cuba and Hispaniola, if not also Puerto Rico, were originally settled by small bands of people during the Lithic age. Kozłowski grouped the Cuban and Hispaniolan finds, which were the only ones known to him, into a regional unit that he named Barrera-Mordán. In my terminology, this translates into the Casimiran subseries.

Three local peoples and cultures can be distinguished within the Casimiran subseries: Seboruco in Cuba, Cabaret in Haiti, and Barrera-Mordán in the Dominican Republic. Recent evidence indicates that the Puerto Rican workshop site of Cerrillo was probably not exploited until the Archaic age.

Two radiocarbon dates have been reported for the Levisa rock shelter in Cuba (Kozłowski 1974, table 10). The earlier one, 4190 B.C., comes from a definitely identifiable Lithic-age deposit; the other, 1510 B.C., from an overlying Archaic-age deposit. Moore (1991) has obtained a date of 3630 B.C. for the Vignier III site in Haiti. This site, which is near the coast, contains a high-enough concentration of shells, relative to flintwork, to suggest that it, too, may have been a place of habitation. Moore (1991; personal communication) has acquired five additional dates ranging from 3320 to 320 B.C. for other Cabaret-culture deposits. Only the last of these dates is later than 2000 B.C., the end of the Lithic age. The Barrera-Mordán sites, across the border in the Dominican Republic, have yielded four dates, three on one sample, from 2610 to 2165 B.C. (Rouse, Allaire, and Boomert 1985, table 4). The overall patterning of the radiocarbon measurements indicates that the Casimiran subseries was in existence during the fourth and third millennia B.C. The two Archaic-age subseries would appear to have developed from it during the second and first millennia.

When Cruxent and I first attempted to establish a cultural chronology for the Hispaniolan preceramic sites in the 1960s, we utilized the artifact typology prevalent at the time in North American archeology (Cruxent and Rouse 1969). In reporting on the Cuban finds in the 1970s, Kozłowski employed the typology of European Paleolithic archeology. He noted that his was "the first study [in the Caribbean area] accomplished by a European prehistorian and thus two schools, a European and an American, meet face to face . . . , the appreciation of the results of this confrontation being left to the reader" (Kozłowski 1974: 5).

To judge from the readers' response, neither approach has been successful. Recently Pantel (1988) has attempted to rectify the situation by studying the flaked-stone tools in their own terms. Instead of classifying them on the basis of typologies developed in the study of cultures far removed from them in time and space, he has analyzed the West Indian flaked-stone collections in terms of the evidences of manufacture on the artifacts themselves, considering the steps in the artisans' procedure, which he calls dimensions, and the norms used in that procedure, which he calls modes. His procedure corresponds to the one I use to analyze West Indian pottery.

Pantel demonstrates that all three local cultures that I have assigned to the Casimiran subseries are characterized by a single tradition of flaked-stone working, in which the artisans collected pieces of flint or other fine-grained rock and struck them with hammerstones to knock off a succession of irregularly shaped flakes. They discarded the cores with which they started and used the flakes as tools with little or no secondary chipping (fig. 16b). Pantel found that the variations from culture to culture reflect differences in the available stone, as well as in local customs.

As in assemblages elsewhere in the world dating from the times when the flaking technique was first used, the Casimiran assemblages contain no other definitely identifiable types of artifacts. There must, however, have been a variety of tools made of perishable materials, which have not survived archeologically. These were gradually supplemented by survivable tools of stone, bone, and shell as the Casimiran cultures evolved into the subsequent Courian and Redondan cultures.

Before turning to the later developments, let us consider the origin of the Casimiran subseries. Previous attempts to answer this question have

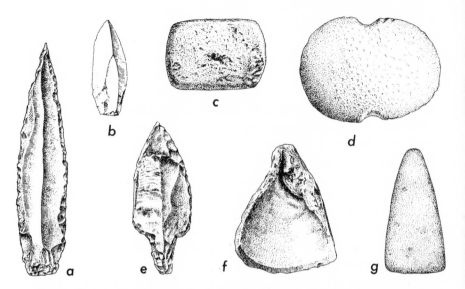

Fig. 16. Casimiroid artifacts: *a*, backed knife; *b*, simple flaked tool; *c*, rectangular hammer-grinder; *d*, double-bitted ax; *e*, stemmed spearhead; *f*, shell gouge; *g*, conical pestle. Figs. *a*, *c–e*, and *g* are from the Couri culture; *b*, from the Casimira culture; *f* and *g* from the Cayo Redondo culture (*a–f*, Yale Peabody Museum specimens; *g*, after Harrington 1921, fig. 101).

been outdated by Richard S. MacNeish's recent discovery of Casimiran-like flaked-stone tools in the middle of a sequence of local cultures extending back into the Lithic age in Belize, Central America (MacNeish and Nelken-Turner 1983, fig. 4). His tools date from about 7500 to 4000 B.C., that is, from immediately before the peopling of Cuba and Hispaniola. By the time that event took place, the inhabitants of Belize had already entered the Archaic age, but other mainland peoples peripheral to them may have remained in the Lithic age and carried the Casimiran tradition of stoneworking into the West Indies.

The most obvious route of migration would have been via the Yucatán Channel and the Cuban countercurrent. Alternatively, the ancestors of the Casimiran peoples could have proceeded along an intermittent chain of islets, known as the Mid-Caribbean Islands, that extends from Nicaragua to Jamaica. This chain was more continuous during the fourth millennium B.C. than it is today, because the sea level was lower at that time (Cruxent and Rouse 1969), but migrants from Central America who took that route would have had to travel against the trade winds and the North Equatorial current. More important, neither Lithic-age nor Archaic-age sites have been discovered on Jamaica at the end of the route despite extensive search for them. A search for Lithic-age sites is needed in Yucatán, too.

Since the above was written, a pertinent computer simulation has come to my attention. Richard T. Callaghan (1990) has compared via computer simulation the possible routes of Lithic-age migration, using winds, currents, and other conditions of the natural environment as variables. He finds that migration from South America would have been the easiest and travel from Central America via the Mid-Caribbean Islands the most difficult. The route from Yucatán to Cuba, which best fits the archeological evidence, falls between these two extremes.

MacNeish concludes that the preceramic peoples of Belize originally lived on upland savannas, where they were able to hunt large land mammals. Then they moved into the major river valleys to exploit the fish and plant foods available there. Finally, they began to migrate seasonally to the coast and nearby islands to supplement their terrestrial diet with seafood. The Casimirans who settled Cuba and Hispaniola would presumably have introduced not only the Belizean peoples' tradition of stone flaking but also their practice of moving up and down the river valleys to obtain land and sea foods. Kozłowski's Cuban finds document the terrestrial part of this practice, and Moore's Haitian finds, the maritime part.

The Casimirans' concentration in Cuba and Hispaniola may be explained by the wealth of resources available on those two islands. They have the largest river valleys and the richest terrestrial resources in the West Indies, including all the sloths except for a few in Puerto Rico and nearly 90 percent of the West Indian freshwater fish (Woods and Eisenberg 1989: 805; Burgess and Franz 1989: 265). They also have much the longest coastlines, with numerous indentations that favor the growth of marine foods (Watters and Rouse 1989: 131–33).

COURIAN SUBSERIES

As already noted, the Casimiroid peoples and cultures of the Archaic age are classified into two subseries: Redondan, which succeeded Casimiran in Cuba, and Courian, which succeeded it on Hispaniola. The distribution of the members of these two subseries is shown in figure 14 between the line marking the end of the Lithic age, whose peoples and cultures were just discussed, and the line marking the start of the Ceramic age.

The Courian subseries is better known. I distinguish two local cultures, El Porvenir in the Dominican Republic and Couri in Haiti. There are twenty-five radiocarbon dates for the former, ranging from 2030 B.C. to 145 A.D., and four for the latter, ranging from 2660 B.C. to 240 A.D.

(Rouse, Allaire, and Boomert 1985, table 4; Moore, personal communication). Both cultures would therefore appear to have been in existence during the second and first millennia B.C.

The El Porvenir culture is widely distributed in river valleys and along the coast (Veloz Maggiolo and Ortega 1976). The Couri culture is known only from two small clusters of sites, one on the northern coastal plain near Fort Liberté (Rainey 1941; Rouse 1941) and the other centering on Ile à Vache, off the southern coast (Moore 1982; Rouse 1982b). The Courian peoples must have continued the Casimiran use of both terrestrial and marine resources. Kozłowski (1980) has raised the possibility that they, too, moved seasonally from the interior to the coast to exploit all available wildlife. It may be inferred from the size of their deposits that they were still organized into bands, which were considerably smaller than the villages of the Tainos and their ancestors.

The Courians elaborated on the Casimiran tradition of stone flaking by preparing prism-shaped cores, from which they were able to strike larger, longer, and narrower flakes, here called blades. They rechipped the edges of these blades to form stemmed spearheads (fig. 16e), backed knives, so called because the edge not used for cutting is blunted (fig. 16a), and end scrapers, which are beveled on one end. These were probably hunting implements, used to kill and butcher sloths in the interior and manatees in the coastal estuaries. That sloths were still available at the time is attested by a radiocarbon date of 804 B.C. for a find in the Cordillera Central. Marcio Veloz Maggiolo and Elpidio Ortega (1976: 160–62) have suggested that the Courians used their new tools so effectively that the animals became extinct.

There was a great variety of ground-stone work. The most distinctive implements were double- and single-bitted axes (fig. 16d), well-formed rectangular hammer-grinders (fig. 16c), and conical pestles (fig. 16g). The grinders and pestles were used on regularly shaped metates (flat stones) and mortars to process food or red ocher, the ocher presumably being used to paint the body, as among the Tainos. The artisans also produced stone bowls, in which food may have been served. Well-finished balls, disks, and objects shaped like daggers, fans, hooks, and pegs may have been used in rituals. Finally, the Courians had surprisingly complex ornaments, including beads and pendants of both stone and shell (fig. 17b,d).

The combination of metates and manos (hand grinders) and mortars and pestles implies extensive consumption of wild vegetable foods. The pollen of guáyiga has been found at the site of El Porvenir, indicating that the cycad was among the plants ground with these implements. Remains of crocodiles, sea turtles, manatees, whales, and a variety of shellfish have also

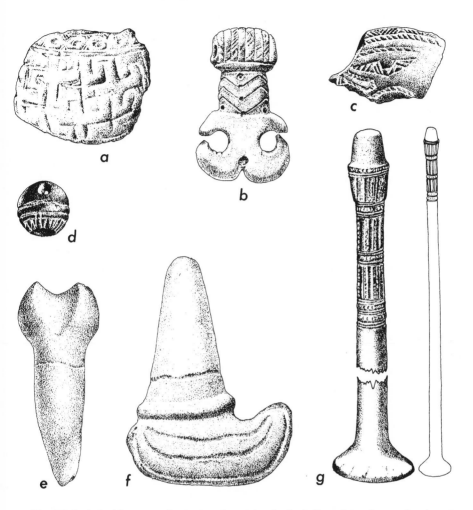

Fig. 17. Casimiroid art: *a, c,* fragments of stone bowls; *b,* shell pendant; *d,* stone bead; *e,* peg-shaped stone; *f,* hook-shaped stone; *g,* wooden baton. Figs. *a–f* are from the Couri culture; *g,* is probably from the Cayo Redondo culture (*a,* after Rouse 1982b, pl. 2e; *b–f,* drawings of Yale Peabody Museum specimens; *g,* after Harrington 1921, fig. 102).

been found there. These foods, combined with the meat obtained through hunting land mammals, should have given the Courians a rich and balanced diet (Veloz Maggiolo 1976: 257–58).

The ground-stone artifacts are larger, bolder, and more massive than the corresponding artifacts made by the Tainos' Saladoid ancestors. Many are ornamented. The butts of single-bitted axes and fan-shaped stones and the bottom of a shell pendant are decorated with ears, some of which resemble those in a fleur-de-lis (fig. 17b). Objects of these types, and also stone bowls, are occasionally engraved or incised with elaborate mazelike designs (fig. 17a,f) or with hatched, crosshatched, and dotted areas (fig. 17a–c). This unique form of art reached its climax in what is now Haiti during the first millennium B.C., to judge from the radiocarbon evidence.

REDONDAN SUBSERIES

My knowledge of archeological research in Cuba since Castro came into power is too poor for me to revise the taxonomy of the local cultures that I previously formulated for that island (see Rouse 1982a, fig. 1). In figure 14, I continue to distinguish only two cultures, Guayabo Blanco and Cayo Redondo, and to group them into a single Redondan subseries. (For an alternative, nonhierarchical classification, see Kozłowski 1974: 73–108.) The two cultures are defined primarily on the basis of research in western Cuba; other local cultures need to be formulated to take their place in the central and eastern parts of the island. My scheme is sequential and developmental. In the earlier culture, Guayabo Blanco, the use of grinding to intentionally shape tools is limited to shellwork; in Cayo Redondo, it is extended to stone artifacts.

The two cultures are assigned to a separate, Redondan subseries because they share the manufacture of shell gouges, each consisting of a triangular piece of the outer whorl of a conch shell that is ground to a bevel at the lower end (fig. 16f). To my knowledge, this type of artifact has not been found anywhere else in the West Indies except in a variant form on the southernmost islands, and there only in the latter part of the Ceramic age. The closest occurrence of the Cuban type of gouge is in the Archaic sites around Cape Canaveral in Florida; that type may have diffused from there (Rouse 1986: 183–84).

Redondan deposits have yielded twenty-four radiocarbon dates, ranging from 2050 B.C. to 1300 A.D. Eleven of the dates are in the Christian era. They reflect the fact that the ancestors of the Tainos were slow to reach Cuba and never did occupy the western end of the island (Rouse, Allaire, and Boomert 1985).

Redondan habitation sites extend from the interior to the coast and range from rock shelters to open-air sites (Harrington 1921). Shell mounds are common along the shore, in marshes, and on adjacent islets. Geometric designs were painted on the walls of caves (Núñez Jiménez 1975).

Corpses were interred in the mounds or in caves, occasionally accompanied by stone balls. The bodies were extended or flexed; in one case a number of crania were arranged in a circle around the rest of the bones. The crania from Redondan burials lack intentional deformation of the fore-head, which is characteristic of the Tainos and their ancestors (Harrington 1921, pl. 108). It is not known whether there are also genetic differences, as there should be if the Casimiroid peoples had come from Middle America.

Like the Courians, the Redondans retained the Casimiran flaked-stone tradition. They did less rechipping, however, and as a result failed to pro-duce such specialized types of tools. Blade tools declined in quality and quantity, presumably because the sloth was becoming extinct in Cuba, as in Hispaniola (Harrington 1921: 409–11).

The ground-stone work of the Redondans also resembles that of the Courians. It reached its peak in eastern Cuba, across the Windward Pas-sage from the Courian climax (compare Rouse 1982b and Hahn 1960). The types include stone rings, not found in Hispaniola. Pendants are less elaborate and decoration less common. The best example of engraving and punctation that I know of is on a wooden baton from the western end of Cuba (fig. 17g).

Two bowls and a pestle of wood from Redondan territory are in the same tradition as the ground-stone work (Veloz Maggiolo 1976: 275–76). They raise the possibility that the Casimiroid peoples developed the tradition in woodwork before they left the mainland and extended it to stonework after they arrived in the West Indies, thereby advancing from the Lithic to the Archaic age. This progression would explain the resemblance be-tween the Casimiroid ground-stone tools and those in Mesoamerica and the southwestern United States (Hahn 1960: 270–71).

CONCLUSIONS

There is reason to believe that the cultures of the original Casimiran subseries diverged to form the Courian subseries in Hispaniola and the Redondan subseries in Cuba. The presence in all three subseries of the Casi-miran tradition of stone flaking and the practice of exploiting interior as well as coastal resources indicates this, as does the location of the climaxes of the later series in the center of their joint distribution, on either side of the Windward Passage area. The presence of similar ground-stone work in the later subseries also attests to local development, as do a common style of art and the lack of this art in the adjacent mainland areas.

All of the Casimiroid peoples were land oriented, like their presumed ancestors in Central America. If they had been oriented toward the sea, like the Tainos and their ancestors, they would have had a more regular distribution than that shown in figure 8, which I organized by passage area in order to trace the Tainos' ancestry. If I had been intending to figure the ancestry of the Casimiroids, I would have organized its columns island by island in order to show the continuities in the distribution of the Lithic-age and Archaic-age peoples.

The Ortoiroid Peoples, 2000–400 B.C.

This series is named after a local culture in Trinidad, just beyond the southern limit of the West Indies; it has also been called Banwaroid after another site of the same culture (Rouse 1953b: 94–96, 106; Veloz Maggiolo 1976: 145). Related local cultures have been found on the adjacent mainland of South America, extending for an indefinite distance on either side of the Orinoco Delta (Rouse and Cruxent 1963: 58–59), and in the West Indies proper, as far north as the Virgin Islands and Puerto Rico.

The series is difficult to define and to divide into subseries because its sites contain small numbers of artifacts, all simple types with so few traces of manufacture that it is hard to find sufficient diagnostic traits. The differences from one culture to another appear to be due as much to the nature of the local resources as to variations in style. Consequently, we have had to base our classification primarily on negative information, that is, on the absence of traits diagnostic of other series.

The best information comes from the northern end of the distribution of the Ortoiroid peoples. Here we can distinguish two local cultures, Coroso in Puerto Rico and Krum Bay in the Virgin Islands, and group them into a Corosan subseries (Lundberg 1989, 1991; fig. 14). Jolly Beach on Antigua, Boutbois on Martinique, and Ortoire in Trinidad are the only other recognizable cultures, and none of them can be assigned to subseries. Single sites have also been located on Saba and St. Kitts, near Antigua, and on St. Vincent, north of Trinidad; in the absence of better data they can be used only to study the distribution of the overall series (fig. 15).

Before discussing the finds, let us consider their radiocarbon dates. The seven measurements obtained at Trinidad sites range from 5230 to 470 B.C. (Rouse, Allaire, and Boomert 1985). There are dates of 1775 B.C. for Antigua, 2150 B.C. for St. Kitts, and 1205 B.C. for Saba. St. Thomas in the Virgin Islands has yielded seven dates between 880 and 225 B.C., and Puerto Rico, seven dates between 1060 B.C. and 190 A.D. This sequence of dates indicates a movement from south to north during the second millennium B.C. By 1000 B.C. the Ortoiroid peoples had apparently reached Puerto Rico and established a frontier with the Casimiroid peoples in Hispaniola.

ORTOIRE PEOPLE

The sites of this culture are found along the beaches of Trinidad and on the edges of swamps extending some distance inland, but not in the river valleys or uplands. The refuse deposits are deep, corroborating the radiocarbon evidence that the Ortoiroid peoples had a long history of development in South America before they entered the West Indies (Rouse 1953b: 108).

The antiquity of the culture is further evidenced by the presence of only freshwater shells in the lower layers in several sites, dating from the time before Trinidad was separated from the mainland by the postglacial rise in sea level. The overlying deposits also contain seashells. Both kinds of shellfish were used only as food; the outpouring of fresh water from the Orinoco River precluded the growth of seashells large enough to be made into tools and ornaments.

Projectile points and barbs, both of bone, are the most distinctive artifacts (fig. 18b,c). The former are bipointed. Only one end of each barb is ground to a point; the other is tapered for attachment to a hardwood spear. Hunters in the upper part of the Orinoco Basin still make projectiles with similar barbs (fig. 18g). The points and barbs were suitable for use in Trinidad because it, too, has continental fauna, dating from the time when it was part of the mainland. Animal teeth were perforated for suspension as ornaments.

Irregularly shaped metates and manos, as well as conical pestles, attest to the consumption of wild vegetable foods. There are also simple stone choppers, hammerstones, pebbles notched for use as net sinkers, and mortars in which red ocher was ground into paint (fig. 18a). The stone flakes of the Casimiroid cultures are replaced by coarse, irregularly shaped chips (fig. 18d). Like the metates and manos, they were presumably selected because they required no modification before being used (Rouse 1960: 10–11; Veloz Maggiolo 1976: 45–47).

BOUTBOIS PEOPLE

This culture is known only from a pair of neighboring sites in the mountainous interior of Martinique. Because no other Ortoiroid finds occur in such a setting, we may presume that the two sites were interior outposts of still-undiscovered coastal settlements. It may be no accident that the local forests are unusually lush. Even though the deposits are small and shallow, they are covered with volcanic debris that has protected them from disturbance (Allaire and Mattioni 1983).

Edge grinders, that is, pebbles with grinding facets on their edges rather

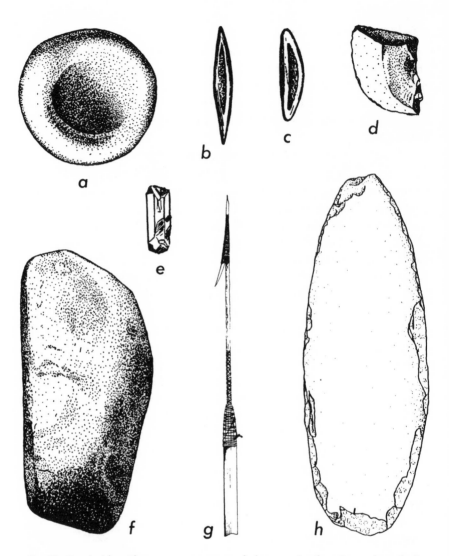

Fig. 18. Ortoiroid artifacts: *a*, stone mortar; *b*, bone projectile point; *c*, bone barb; *d*, stone chip; *e*, quartz crystal; *f*, edge grinder of stone; *g*, hafting of bone barb; *h*, stone celt. Figs. *a–e* and *g* are from the Ortoire culture; *f*, from the Coroso culture; *h*, from the Krum Bay culture (*a–f*, after Rouse 1960, figs. 5*a,g,h,c,f* and 7*b*; *g*, after Rouse and Cruxent 1963, fig. 7*g*; *h*, after Lundberg 1989, fig. 21).

than their sides (fig. 18f), are a dominant feature of the assemblages. By themselves, they do not allow the culture to be assigned to the Archaic age, for their facets are the result of use rather than manufacture. That age, however, is indicated by a fragment of a ground-stone celt. There are also hammerstones, metates, and a number of stubby, irregularly shaped flakes struck off unprepared pebbles, the last too crude to be considered Casimiroid.

JOLLY BEACH PEOPLE

The twenty-four sites of this culture are situated along the coast of Antigua, mostly on its northern half, where conditions are more favorable for fishing and for gathering shellfish (Davis 1982). There is no evidence that the resources in the interior of the island were being exploited. All of the sites except one are shell heaps. The exception is a workshop like those in the Casimiroid cultures. It is on an islet offshore, where a good supply of flint exists. No traces of habitation have been found there.

The flinty tools obtained from the workshop and from the dwelling sites are in the Casimiroid tradition. They include broad, well-shaped flakes struck off pebbles, and narrow blades obtained from prepared cores. None have been rechipped into artifacts designed to serve specific functions. In this respect Jolly Beach flintworking resembles that of Cerrillo in Puerto Rico, discussed below.

The Jolly Beach culture clearly dates from the Archaic age. Its diagnostic tools are shell celts, formed by grinding the ends of the thick lips of conch shells. They are accompanied by a few ground-stone artifacts, including a celt, simple beads and pendants, and a conical pestle decorated with ears (Davis 1974, pl. 3). The pestle recalls types of stone artifacts in the Casimiroid series. Also found are the usual nondescript tools battered or ground through use, such as hammer-grinders, metates and manos, and artifacts crudely shaped through chipping, such as net sinkers (Davis 1982, fig. 3g,h).

COROSAN SUBSERIES

The authorities disagree on the boundary between Krum Bay and Coroso, the two cultures of this subseries. The Virgin Island archeologists draw the line through the sound that separates Vieques Island from Puerto Rico proper, thereby incorporating the Vieques remains into the Krum Bay culture of the Virgin Islands (Lundberg 1989: 165–69). Their Puerto Rican counterparts follow the modern political boundary, which runs through the passage between Vieques Island and the Virgins, thereby assigning the Vieques finds to the Coroso culture in their own country

(Rouse and Alegría 1990: 77–80). Here I follow the Virgin Islanders, for their classification better accords with all the evidence. Prehistoric peoples and cultures should not be delimited in terms of our political boundaries.

Both cultural groups lived on or near the shore, the Krum Bay people only in the open, the Coroso people in caves as well (Lundberg 1989: 165–71). The sites consist of clusters of small heaps of shells containing evidence that they moved from place to place to perform different activities. Their range of movement was small, however; even in Puerto Rico they apparently did not make seasonal trips up and down the rivers like the Casimiroid peoples in Cuba and Hispaniola. They remained near beaches and mangrove swamps, where seafood was readily available.

Corpses, with the bodies extended, were put directly in the refuse. So far as I am aware, the bones from the burials have not yet been studied by physical anthropologists (Rouse and Alegría 1990: 17).

Edge grinders are diagnostic of the subseries (fig. 18f). Both cultures also contain a few simple beads and pendants of stone, bone, or shell. In addition, the Krum Bay culture has chipped, and in some cases partially ground, stone celts. The Coroso culture lacks this type of artifact; most of its sites have yielded only pieces of stone, bone, and shell that show traces of use rather than manufacture, such as choppers, hammerstones or grinding stones, sharp-edged flakes of igneous rock, and shell picks and scrapers. These objects have little diagnostic value, for they are difficult to distinguish from natural objects. To be sure, flaked flint tools have been found at several Coroso sites, conical pestles at one and a stone bowl at another, but they may be the result of Casimiroid influence.

CONCLUSIONS

The Ortoiroid peoples were oriented toward the sea rather than the land. Their territory did not favor the exploitation of terrestrial resources; it was drained by short, narrow river valleys that offered too few natural resources to support seasonal movement like that of the Casimiroid peoples. Puerto Rico is the exception that proves the rule. The Coroso people would presumably have taken advantage of the abundant resources available deep in the interior of that island if they had not been constrained by a previous tradition of living on or near the coast.

All the Ortoiroid-settled islands, including Puerto Rico, have such short coastlines that they could have supported only small populations. The inhabitants must have had difficulty recovering from natural disasters like hurricanes and must have constantly been in danger of overexploiting the local resources. Consequently, David R. Watters (1980: 297) and

William F. Keegan (1985: 51–53) have hypothesized that the Ortoiroid settlements were transient and intermittent.

The Ortoiroid peoples did little flaking of flint except in Antigua and Puerto Rico. Their grinding differs from that of the Casimiroid peoples in three ways. First, the technique was used to make tools of bone, not just tools of stone and shell. Second, the artisans had no interest in overall shapes; they ground only as much of the surfaces of the artifacts as was needed to improve their utility. Finally, they had no interest in art. The eared pestle from Jolly Beach is another exception that proves the rule, as noted below.

The kinds of tools produced by grinding are irregularly distributed. Each culture has its own distinctive type: bone projectile points and barbs in the Ortoire culture, edge grinders of stone in Boutbois, shell celts in Jolly Beach, stone celts in Krum Bay, and edge grinders again in Krum Bay and Coroso. The edge grinders are widespread enough to be considered a diagnostic of the Ortoiroid series overall. So also are partially ground celts of either stone or shell; they occur in all the cultures of the West Indies proper except Coroso, although not in great numbers.

The Ortoire people's emphasis upon bone projectile points and barbs may reflect the hunting possibilities on Trinidad: the island is favored with a continental fauna containing many terrestrial mammals. The Ortoiroid peoples who expanded into the oceanic islands of the Lesser Antilles would have had less bone suitable for making projectile points and barbs and less need for them because of the absence of large game.

The irregular distribution of types of flint, ground-stone, and shell tools is more difficult to explain. It, too, may reflect differences in the availability of materials from island to island; for example, Trinidad lacks fine-grained stone and large conch shells from which implements could have been ground. The tendency for frontier cultures to be simpler than central cultures may also have been a factor in Puerto Rico.

The Ortoiroid-Casimiroid Frontier, 1000–400 B.C.

The Ortoiroids of Puerto Rico and the Casimiroids of Hispaniola faced each other across the Mona Passage, so they must have interacted. Too little is known about the chronology of the local Archaic-age peoples and cultures to determine the extent of trade and diffusion across the passage, but I can propose several hypotheses.

The direction of diffusion seems to have been entirely from northwest to southeast. Evidence of a possible spread of the Casimiroid tradition of flintworking from Hispaniola to Puerto Rico has been found at the work-shop site of Cerrillo, on the western end of Puerto Rico. It has yielded a radiocarbon date of 624 A.D., which places it in the Ceramic age, but the exploitation of its flint nodules may have begun during the Archaic age (Lundberg 1989: 171).

From Puerto Rico the Casimiroid tradition of flintworking may have spread to Antigua. Dave D. Davis comments on its occurrence there: "It is my feeling . . . that the [Barrera-Mordán] complex, or a culture derived from it is the forebear of the earliest occupation of Antigua. . . . The pri-mary cultural affinities of the occupants of Jolly Beach appear to be with the areas north and west, although some period of contact with the late Manicuaroid peoples [east of the Ortoiroids on the coast of Venezuela] seems likely" (1974: 69–70).

In my terminology, Jolly Beach can be considered a dual culture, com-parable to that of the Island-Caribs. One side of the duality is obviously Casimiroid, but the other side cannot be Manicuaroid, for the pertinent part of the latter series is more recent than Jolly Beach (Rouse and Cruxent 1963, fig. 6). The other side of the duality is more likely to have been a local, Ortoiroid development. Its shell celts are, in my opinion, a variant on the stone celts of the Boutbois and Krum Bay cultures, rather than an offshoot of the Manicuaroid series, as Davis thought.

Among the artifacts on the Casimiroid side of the duality is a conical pestle with ears that are reminiscent of those on the axes and fan-shaped stones of the Casimiroid cultures. This specimen raises an interesting pos-sibility. St. Vincent and several other Windward islands have yielded eared stone artifacts, which cannot be assigned to ages and cultures because none has been found in excavated assemblages. The context of the Jolly Beach pestle suggests that these eared objects may also date from the Archaic age and may be the result of Casimiroid influence across the Puerto Rican frontier.

The Cayo Cofresí site, on the southern coast of Puerto Rico, offers another possible example of Casimiroid contact with the Ortoiroid series. Emily R. Lundberg (1989, 1991) regards that find as representing a sepa-rate culture within the Corosan series because it contains flint blades and conical pestles. The rest of its artifacts are typically Ortoiroid, so I view it instead as a frontier variant on the Coroso culture, resulting from Casi-miroid influence. Indeed, some of the artifacts may be trade objects from Hispaniola.

The Ortoire culture of Trinidad also contains conical stone pestles. Since the fine-grained stone of which they are made is not available locally, they are likely to have been imported from farther north. In this connection, it is worth noting that many of the Ortoiroid peoples possessed quartz crystals (fig. 18*e*). They are presently used as charms by the Warao Indians in the Orinoco Delta. Lundberg (1991) suggests that they were traded from island to island.

Conclusions

In the previous chapter I traced the ancestries of the Tainos back from the Historic age into the Formative and Ceramic ages. Here I have moved forward from the beginning of prehistory, that is, from the Lithic to the Archaic age, in an attempt to reconstruct the peopling of the West Indies.

My generation of archeologists was trained to proceed solely in terms of artifacts and the cultures to which they belonged. Here I have also taken into consideration the peoples who possessed the cultures by examining the ways in which they made and used their artifacts, by trying to reconstruct the nonartifactual aspects of their cultures, and by paying attention to the societies into which they were organized and through which they adapted to their environments. In considering each people, I have given as much weight to the sites it occupied, that is, to the context in which its remains were found, as to the remains themselves. I began with the people's settlement pattern, moved on to its artifacts and subsistence, and concluded with the more abstract aspects of its culture. I discussed the Tainos' culture in the same way in chapter 1 in order to facilitate comparison.

The West Indies were evidently peopled in two directions, first by Casimiroid Indians from Middle America and then by Ortoiroid Indians from South America. The former migration began about 4000 B.C. and the latter about 2000 B.C. It appears likely to me that the Casimiroids originated among peoples in Yucatán peripheral to the Lithic- to Archaic-age series recently discovered by MacNeish in Belize. They took advantage of the Cuban countercurrent to move into Cuba and Hispaniola but did not colonize any of the other islands. Apparently, they preferred the two largest islands because they were richer in terrestrial and marine resources and were better suited to the practice of seasonal movement from the interior to the coast, which they appear to have brought from Middle America.

Present evidence indicates that the Ortoiroids were coastal peoples. They arose in Trinidad while it was still attached to the mainland, advanced through the Lesser Antilles and the Virgin Islands, and halted in Puerto Rico. There they established a frontier with the Casimiroid peoples, which lasted from circa 1000 to 400 B.C., that is, until the arrival of the Saladoid forebears of the Tainos.

The Saladoids who reached the West Indies were probably not moving into unknown territory when they crossed the water gap between Trinidad-Tobago and the Lesser Antilles. They must have learned about the existence of islands beyond the gap from Ortoiroid Indians, who had been trading across it for crystals and other rare commodities, such as conical pestles. The land north of the gap would have been especially attractive to farmers like the Saladoids because its agricultural potentialities and other terrestrial resources had not been tapped by their predecessors. Some of the marine resources may have been depleted, but these would have been of less interest.

The newcomers must have had little difficulty occupying the islands. The previous population was so small and so widely dispersed as to be easily displaced or assimilated. When the Saladoids reached the frontier in Puerto Rico, however, they encountered very different conditions. The Casimiroid peoples who lived beyond the frontier had been exploiting the interior as well as the coastal habitats and had apparently caused the extinction of some attractive interior resources, such as the sloth. The Casimiroids were not sitting ducks like the Ortoiroids. They could retreat into the interior of Hispaniola and use it as a base from which to defend their territory.

Their larger population and more advanced culture must have enhanced their chances of success. Their surviving technology and weapons, for hunting if not for warfare, are superior to those of the Ortoiroid Indians, and they may also have been organized into more complex societies. It is not surprising that they were able to halt the advance of the Saladoid peoples at the Puerto Rican frontier and to fall back to other frontiers when subjected to even greater pressure by the Ostionoid descendants of the Saladoids, thereby continuing to retain a separate identity.

T H E   F I R S T

R E P E O P L I N G

We have seen that the West Indies were peopled from both the northwest and the southeast. During the Lithic age, Indians from Yucatán moved into Cuba, Hispaniola, and western Puerto Rico, where they developed the Casimiroid series of cultures. During the Archaic age, peoples of an Ortoiroid series migrated from the mouth of the Orinoco River through the Lesser Antilles and the Virgin Islands into Puerto Rico. The two groups met at the Mona Passage, between Puerto Rico and Hispaniola.

Saladoid Indians subsequently arrived from the interior of South America, introducing the Ceramic age. They descended the Orinoco Valley to the coast and proceeded out into the West Indies as far as Puerto Rico, where they halted at the Ortoiroid-Casimiroid frontier. The newcomers originally possessed cultures belonging to the Ronquinan Saladoid subseries. Upon reaching the coast, they developed a new subseries, called Cedrosan Saladoid, which they carried into the Antilles. There it eventually gave rise to the culture of the Taino Indians. They also appear to have introduced the linguistic and biological heritages of the Tainos.

The Cedrosan Saladoids spread too widely to interact closely with one another, and so they grew apart, diverging into separate subseries and series. By the middle of the Ceramic age they had diversified into four regional lines of development: (1) on the mainland, including the islands of Trinidad and Tobago, (2) in the Windward Islands, (3) in the Leeward and Virgin islands, and (4) in the rest of the Greater Antilles and the Bahamian Archipelago. Guadeloupe was transitional between Regions 2 and 3, and Puerto Rico between 3 and 4.

Although the later inhabitants of the four regions retained many of the traits they had inherited from their Saladoid ancestors, they also developed distinctive customs of their own, some in adaptation to features of the local environments and others in response to influences from neighboring peoples. Still other differences are idiosyncratic; they would not have arisen if the migrants had been able to interact more closely. The developments in the four regions may be summarized as follows.

1. *Mainland.* During the middle of the Ceramic age, the Cedrosan Saladoids who inhabited the high land surrounding the Orinoco Delta gave way to new peoples belonging to the Barrancoid series, who were in turn succeeded by peoples of the Arauquinoid and Guayabitoid series. The Barrancoids and Arauquinoids seem to have expanded from the lower Orinoco area into the northern part of the Guianas. The corresponding changes farther west were likely due to acculturation, resulting from interaction with the Barrancoids and Arauquinoids who had invaded the Guianas. Toward the close of the Ceramic age, other peoples intruded from the Orinoco Valley and western Venezuela; for example, Caribs from the interior interpenetrated the coastal population (fig. 9).

2. *Windward Islands.* The Cedrosan Saladoid inhabitants of the adjacent islands likewise evolved through several series of cultures, Troumassoid during the middle of the Ceramic age and Suazoid during its latter part (fig. 8). Again, the new series appear to be products of divergence and interaction with neighboring peoples, rather than population movement. The rise of Island-Carib culture illustrates the two processes. Whereas this rise was touched off by an invasion from the mainland, the newcomers only succeeded in modifying the local Igneri culture and language, not in replacing them.

3. *Leeward and Virgin islands.* The Cedrosan Saladoid peoples of Regions 3 and 4 jointly developed a new Ostionoid series of cultures, the local form of which is known as Elenan (fig. 8). Its earlier remains are simple, apparently reflecting a considerable degree of isolation from the neighboring regions. Late in the Ceramic age, the Elenan cultures of the Virgin Islands and the northern Leewards came under the influence of the Chican cultures in Hispaniola and Puerto Rico (Hatt 1924: 33; Hofman and Hoogland 1991). This conjunction of Ostionoid heritage and Chican influence has led Louis Allaire (1985a,b) to identify the protohistoric inhabitants of Region 3 as Eastern Tainos.

4. *Greater Antilles and the Bahamas.* The Cedrosan Saladoid peoples

who lived on the frontier between the Ceramic and Archaic ages in Puerto Rico developed a more conservative, Ostionian division of the Ostionoid series. They and their descendants resumed the Saladoid migration, advancing the frontier to the eastern tip of Cuba and then to its historic position in the western part of that island (fig. 10). With the passage of time, they diverged into two new subseries, Chican in their heartland and Meillacan on the frontier, and into a separate Palmetto people in the Bahamian Archipelago, which may be considered an offshoot of the Ostionoid series. The Chican peoples were ancestral to the Classic Tainos; and the Meillacan and Palmetto peoples, to the Western Tainos (fig. 8).

In this chapter I focus on the Saladoid and Ostionoid peoples, the forebears of the Tainos, and examine their movement through the West Indies.

Several problems of terminology should be clarified. The migrations of the Saladoid and Ostionoid peoples constitute a population movement, so called because the Saladoids replaced the previous Ortoiroid population, and the Ostionoids almost completely eliminated the Casimiroids. The two invading series caused almost as radical a change in the population of the West Indies as did the original peopling of the islands, hence my use of the term *repeopling* in the title of this chapter.

Population movement, or repeopling, should not be confused with colonization and immigration. In colonization an invading people occupies part of a new area but leaves the rest of it to the previous population. Immigration takes place when the invaders arrive in such small numbers that the local population eventually absorbs them. The Carib expansions into Regions 1 and 2 are cases in point. Caribs from the interior of the Guianas colonized parts of the land around the mouth of the Orinoco River (1), leaving the rest of it to the Arawaks. When they continued into the Windward Islands (2), they became immigrants rather than colonizers. They were apparently assimilated into the local Igneri population, though they succeeded in changing the name of that population to Island-Carib and in modifying its culture and language.

Population movement and colonization differ only in degree. In both cases individuals leave their home societies and organize new societies elsewhere. With population movement the invading people's societies take over an entire area, replacing the societies of the previous inhabitants. With colonization the previous people's societies survive alongside those of the invaders.

Immigration differs in kind. Immigrants join the societies already in existence within their new homeland. They may come as conquerors and impose their rule on the local societies, as the Mongols did in China, or they may play a subordinate role, as the immigrants to the United States have. In either case, they eventually lose their separate identity.

Population movement and colonization are territorial processes. They have been likened to waves, which flood beaches, obliterating shorelines and forming new ones. Immigrants, in contrast, penetrate territories. They are analogous to the passengers on a train, who move from one place to another without disturbing the boundaries of the places they pass through (Rouse 1986: 176–80). Students of population movement and colonization must proceed in terms of whole cultures and trace their distribution from one area to another, paying due attention to their frontiers with other cultures. Students of immigration, on the other hand, work with individual traits or clusters of traits, and trace their diffusion across the boundaries that separate one culture from another.

Immigration and its counterpart, emigration, are only one of several mechanisms whereby traits may diffuse across boundaries. Others include intermarriage, travel, and trade. Areas that are closely interconnected in these ways are known as interaction spheres.

Some who study the repeopling of the West Indies have confused population movement and colonization with immigration and other kinds of interaction. They have used the distribution of traits and trait-complexes to trace the repeopling, instead of studying the spread of whole cultures as I do. The research of the Circum-Caribbeanists is a good example; other examples are cited below.

Because the Saladoid and Ostionoid peoples are territorial units, they have to be traced in terms not only of their cultures but also of their geographical and temporal boundaries, especially the boundary between the Ceramic and Archaic ages (figs. 9, 8). Indeed, that line of demarcation is the only marker common to the entire repeopling process. Were we to ignore it, we would be studying the diffusion of individual cultural traits inherited by the Tainos rather than the movement of the Tainos' ancestors and their cultures.

The Saladoid Peoples, 2000 B.C.–600 A.D.

The movement of the Saladoid peoples can be traced in their successive subseries, from the Ronquinan to the Cedrosan to a newly discovered La Hueca people, whose affiliation is currently under debate. We shall consider each unit's geographical and temporal limits and then discuss its characteristics, not only in the center of its distribution but also on its frontiers.

RONQUINAN SALADOID SUBSERIES

This culturally defined population extended from the head of navigation in the Orinoco River, just above its juncture with the Río Apure, to the top of the delta. Its radiocarbon dates range from 2140 to 620 B.C. (Rouse, Allaire, and Boomert 1985, table 1). Notwithstanding problems with many of the dates, it cannot be doubted that the Ronquinan Saladoids lived in the Orinoco Valley during the second millennium B.C. (Roosevelt 1980: 193–96).

The upper limit of the subseries varies from place to place. If the latest hypothesis is correct (Rouse 1978), Ronquinan Saladoid people in the lower-middle Orinoco Valley, that is, in the center of the distribution of the series, developed a new, Barrancoid series around 1500 B.C. The peoples on the frontiers in the upper middle and the lower parts of the valley remained Ronquinan Saladoid until 1000 B.C. or so, after which the coastal part of the series evolved into the Cedrosan Saladoid series.

The principal sites of the subseries are on natural levees along the banks of the Orinoco River. These levees were islands during the rainy season, which corresponds to the North American summer, but became part of the alluvial plain when the river fell thirty to forty feet during the dry season. The levees were covered with woodlands, which the Ronquinan Saladoids are believed to have slashed and burned to practice agriculture. Like the Historic-age Indians, they probably also raised crops on the treeless land uncovered when the river fell during the dry season, thereby taking advantage of soil whose fertility was renewed by an annual deposit of silt, as in the Nile Valley.

To judge from the extent of their refuse, they lived in villages comparable to those of the Tainos. The largest and most permanent settlements were on the levees; others were situated on high ground back from the river (Roosevelt 1980, maps 4, 5). The houses were built of perishable materials; their configuration is unknown.

Ronquinan pottery consisted typically of bell-shaped bowls with an unusual variety of decoration: geometric designs painted red or white on red; sequences of predominantly short, curvilinearly incised lines; wedge-shaped lugs; and modeled-incised figures on lugs, strap handles, and vessel walls (fig. 19). The painted designs include simple crosshatching, which gives the impression of having been copied from zoned-incised crosshatching, which does not occur in the Orinoco Valley.

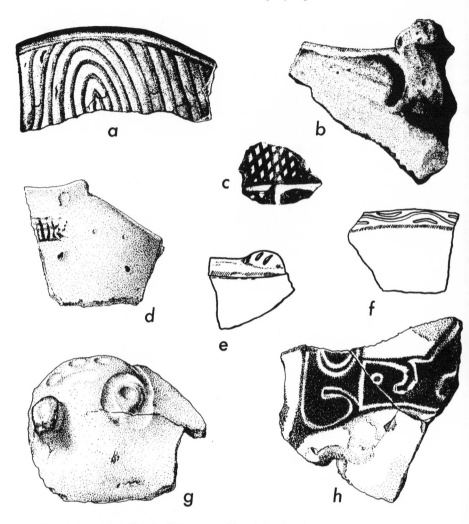

Fig. 19. Ronquinan Saladoid pottery: *a, f,* bowl sherd with curvilinear incision; *b,* strap handle with modeled lug; *c, d,* bowl sherd with red-painted crosshatching; *e,* wedge-shaped lug with incision; *g,* modeled-incised and punctated body of a vessel; *h,* bowl sherd with white-on-red painting. Figs. *a–f* are from the Saladero culture; *g* and *h,* from the La Gruta culture (*a–c, e, f,* after Rouse and Cruxent 1963, fig. 29*a,i,d,g,c; d, g, h,* after Rouse 1986, fig. 25*c,a,b*).

The assemblages also contain clay griddles (fig. 20), whose resemblance to the ones used by the Tainos to bake cassava bread implies the presence of agriculture. The griddles were not supported over the fire by stones, as among the Tainos, because the levees do not contain suitable stones. Instead, the Ronquinan Saladoids used baked clay cylinders, which are known today as topia. In the absence of stone, most tools and ornaments had to be made of perishable materials.

Through much, if not all, of the second millennium B.C., Ronquinan Saladoids faced the Ortoiroids across a frontier at the head of the Orinoco Delta (fig. 10). The Barrancoid peoples, who appear to have developed in the lower-middle part of the valley during this time, expanded downstream at the beginning of the first millennium B.C., pushing the contemporaneous Saladero people past the delta to the coast.

The Saladero people had been slower to change than their relatives upstream, as frontier peoples often are. Upon reaching the coast, they finally diverged from the ancestral subseries and formed a new, Cedrosan subseries of Saladoid cultures.

CEDROSAN SALADOID SUBSERIES

The remains of the new subseries have the broadest geographical distribution in the Caribbean area. They extend for six hundred miles along the northern coast of South America, from the Wonotobo Valley in Suriname to Margarita Island in eastern Venezuela, and for another thousand miles from Trinidad to Puerto Rico and the eastern tip of Hispaniola. Their radiocarbon measurements also have an unusually broad range, from 530 B.C. for Horizon I in Martinique to 655 A.D. for the El Mayal culture in the Carúpano area, on the eastern coast of Venezuela (Rouse, Allaire, and Boomert 1985, table 4; Rouse 1989a, tables 1, 2). Varying greatly from place to place as they do, the dates have given rise to much controversy. A pattern is beginning to emerge, however, and it is supported by the sequence of dates for correlated volcanic eruptions on Martinique (Allaire 1989).

When the migrants arrived on the coast, they replaced Ortoiroid peoples on both sides of the Orinoco Delta, including the island of Trinidad, which lies to the northwest. The Archaic-age inhabitants who lived within the delta do not seem to have been affected; they continued to resist the advent of the Ceramic age until the arrival of Europeans.

The migrants could have traveled by way of the Boca Grande, which flows along the east side of the delta, separating it from the Venezuelan part of the Guianas. Alternatively, they could have descended the Caño Mánamo, which flows along the west side of the delta, in which case they would have settled around the Gulf of Paria, a virtually landlocked body of water cupped by Trinidad and the Peninsula of Paria.

Archeologists have long assumed that the migration proceeded down the west side of the delta; they overlooked the eastern route because no Cedrosan remains had been found there. The discovery of Cedrosan assemblages beneath Barrancoid refuse at the Wonotobo Falls site in Suriname (Boomert

1983) has forced them to reconsider. Dutch excavators have obtained a radiocarbon date of 50 A.D. for the underlying assemblages, which is within the range of the dates for Cedros, the type site for the Cedrosan subseries in Trinidad on the other side of the delta and which precedes the dates for all the other Cedrosan sites on that side of the delta (Rouse, Allaire, and Boomert 1985, table 2).

According to Aad Boomert (personal communication), Dutch geologists have obtained evidence that the Caño Mánamo may have been closed at the time of the Saladoid movement from the Orinoco Valley to the coast. If so, the migrants could only have gone down the Boca Grande. They would have been drawn into the network of rivers extending eastward to the Northwest District of Guayana, would there have developed their new, Cedrosan subseries, and would subsequently have carried it across the mouth of the delta to Trinidad and the Gulf of Paria.

Thanks to the research of Venezuelan and Trinidadian archeologists, much more is known about the latter part of this presumed movement than its initial part. Wonotobo Falls is still the only well-identified find on the eastern side of the delta. Further fieldwork is urgently needed in Suriname, Guyana, and Venezuelan Guiana to test the hypothesis that the Cedrosan subseries developed there before spreading westward. The eastern route would have been more attractive to migrants from the Orinoco Valley because it led into the same kind of terrain to which they had been accustomed inland: flood plains drained by large rivers that were bordered with natural levees. As in the Orinoco Valley, they could easily have farmed by making clearings in the woodlands on the levees. Later Indians in the Guianas supplemented the levees by building ridged fields (Boomert 1978), which had the same advantages as the Tainos' mounds. There is no evidence that the Cedrosans made either kind of structure.

Once established in the interior of the Guianas, the Cedrosans could easily have expanded across the seasonally flooded lowlands to the sandy ridges that extend along the coast. On these beach ridges, which would have offered an environment similar to that on the river levees, the Cedrosans could have developed the skills they needed to exploit the coastal resources and to follow the South Equatorial Current to Trinidad. Alternatively, they may have learned these skills from their Ortoiroid predecessors.

The southern half of Trinidad must have seemed attractive to them. It includes beaches, sandy ridges, and low hills, interspersed among poorly drained areas like those in the Guianas. Conditions are different in northern Trinidad and on the Peninsula of Paria, just to its west, where mountains come directly down to the sea and are drained by small rivers that have few, if any, flood plains and natural levees. It is reasonable to assume that

Cedrosans from southern Trinidad bypassed this area, proceeding directly to the satellite island of Tobago farther north and continuing from there into the West Indies.

As they moved northward through the Lesser Antilles and the Virgin Islands to Puerto Rico and eventually established a foothold on the eastern tip of Hispaniola, they were faced with an even greater variety of local conditions. Their earliest remains have been found only on the higher islands, such as Grenada, Martinique, Guadeloupe, and Antigua in the Lesser Antilles, St. Croix and St. Thomas in the Virgin Islands, and Puerto Rico and the eastern tip of Hispaniola in the Greater Antilles. The original migrants appear to have bypassed the low islands, such as Barbados and Anguilla, presumably because these islands lacked mountains to trap the rain clouds and permit the formation of large forests (Watters 1980: 330–41; Drewett 1989: 82–83). In effect, the Cedrosans colonized the islands that suited their ecological needs and bypassed the other islands.

Caribbeanists have made much of the fact that the colonists were more interested in forest resources than their Ortoiroid predecessors had been (see Barrau and Montbrun 1978). Their sites are limited to the coastal plains, mostly on the northern and eastern sides of the islands, which had luxuriant forests because of their exposure to the trade winds. Wherever possible, they chose to settle on rivers a short distance back from the shore, where access to the heart of the forest was easiest, but in the absence of large streams they lived along the shore on the edge of the forest (compare, for example, Hacienda Grande and Maisabel on the northeastern coast of Puerto Rico; see Rouse and Alegría 1990: 63 and Siegel 1989).

They would have been unable to settle on the windward sides of the islands if they had not become familiar with the sea. They sought out localities that were protected from the trade winds by coral reefs and exploited the resources available on the reefs, on nearby beaches and rocky shores, and in the mangrove swamps (Roe and others 1986). Thus they combined the strategies they had inherited from their ancestors in the Orinoco Valley and along the Guianan rivers with the practices they had developed after reaching the coast (Wing 1990).

The time of their arrival in the Lesser Antilles and Puerto Rico is still uncertain. Recent radiocarbon measurements have pushed it back from around 200 A.D. to no later than 250 B.C., which is the time shown in figure 14, but there are also earlier dates of 530 and 265 B.C. for the Vivé culture in Martinique; 440, 440, and 260 B.C. for the Trant culture in Montserrat, 325 and 300 B.C. for the Cedrosan component of the Hope Estate site on St. Martin; and 430 B.C. for the Hacienda Grande culture in Puerto Rico (Rouse 1989a, table 1; David R. Watters, personal communication; Haviser 1991; Narganes Storde 1991, table 5). The Cedrosan Saladoid movement into the Antilles may therefore have begun as early as the middle of the first millennium B.C.

During the first part of the Christian era, the Cedrosans who remained behind in the Gulf of Paria expanded through the Carúpano area on the eastern Venezuelan coast to nearby Margarita Island. Because the resources were not as attractive as in the West Indies, they were slow to occupy these areas to the west, nor did they expand far; as they approached the lowlands (Llanos) at the end of the eastern Venezuelan mountains, they encountered drier and less forested conditions, which were not to their liking (Rouse 1986: 139).

If the radiocarbon dates are correct, their westward movement was contemporaneous with their colonization of the low islands in the Lesser Antilles, which were also bypassed by the initial migrants. Both movements were probably touched off by local population growth. Another factor may have been the expansion of Barrancoid peoples down the eastern side of the delta into the northwestern part of Guyana, following in the footsteps of the previous Saladoid invaders (fig. 9).

Caribbean archeologists have paid less attention to the internal composition of sites than to their external context. Except when studying Formative-age ball courts and dance courts (see Alegría 1983), they have treated their sites merely as receptacles from which to collect artifacts, food remains, and burial remains, digging almost exclusively in middens (refuse deposits), where these objects are most numerous. Now they are beginning to search between and beneath the middens for post molds and other traces of structures and for areas in which activities other than the deposition of refuse took place.

At Maisabel in Puerto Rico, which dates back to the beginning of the Cedrosan Saladoid period, Peter E. Siegel (1989, fig. 3) has found a central burial ground surrounded by a ring of mounded middens. There are traces of house structures beneath the midden deposits, but their shapes could not be determined. The cemetery area contains little refuse. Siegel (1990) suggests that it was a sacred place, around which the daily and ritual life of the community revolved. The grave goods in the cemetery show no sign of the differences in rank and wealth present among the Classic Tainos. The central area might possibly have functioned as a dance ground and ball ground, like the central plazas of the Western and Eastern Tainos in Columbus's time, but I know of no way to determine whether it did. Siegel encountered no evidence of artificially constructed dance and ball courts like those among the Classic Tainos.

At Golden Rock, a site on the tiny island of St. Eustatius in the Leeward group that dates from the close of the Cedrosan Saladoid period, the Dutch archeologist Aad H. Versteeg (1989) has uncovered post molds from two small circular houses. These were succeeded by a larger structure, also circular, that resembles the caneys among the Tainos. Toward the center of the site, he encountered a smaller, rectangular building reminiscent of the bohíos of the Tainos. Wind screens extended from both types of structures.

Unfortunately, the center of the site had been destroyed by construction of an airport. Behind the rectangular building and in front of the circular houses was a ceremonial area, containing caches and burials with grave goods. In back of the houses were mounded middens and more carelessly prepared burials without grave goods. This settlement pattern foreshadows the one at the ball-court site of Salt River on St. Croix, which dates from the time of Columbus.

Cedrosan Saladoid pottery is characterized by a duality of white-on-red painted ware and zoned-incised crosshatched ware, names that are commonly shortened to painted ware and zic ware. Descriptive terms are used to avoid confusing these wares with the Cedrosan styles within which they occur. That the names for the two wares refer to decoration is not significant; each is characterized by a different set of modes for material, technology, shape, and decoration.

Painted ware, which is dominant in the duality, includes most of the pottery in the Cedrosan assemblages. It appears to be directly derived from the pottery of the Ronquinan Saladoid peoples. It is characterized by bell-shaped bowls with light-colored paste and plain or flanged rims, to which D-shaped strap handles are often attached, as in the Ronquinan assemblages (fig. 19b). The white-on-red and red-painted decoration of Ronquinan pottery is now accompanied by polychrome designs, containing black or orange paint. The range of colors was further expanded by leaving parts of the vessel surface unpainted. The designs are mostly areal (fig. 20a). Linear painting like that which accompanies areal painting on Ronquinan pottery does not become common until toward the end of the Cedrosan subseries.

Equally important on the painted ware is a distinctive kind of incision, in which continuous curved and straight lines are used either to outline the painted areas or to form purely incised designs. In a variant ware developed in Puerto Rico, curvilinear lines are incised through a red slip and filled with white paint (fig. 20b). Other motifs are modeled and incised on flanges, on tabs projecting from the rims or flanges, and on lugs, where they portray animal or human heads (fig. 20f,g). The heads may represent zemis, as they did among the Tainos. Most of these modes of decora-

Fig. 20. Cedrosan Saladoid artifacts: *a*, white-on-red bowl; *b*, red-slipped sherd with curvilinear incision overlaid with white paint, where the paint is used not only to form designs but also to fill the incisions; *c*, clay griddle; *d*, zic design; *e*, stone three-pointer; *f*, modeled-incised head lug; *g*, turtle-shaped bowl with zic incision; *h*, incense burner showing Barrancoid influence. Fig. *a* is from the Cuevas culture; *b* and *e*, from the Hacienda Grande culture; *c* and *h*, from Martinique; *d* and *f*, from the Morel 1 culture; *g*, from the Morel 2 culture (*a, c, g, h, b, e*, after Rouse 1986, figs. 26, 28*a*, 27*b*; *d, f*, after Rouse 1964, fig. 11).

tion may be regarded as elaborations on Ronquinan Saladoid incised and modeled-incised designs.

The material, technology, shape, and decoration of zic ware is different. The typical vessel is a hemispherical bowl made of darker paste than the painted ware is. It has *D*-shaped handles, rim flanges, and modeled-incised lugs like those of the painted ware but lacks the painted designs of the latter. They are replaced by areas filled with the eponymous fine-line zic decoration and by broad-line, rectilinearly incised designs (fig. 20*d,g*).

Zic ware is definitely secondary to the painted ware in the ceramic mix, just as the men's pidgin was in the Island-Carib duality. It must, however, be considered an integral component of all the Cedrosan cultures. The Cedrosan potters began to make it while still in their presumed Guianan homeland and carried it with them throughout their whole migration, abandoning it only toward the close of the Cedrosan period as part of the general decline in ceramic decoration that took place at that time. It may have been produced for use in special activities such as rituals and trade (Rouse and Alegría 1990: 84–85).

Not only do the two wares share many traits of material, shape, and decoration but also, as Peter G. Roe (1989) has shown through grammatical analysis, their shapes and designs are variations on a single theme. For example, both have areal as well as linear designs, but the areas are painted in one ware and filled with zic patterns or punctation in the other. There can be no doubt, therefore, that both were brought into the West Indies by the Cedrosan Saladoid peoples.

The zic technique, considered by itself rather than as a diagnostic of zic ware, is another matter. It is unlikely to derive from the painted crosshatching on Ronquinan Saladoid pottery because that appears to be a copy of it. The zic technique may have diffused either from the contemporaneous Ceramic-age peoples in the western part of South America or from those in Amazonia, where areas were being zoned by incision, punctation, and/or stamping about the same time. A western origin is precluded by the late date of Cedrosan pottery on the Caribbean coast of Venezuela (Cruxent and Rouse 1958–59, 1:37). The new evidence indicating that the Cedrosans came from the eastern side of the Orinoco Delta lends more credence to the hypothesis that zic incision originated in Amazonia. The trait would have had to diffuse via the Guianas, for it does not occur in the Orinoco Valley.

As the Cedrosans expanded from their presumed Guianan homeland to Trinidad and Tobago, and out into the West Indies, they elaborated their pottery by adding new types, including jars, bottles, effigy vessels, incense burners, and bowls provided with tubes, supposedly for inhaling snuff during the worship of zemis (fig. 21*e*; Mattioni and Nicolas 1972; Rouse and Alegría 1990: 71–73). We do not yet know enough about the nature of the local Cedrosan styles to determine where each of these types originated.

The Cedrosan potters also began to produce large hollow figurines, masks like the Tainos' guaíza, and three-pointed objects (fig. 20*e*). The last type, which was also made of stone, shell, or coral, appears to have diffused eastward from Colombia via the Circum-Caribbean route. Though much smaller and plainer than the Taino three-pointers, the Cedrosan examples are enough like them to confirm the hypothesis that the Cedrosans introduced the worship of zemis into the Antilles.

Like their Ronquinan ancestors, the Cedrosans used clay griddles, apparently to bake cassava bread (fig. 20c). Thus they may also be credited with the introduction of agriculture. When they reached Puerto Rico, they were still making clay cylinders (topia) on which to support their griddles over the fire (Rouse and Alegría 1990: 50). They did not replace these cylinders with stones, which were readily available in the islands, until toward the close of Cedrosan time.

While colonizing the Windward Islands, they acquired a taste for eating land crabs and retained it until they reached Puerto Rico. There is reason to believe that they exhausted the supply of that animal in the small islands of the Lesser Antilles (Goodwin 1979).

From the start, they manufactured stone celts, using materials that had become available to them on the coast. In the Lesser Antilles, they supplemented these with shell celts, possibly under influence from the previous Ortoiroid peoples. In the Virgin Islands and Puerto Rico, they began to produce finely made stone adzes. They also developed a broad array of ornaments carved from stone, bone, and shell and by the time they reached Puerto Rico were inlaying pieces of mother-of-pearl in wooden objects and overlaying them on clothing (Rouse and Alegría 1990: 73). Another trait that foreshadows Taino culture is pendants made by drilling human teeth. This testifies to the presence of the Taino and Island-Carib practice of acquiring power by co-opting the zemis or personal spirits resident in ancestors, friends, or enemies (Roe 1991).

The Cedrosans who remained on the mainland participated in an interaction sphere at the mouth of the Orinoco River. This sphere came to my attention in connection with a study I made of the ethnohistory of that area (Rouse 1983). The European explorers document the existence of trade, intermarriage, political relations, warfare, and other kinds of contact between the Indians in the Guianas, the lower part of the Orinoco Valley, Trinidad and Tobago, and the Peninsula of Paria. Seeking to project this situation back into prehistory, I searched for and found evidence of its existence among the Barrancoid and Cedrosan Saladoid peoples who lived side by side during the first part of the Christian era, the former in the Orinoco Valley and Guyana and the latter farther west along the coast. Cedrosan trade pottery, including both painted and zic wares, has been found in assemblages excavated from Barrancoid sites in the lower part of the Orinoco

Valley, and there is Barrancoid trade pottery in Cedrosan Saladoid assemblages from Trinidad, Tobago, and the adjacent coast of Venezuela (Rouse 1989a: 387).

The Barrancoid peoples apparently led in trade within the sphere. The occurrence of an unusually large number of purely Barrancoid potsherds in late Cedrosan Saladoid sites on Tobago raises the possibility that villages on this island may have served as ports of trade from which Barrancoid designs spread to the Cedrosan potters of the Windward Islands between circa 300 and 500 A.D. The ceramics of that area and period are often called Saladoid-Barrancoid, which is a shorthand way of saying "Cedrosan Saladoid pottery that exhibits Barrancoid influence."

From the beginning, the Cedrosans in the West Indies traded widely for ornaments or for the materials from which they were made. Sites of the Prosperity culture on St. Croix have yielded animal figures carved from naiad shells identified as species native to the Orinoco River (Vescelius and Robinson 1979: 5–6). Other beads and pendants manufactured from exotic gemstones are distributed throughout the islands from the Pearls site on Grenada to Hacienda Grande in Puerto Rico (Cody 1991; Rouse and Alegría 1990, fig. 12). A concentration of them is on Montserrat at the entry into the Leeward Islands, where there may have been another port of trade (Harrington 1924). The materials from which the ornaments are made do not occur locally; Sven Lovén (1935: 476–77) traces them back to the Guianas, Venezuela, and Colombia.

LA HUECA PEOPLE

When the Cedrosan Saladoids reached the Leeward Islands, they were faced with a choice of routes. They could either have proceeded along the line of islands on the Atlantic side of that chain, through St. John and St. Thomas in the Virgin Islands and on to the northern coast of Puerto Rico, or they could have expanded along the line of islands on the Caribbean side, through St. Croix and Vieques and on to the eastern coast of Puerto Rico. Given their penchant for living on the windward sides of the islands, facing the Atlantic Ocean, one might expect them to have favored the first route, and they appear to have done so. Most known sites of the Hacienda Grande culture, the original member of the Cedrosan Saladoid subseries on the main island of Puerto Rico, are along the Atlantic coast (Rouse and Alegría 1990: 63).

Recent research at two sites at the western end of the Caribbean route indicates that a divergent La Hueca people may have colonized the land at the end of that route. Luis A. Chanlatte Baik (1981, 1983) has discovered remains of the La Huecans and their culture at the Sorcé site on the south-

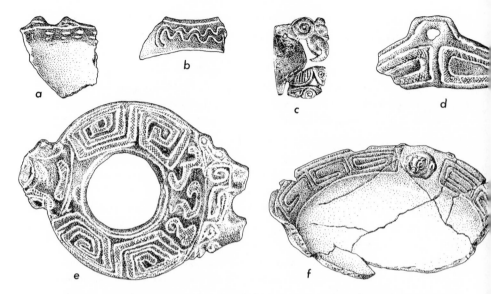

Fig. 21. La Hueca artifacts: *a*, sherd with punctation and wedge lugs; *b*, sherd with curvilinear incision; *c*, bird-head pendant of stone; *d*, tabular lug and zic design; *e*, small inturned bowl with a modeled head lug at one end and a pair of snuffing tubes at the other—the incisions filled with white paint, as in fig. 20*b*; *f*, open bowl decorated with a modeled head lug and curvilinear incision. All are from the Sorcé site on Vieques Island (*a–b*, *d–f*, after Chanlatte Baik 1983: 23, 68, 70; *c*, after Rouse 1986, fig. 27*a*).

ern side of Vieques Island, and Miguel Rodríguez (1991) has obtained additional assemblages at Punta Candelero, just across the Vieques Sound on the eastern coast of Puerto Rico.

When Chanlatte first reported finding the La Hueca culture at the Sorcé site, I considered it to be a local variant on Hacienda Grande culture. Its settlement and subsistence patterns are similar, its pottery shares zic ware, and its assemblages have yielded almost all of the same types of artifacts, for example, snuffing vessels, three-pointers, and similar kinds of simple carved stone pendants. The La Hueca assemblages do lack painted ware, which is the other side of the Hacienda Grande duality, but its potters rubbed white or red paint into their zic incisions (fig. 21).

The subsequent finds at Punta Candelero changed my mind. They indicate that there was a separate La Hueca culture at the end of the migration route on the Caribbean side of the islands, paralleling the Hacienda Grande culture at the end of the route on the Atlantic side, and suggest that this culture or an ancestor diverged from the Cedrosan Saladoid subseries somewhere back toward South America. My principal reason for this conclusion is the apparent transfer of certain modes typical of Cedrosan Saladoid painted ware to the La Hueca zic ware. The presence of white or red paint in the incisions is one example. Another is the occurrence on La Hueca zic ware of crudely curvilinearly incised designs that appear to be copies of the incised designs on Cedrosan Saladoid painted ware (fig. 21*b,f*). Third, the La Hueca potters expanded the placement of their punctated and zic designs into areas occupied by painted designs in Cedrosan Saladoid pottery (fig. 21*a,d*), as if they were attempting to substitute them (Rodríguez, personal communication).

Sorcé and Punta Candelero, the two sites of the La Hueca culture, are also characterized by bird-head pendants elaborately carved from an exotic kind of stone (fig. 21*c*). Rodríguez (personal communication) has obtained evidence that they were made at Punta Candelero. The only other West Indian example known to me comes from Prosperity, a Cedrosan Saladoid site on St. Croix (Linda S. Robinson, personal communication). One occurrence in South America has also come to my attention: a stone pendant from an indeterminate context in Trinidad (Fewkes 1907, pl. 56*b*). A bird-head pendant of the La Hueca style has been reproduced in gold metal for sale in North American museum shops (Birgit F. Morse, personal communication).

It is probably no accident that this type of pendant resembles bird figures modeled and incised on Barrancoid pottery from the lower Orinoco area (José R. Oliver, personal communication). The type was presumably distributed by means of the long-distance trading system, in which the Barrancoid peoples played a leading role. In effect, that system foreshadows the Tainos' trade for guanín.

The Sorcé site may well have been a port of trade, like the ones postulated for Tobago and Montserrat islands. It sits at the entry to the Greater Antilles, just as the Tobago and Montserrat ports sit at the entries to the Windward and Leeward islands.

Punta Candelero is directly on the beach within sight of Vieques Island, where Sorcé is situated. Rodríguez (personal communication) has suggested that it was a satellite village, established by people from Sorcé to exploit the local resources. If so, it would be an early example of the Taino orientation toward water passages.

The La Hueca and Hacienda Grande cultures, at the ends of the two migration routes through the Leeward Islands, apparently began about the same time. The Punta Candelero site has yielded radiocarbon dates of 170 and 70 B.C., which are somewhat later than the earliest dates for the Hacienda Grande culture (Rouse and Alegría 1990, table 9). Seven additional dates for La Huecan assemblages from that site, between 640 and 1260 A.D., are obviously too late and may be attributed to the disturbance of the original assemblages by later inhabitants of the site (Rodríguez 1991, table 1). Similarly, only thirty-two of the sixty-eight dates reported for the La Hueca component of the Sorcé site fall within the expected range for the La Hueca culture (Narganes Storde 1991, tables 1, 2). The others overlap a sizable number of dates for assemblages laid down when that site was subsequently inhabited by Hacienda Grande peoples and their successors. Comparing all the available dates, Ricardo E. Alegría and I (1990: 54–62) have concluded that the La Hueca occupation of the site was succeeded by a Hacienda Grande occupation about 200 A.D.

What caused this replacement? Hacienda Grande people may have expanded back from their forward position on the main island of Puerto Rico and assimilated the La Hueca population, or else they may have influenced the La Hueca potters to resume the production of painted ware. The second alternative is favored by the overlapping in radiocarbon dates for the two styles at the Sorcé site and by the survival of bird-head pendants into the Hacienda Grande period at Sorcé (Chanlatte Baik 1983, pl. 47-A).

Only one other currently known style of pottery is comparable to La Hueca: Río Guapo in the Río Chico area of the central Venezuelan coast, which is in the Llanos (lowlands) beyond the end of the westward radiation of the Cedrosan Saladoid peoples (Rouse and Cruxent 1963: 108–10). The nature of this style is open to question. According to its discoverer, José M. Cruxent (personal communication), the Río Guapo pottery may have had painted designs, which were subsequently destroyed by locally high ground water, as has happened elsewhere in the Llanos. However, we found no traces of painting on the Río Guapo sherds.

Assuming that the ware was never painted, Chanlatte (1981: 15) has classified the Río Guapo style with La Hueca and has inferred that there was a "Guapoid" or "Huecoid" migration from the central Venezuelan coast to Vieques Island. Such a migration must have proceeded directly across the Caribbean Sea, for no comparable pottery has been found on any of the intervening islands. I doubt that the Río Guapo people possessed either the ability or the incentive to travel so far overseas without sails, which made long voyages possible in other parts of the world (Watters and Rouse 1989: 134–35).

More important, the Río Guapo style has a radiocarbon date of 320 A.D., which is confirmed by measurements of 310 and 335 A.D. for the deposits of El Palito–style pottery farther west that have yielded zic-ware trade sherds (Rouse 1989a, table 3). Río Guapo is thus too recent to be ancestral to La Hueca.

Migration and the erosion of painted designs are not the only possible explanations for the similarities between the Río Guapo and La Hueca pottery. The two styles may have developed independently at the ends of the westward and northward radiations of the Cedrosan Saladoid subseries as a result of the process known as the founders' effect, which causes migrants to drop traits such as painted ware (Rouse 1986: 10). Further research in the Río Guapo area is needed to test the hypothesis of abandonment in the west. The question of abandonment in the north is currently being investigated at the Hope Estate site on St. Martin. Whereas most of this site has yielded typically Cedrosan Saladoid assemblages, several parts of it have been found to contain only zic ware (Haviser 1991). Both kinds of assemblages are currently being radiocarbon-dated to determine whether they are contemporaneous.

The Hope Estate excavations are still in their infancy, and the assemblages obtained to date contain too few examples of the two wares to yield definitive results. The differential distribution of zic ware, if validated, would indicate that one or more social groups resident at the site had abandoned painted ware and were creating a new subculture, which they subsequently carried to Vieques Island and transformed into the La Hueca culture. Alternatively, the abandonment of painted ware could have taken place farther down the island chain toward South America.

CONCLUSIONS

The Cedrosan Saladoid potters obviously carried their duality of painted and zic wares with them as they radiated from Trinidad and Tobago, northward into the West Indies and westward along the coast of Venezuela. The painted ware may have been dropped from the ceramic mix at both ends of the radiation. In the West Indies, the abandonment of painted ware has been clearly demonstrated only for the La Hueca culture, which is at the end of an alternate route through the Leeward Islands to Puerto Rico along the Caribbean side of that island chain, and it is limited to the period immediately before and after the time of Christ. The Hacienda Grande people, at the end of the main migration route on the Atlantic side of the chain, continued to use both wares until circa 400 A.D., after which they successively abandoned zic and painted wares as the Cedrosan Saladoid subseries came to an end.

These conclusions are supported not only by the similarities between the La Hueca and Hacienda Grande cultures in their pottery, settlement and subsistence patterns, and other lifeways but also by the lack of any non-Cedrosan remains from which the La Hueca culture could have developed. In the absence of such remains, it seems reasonable to conclude that the ancestors of the La Hueca culture diverged from the ancestors of the Hacienda Grande culture somewhere along the dual migration route through the Leeward and the Virgin islands. It would be advisable to search along these routes for additional cultures resembling La Hueca, especially at the Hope Estate site on St. Martin and at the Prosperity site on St. Croix. Pending such a search, I tentatively assign the La Hueca and Río Guapo pottery to a divergent, Huecan Saladoid subseries (fig. 14). That the divergence would have taken place at opposite ends of the Cedrosan Saladoid radiation and at different times does not seem to me to nullify this hypothesis.

The Saladoid-Casimiroid Frontier, 200 B.C.–600 A.D.

The westernmost occurrence of the Hacienda Grande style is at La Caleta near La Romana, across the Mona Passage from Puerto Rico. A radiocarbon date of 240 A.D. or so (Rouse, Allaire, and Boomert 1985, table 4) indicates that Hacienda Grande people settled there about the same time that their style spread back to Vieques Island. The forward expansion of the style must be due to population movement, for the La Caleta site has yielded no traces of admixture with the previous cultures in the area.

The people displaced by the Hacienda Grande colony also had pottery, belonging to a rudimentary style known as El Caimito. It is limited to poorly made and roughly finished hemispherical bowls (Veloz Maggiolo, Ortega, and Pina P. 1974: 14, 18–20). Its decoration consists of simple strap handles, crude modeling, and incised lines sometimes ending in punctations (fig. 22). Five radiocarbon dates have been obtained, ranging from 305 B.C. to 120 A.D. (Rouse 1989a: 390–91).

The El Caimito style has been an enigma. I originally deferred judgment on it because its dates were much earlier than the ones then accepted for the first appearance of pottery in Puerto Rico and because I did not know of any other reasonable source (Rouse 1982a, fig. 1). Betty J. Meggers and Clifford Evans (1983, fig. 7.11), in contrast, thought it might be an offshoot of a ceramic series on the South American mainland. They assumed that Malamboid people from Colombia had established a colony on the island of Hispaniola or had transmitted elements of their style to the Hispaniolan Indians by interacting with them. Neither assumption made sense to me because both would have required long overseas voyages against the prevailing winds and currents.

Recently I reevaluated the El Caimito style in the light of the newly obtained radiocarbon dates for the beginning of the Ceramic age in Puerto Rico (Rouse 1989a: 390–91). These dates make the Hacienda Grande and El Caimito styles contemporaneous and raise the possibility that the similarities between the two are due to transculturation from the Hacienda

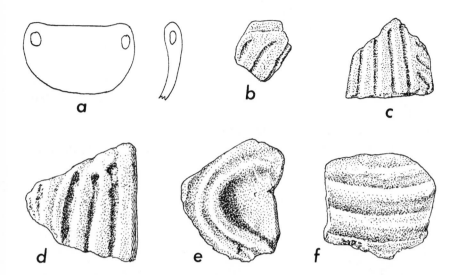

Fig. 22. El Caimito pottery: *a*, bowl with strap handle; *b*, sherd with curvilinear incision; *c*, sherd with rectilinear incision; *d*, sherd with lines ending in punctations; *e*, sherd with modeling; *f*, sherd with curvilinear incision. All are from the type site in the eastern part of the Dominican Republic (after Veloz Maggiolo, Ortega, and Pina P. 1974: 14, 19).

Grande people to the El Porvenirs of the Courian Casimiroid subseries, who preceded the El Caimito people and survived alongside them in the rest of Hispaniola.

Transculturation seems to me to explain the similarities better than overseas diffusion from Colombia. The Hacienda Grande style of pottery contains all the traits of the El Caimito style noted above. These traits appear in cruder form on El Caimito pottery, as if they had been copied by novices (compare figs. 20 and 22). If the El Porvenir artisans were the copiers, they would have been predisposed toward pottery in general and incision and punctation in particular by their tradition of making, incising, and punctating stone vessels, which had begun centuries earlier according to the radiocarbon measurements.

The stone, bone, and shell artifacts found with the El Caimito pottery are all Courian Casimiroid types. They include long flint blades, double-bitted stone axes, and a stone vessel decorated with rectilinearly incised designs and punctations. The only Hacienda Grande–type artifacts known to me are stone celts, which the El Caimito people may have obtained by trade with the Hacienda Grande people (Veloz Maggiolo 1980: 75–92; Rouse 1989a: 390–91). Furthermore, the El Caimito people exhibit the same settlement and subsistence patterns as their presumed El Porvenir forebears. Their sites are equally small and are often situated in the interior on rocky escarpments rich in wild plants and animals. Griddles, which would indicate the presence of agriculture, are lacking (Veloz Maggiolo, Ortega, and Pina P. 1974: 1–2). It would seem, then, that the makers of El Caimito pottery were El Porvenir people who copied Hacienda Grande–style pottery, thereby creating a dual culture. Because their El Porvenir heritage was dominant and their ceramics was borrowed, I have assigned them to the Courian Casimiroid subseries in figure 14.

No evidence of diffusion or trade back across the frontier, from either the El Porvenir or the El Caimito people to the Hacienda Grande people, has come to my attention. The Hacienda Grande artisans apparently did adopt the use of edge grinders from the Corosos of the Ortoiroid series, who preceded them in Puerto Rico (Rouse and Alegría 1990: 50, 66), but no Casimiroid types of artifacts are known to occur in their assemblages.

The Western Ostionoid Peoples, 600–1500

If my inferences are correct, Cedrosan Saladoid peoples from South America reached the northern, western, and southern coasts of Puerto Rico around 200 B.C. and there established a frontier with the Courian Casimiroid peoples living across the Mona Passage in Hispaniola (fig. 10). Finding them more difficult to conquer than the Ortoiroids, they halted at Mona Passage until around 250 A.D., after which they succeeded in colonizing the eastern tip of Hispaniola. With that act of settlement, they established a new interaction sphere, comparable to the one the La Hueca people had initiated on Vieques Sound at the other end of Puerto Rico.

Throughout the new sphere, extending from Vieques Island to eastern Hispaniola, the Hacienda Grande culture evolved circa 400 A.D. into Cuevas, which is the final culture in the Cedrosan Saladoid subseries. Around 600 A.D. it was succeeded in the Mona Passage area by Ostiones, the eponymous culture of the subsequent Ostionoid series. So far as I am aware, both events took place without any further population movement. Habitation continued uninterrupted at the major sites, such as Sorcé, Hacienda Grande, and Maisabel (Rouse and Alegría 1990; Siegel 1990), and there was no appreciable change in the morphology of the human skeletal remains.

There were, however, gradual changes in ceramic style and in artifact typology. Zic ware and polychrome painting disappeared at the end of the Hacienda Grande period, and white-on-red decoration was abandoned in the middle of the Cuevas period, leaving only designs composed of crude linear bands colored red (fig. 23c). They were joined at the beginning of

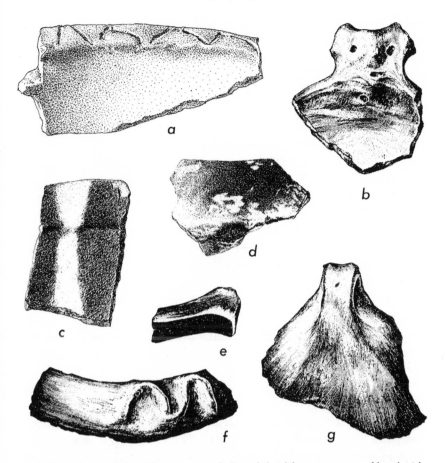

Fig. 23. Ostionan Ostionoid pottery: *a*, red-slipped sherd from an outturned bowl with incision on a beveled rim; *b*, simply modeled head lug with a hole for suspension beneath it; *c*, red-painted designs of vertical bands; *d*, red-slipped sherd from an inturned bowl; *e*, flipper from a red-slipped turtle-shaped bowl, presumably like the bowl in fig. 20g; *f*, sigmoid design modeled on a vessel shoulder; *g*, loop handle. Figs. *a* and *b* are from the modified Ostiones culture; *c–g*, from the Ostiones culture (*a*, Yale Peabody Museum specimen; *b*, *e–g*, after Rouse 1964, fig. 12; *c*, *d*, after Rouse 1986, fig. 28c, b).

the Ostiones period by black-banded designs produced through smudging rather than painting (Oliver, personal communication). The potter coated the surface on either side of the bands with a resin and smothered it during the firing process, so that the carbon from the fire was deposited instead of being combined with oxygen and carried off in the form of carbon dioxide. The resin melted off, removing all the carbon except on the bands themselves.

The red paint was superseded by a more orangy one at the beginning of the Ostiones period. Both the Cuevas and Ostiones potters continued the Hacienda Grande practice of limiting the color to bases, shoulders, rims, and other parts of the pot, and they now began to extend that slip over the entire surface of the vessel (fig. 23a,d,e). The resultant pottery, known as redware, replaced the more elaborate white-on-red painted ware of the Saladoid series (Rouse 1982a).

Curvilinear incision and modeled-incised head lugs likewise died out at the end of the Hacienda Grande period, giving way to slightly modeled face lugs, which persisted through the Cuevas period into the first half of the Ostiones period (fig. 23b). Vessel forms also became simpler. Flanges disappeared at the end of the Hacienda Grande period, and bottles at the end of the Cuevas period.

No rectangular adzes and few ritual artifacts were produced after the end of the Cuevas period, and few ritual artifacts after early Cuevas time. Enough of the latter have been found, however, to indicate that the worship of zemis persisted.

Agriculture also continued throughout the three periods. The consumption of land crabs declined during the Cuevas period, possibly because of overexploitation, as in the Lesser Antilles. Where possible, the subsequent Ostiones people relied more upon marine shellfish, especially large clams and oysters.

As already noted, all Hacienda Grande sites are situated on the coastal plain. Cuevas sites also occur on the beaches and in the foothills, and by Ostiones time the population of Puerto Rico had spread into the principal mountain valleys (Rouse 1952: 526–71). It may be inferred from this distribution that the late Saladoid and early Ostionoid peoples of Puerto Rico gradually acquired the ability to people the interior of the island. There is, however, no evidence of seasonal movement to and from the interior, like that postulated for the Casimiroid Indians. The earliest interior sites contain so few seashells as to indicate that marine shellfish were not obtained by regularly returning to the coast for the purpose (Rouse 1952: 520–21).

These developments prepared the way for the Ostionoids to resume the Saladoid movement westward. Peoples of the Ostionan subseries advanced through Hispaniola and established colonies on the eastern tip of Cuba and the southern coast of Jamaica. Members of the subsequent Meillacan subseries occupied central Cuba and the rest of Jamaica, and an offshoot known as Palmetto peopled the Bahamian Archipelago.

OSTIONAN SUBSERIES

The Ostionans appear to have followed two routes in advancing from their original foothold on the eastern tip of Hispaniola, one through the

Cibao Valley north of the central mountain range and the other along the southern coast of the island. The Cibao Valley route brought them from Samaná Bay, on the eastern end of the island, to the northern shore at the present boundary between the Dominican Republic and Haiti, whence they were able to proceed along the northwestern peninsula of the island and across the Windward Passage to the eastern tip of Cuba. The route along the southern coast took them past the southwestern peninsula of Hispaniola and across the Jamaica Channel to the southern part of Jamaica. Their experience in settling the interior of Puerto Rico must have facilitated their advance along the northern route, and the maritime skills inherited from their Saladoid ancestors must have helped them to cope with the Cuban countercurrent, which flowed against them along the southern route.

The evidence for movement along both routes is almost entirely ceramic. Too little is known about the settlement patterns, stone, bone, and shell artifacts, and behavior of the individual peoples within the Ostionan subseries to be able to bring these aspects of their cultures to bear on the problem.

Ostionan pottery is well distributed along the two migration routes (fig. 14). It underlies Meillacan pottery at two sites in the Cibao Valley (Veloz Maggiolo, Ortega, and Caba Fuentes 1981). At the Macady site in northeastern Haiti, it has been found in association with Meillacan sherds. Clark Moore (personal communication) has recently discovered a purely Ostionan deposit at a nearby site on Isle Boucanier, which better exemplifies the style.

Nineteen radiocarbon dates for Anadel, the Ostionan style in the Dominican Republic, range from 695 to 1245 A.D., and three dates for Arroyo del Palo, the corresponding style in eastern Cuba, from 930 to 1190 A.D. The only dates for the Macady style in northeastern Haiti and the Little River style in Jamaica are 860 and 650 A.D., respectively (Rouse, Allaire, and Boomert 1985, table 4; Moore, personal communication). These figures indicate that the Ostionan expansion along both migration routes took place during the latter part of the first millennium A.D.

Ostionan pottery is often called redware because of its holdover of red, though not white, painting from the Saladoid series. The red still serves primarily as a background, covering part or all of the vessel surface instead of delineating designs. Red is the only ware; the Cedrosan plurality of painted and zic wares had long since disappeared.

The pottery is thin, hard, and smooth surfaced. Straight-sided, open bowls replace the bell-shaped bowls of the previous Saladoid pottery, and loop handles, raised above the rim, take the place of D-shaped handles (fig. 23g). Decoration is rare; in its original form it consists only of red-painted or smudged areas and bands, accompanied by simply modeled lugs and geometric figures modeled on vessel walls (fig. 23*b,c,e,f*).

The Ostionan expansion was obviously a population movement, for it resulted in displacement of the previous Casimiran population. Jamaica may be an exception; because no Casimiroid remains have been found there, the Ostionans would appear to have been the original settlers of that island.

I know of only one possible piece of evidence of contact between the Ostionans and the Courians whom they replaced in Hispaniola. A fragmentary stone vessel from a Courian site in northern Haiti looks as though it had been copied from an Ostionan pot (fig. 17*c*). It has the same thinness and elements of shape but is incised with a typically Courian design. Presumably it dates from the time when the Ostionans occupied the Cibao Valley but had not yet reached the Haitian coast.

One consequence of the Ostionan expansion was to advance the frontier of the Ceramic/Archaic age from the eastern tip of Hispaniola to the eastern tip of Cuba and the southern coast of Jamaica (fig. 10). Another may have been the establishment of four new interaction spheres, centering on the Cibao Valley and the Windward Passage along the northern route and on the southeastern coast of Hispaniola and the Jamaica Channel along the southern route. The new spheres would have intensified the trend toward diversity as the repeopling process continued.

MEILLACAN SUBSERIES

The Meillac people, after whom this subseries is named, lived in the Cibao Valley interaction sphere, including the northeastern corner of the present Republic of Haiti. Other Meillacan peoples have been identified in the Windward Passage area, at the end of the northern migration route, and beyond it in central Cuba. None occur in the southern part of the present Dominican Republic, along the main part of the alternative route, but they do appear in the Jamaica Channel area, at its end, including the entire island of Jamaica.

These distributions imply that the Meillacan peoples arose in the Cibao Valley, expanded into the Windward Passage area, and radiated in two directions from that area, westward into central Cuba and southward along the Hispaniolan and Cuban coasts to Jamaica. In the process, they moved the Ceramic/Archaic-age frontier to its final position in the time of Columbus and completed the peopling of Jamaica.

These events probably took place at the end of the first millennium A.D.; nine radiocarbon measurements for sites in the Dominican Republic range from 825 to 1220 A.D., thirteen for Cuba from 830 to 1460 A.D., and fifteen for Jamaica from 880 to 1490 A.D. (Rouse, Allaire, and Boomert 1985, table 4). The difference in terminal dates between Meillac and the other Meillacan cultures reflects the fact that the former gave way to Chican cultures about 1200 A.D., whereas most of the latter survived until the time of Columbus.

Dominican archeologists have encountered remains of the Meillac culture on top of Ostionan refuse at two sites in the Cibao Valley interaction sphere (Veloz Maggiolo, Ortega, and Caba Fuentes 1981). Its pottery is similar in both material and shape to the preceding Ostionan pottery, being thin, hard, and fine and tending toward bowls with inturned shoulders rather than outsloping sides. Painting has disappeared, however, and with its loss the Meillac potters began to roughen the surfaces of their vessels. Decoration now consists primarily of punctations on ridges just beneath the rims and of incised, applied, and punctated designs on vessel shoulders—both places that Ostionan potters had covered with a smooth red slip. The designs are rectilinear; they feature hatching and crosshatching, incised or applied in rectangular panels extending horizontally around the vessel. Small geometric and zoomorphic lugs with incised, punctated, and appliqué features, including limbs that extend from the bases of the lugs, are also diagnostic (fig. 24).

The Meillac potters may be said to have had only a single, rectilinearly incised ware, which was also characterized by appliqué work and punctation. In effect, this incised ware replaced the redware of the Ostionan styles. There is no ceramic duality, like that between the painted and zic wares in the previous Cedrosan Saladoid styles.

What caused the change? The abandonment of painting may be considered the culmination of a trend begun when polychrome painting died out at the end of the Hacienda Grande period. Its replacement by incision is another matter. Marcio Veloz Maggiolo, Elpidio Ortega, and Angel Caba Fuentes (1981) attribute the replacement to diffusion from the Guyana highlands in South America. The similarities with that area appear to me superficial, however; and to my knowledge nothing like them has been found along the Guyana coast or in the Lesser Antilles, where they should occur if diffusion took place. Courian Casimiroid art offers a source closer to home. Like Meillac ceramic decoration, it combines incision and punctation, is rectilinear, includes both hatched and crosshatched panels, and has lines in the hatched panels that are alternately aligned in different directions. Further evidence of contact between the two cultures is provided by the Courian stone vessel mentioned earlier and by the presence in Meillac assemblages of typically Courian flint blades (Veloz Maggiolo, Ortega, and Caba Fuentes 1981: 358–60). Local Courians possibly became assimi-

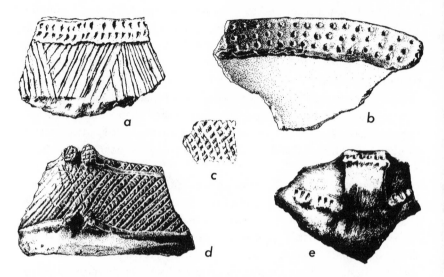

Fig. 24. Meillacan Ostionoid pottery: *a*, alternating panels of incised hatching beneath a punctated ridge on the shoulder of an inturned bowl; *b*, punctated ridge on the interior of an outturned bowl; *c*, crosshatched design in appliqué work; *d*, crosshatched design in incision beneath a pair of geometric lugs; *e*, strap handle decorated with a ridge and flanked by wedge-shaped, punctated lugs. All are from the Meillac culture (*a, c, e,* after Rouse 1964, fig. 14; *b, d,* after Rouse 1986, fig. 28*a, d*).

lated into the invading Ostionan population and caused the change from Ostionan to Meillac pottery. Alternatively, the invaders may have picked up artifacts from Courian sites and copied them, as modern Pueblo potters have done in the southwestern United States.

The Meillac artisans continued to produce clay griddles and stone, bone, and shell artifacts in the Ostionan tradition. In the Cibao Valley they improved upon the previous agriculture by developing the system of mounded fields that Columbus encountered among the Classic Tainos. On the northern coast, however, they relied more on catching fish and collecting shellfish (Veloz Maggiolo, Ortega, and Caba Fuentes 1981: 351–53). The worship of zemis continued as before.

Turning from the Meillac people themselves to the rest of the Meillacans, let us first consider the situation in the areas previously conquered by Ostionans, that is, the land on either side of the Jamaica Channel and Windward Passage areas, which comprised the Ceramic/Archaic-age frontier of the time. The pottery along this frontier indicates that the inhabitants became acculturated to the Meillacan subseries: they replaced their redware with simplified versions of the incised ware developed by the Meillac potters behind the frontier.

No changes in the previous agricultural practices or in the worship of zemis are indicated, but the settlement pattern is different. Whereas the coastal Ostionan villages were on beaches or islets, the coastal Meillacan sites tended to be on high ground back from the shore (Rouse and Moore 1985: 18). The reasons for this change are unknown.

The Meillacan advances beyond the frontier into central Cuba and northern Jamaica must have been population movements, for the migrants replaced Redondan Casimiroid peoples in Cuba and presumably occupied virgin territory in Jamaica. They introduced agriculture, pottery, and zemism to both areas.

PALMETTO PEOPLE

The Indians encountered by Columbus in the Bahamian Archipelago are known archeologically as Palmetto people and ethnohistorically as Lucayan Tainos. Their remains are distributed throughout both parts of the archipelago, the Turks and Caicos and the Bahama islands.

Palmetto pottery is technologically inferior to the rest of the pottery in the West Indies, doubtless because of the poor quality of the clay in the Bahamian Archipelago. Thick, crude, and mostly shell-tempered, it is so friable that it breaks into tiny sherds. The remains come from hemispherical bowls, which are rarely decorated. As in the Meillacan styles, there are examples of appliqué work and punctation, as well as simple rectilinear designs. An occasional rim bears a wedge-shaped or head lug, less complex than those on Meillacan pottery. Mat impressions often occur beneath the decorated areas (fig. 25).

Clay griddles, some of which also bear mat impressions on their lower sides, testify to the presence of agriculture. They are limited to the southern and central islands; winter frosts precluded the growth of cassava in the north (Sears and Sullivan 1978: 18–20). The stone, bone, and shell artifacts are comparable to those in the Ostionan and Meillacan cultures.

Palmetto pottery is too different from the Ostionan and Meillacan ceramics to be assigned to either of those subseries. It cannot, however, be placed in a subseries of its own because it is the only style of its kind. I therefore leave it unaffiliated in figure 14.

Its origin is under dispute. Shaun D. Sullivan (1978) has found evidence that Meillac Indians from northeastern Haiti began to make seasonal visits to the Turks and Caicos islands around 800 A.D., apparently to obtain salt and perhaps also to exploit the local shellfish. He hypothesizes that the

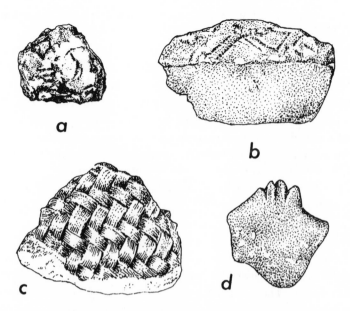

Fig. 25. Palmetto pottery: *a*, plain, badly eroded sherd; *b*, inturned bowl sherd with a crude incised design; *c*, mat-impressed sherd; *d*, outturned bowl sherd with a wedge-shaped lug. All are from the Palmetto culture (*a*, after Rouse 1986, fig. 10*f*; *b–d*, after Sears and Sullivan 1978, fig. 4*i*, *m*, *a*).

Meillac visitors began to settle permanently in the Caicos Islands around 900 A.D., developed the Palmetto style there in adaptation to the locally available materials, and subsequently carried that style through the rest of the Bahamian Archipelago, moving from southeast to northwest.

Other archeologists (for example, Keegan 1985: 297–99) derive the Palmetto people from the Meillacans of the northwestern tip of Hispaniola or the northeastern end of Cuba. Many assume that population pressure, rather than the exploitation of scarce resources, was the motivating factor. They postulate a migration into the southern Bahamas and a radiation southeastward from there to the Turks and Caicos islands and northwestward to the rest of the Bahama Islands. Our present knowledge of the local chronology has not been sufficient to decide between the alternative hypotheses.

Since writing the above, I have learned of a new discovery pertinent to the problem. At the Three Dog site on San Salvador Island in the Bahamas proper, Mary Jane Berman and Perry L. Gnivecki (personal communication) have found a mixture of Ostionan and Palmetto pottery underlying purely Palmetto remains. It recalls the mixture at the Macady site in northern Haiti, where Ostionan pottery is accompanied by Meillacan, and raises the possibility that the Ostionan style was evolving into Palmetto in the southern Bahamas while it was changing into Meillacan in northern Haiti. Berman and Gnivecki have obtained four radiocarbon dates for the mixed deposit in Three Dog site, ranging from 660 to 865 A.D. These approximate the time when the change from Ostionan to Meillacan was taking place in northern Haiti (fig. 8).

The Three Dog finds imply that the Bahamian Archipelago was peopled by Ostionians rather than Meillacans. They could have come from either Haiti or Cuba, that is, from either side of the Windward Passage, for Ostionan remains have been found in both places. The migrants would presumably have developed the Palmetto style after they reached the southern Bahamas, through a combination of adaptation to local conditions and influence from the Meillacans, who were emerging at that time in northern Hispaniola and Cuba.

Whatever the case, the Palmettos appear to have completed their peopling of the Bahamian Archipelago by the twelfth century A.D. Fourteen radiocarbon dates place them between 1110 and 1560 A.D. (Berman and Gnivecki, personal communication).

Conclusions

In writing this chapter, I would have preferred to proceed in terms of the local peoples who participated in the repeopling process, as I did in chapter 3, examining the changes that took place as each people's culture evolved into its successor. Limitations of space and knowledge have required me to proceed on the level of subseries, descending to individual peoples only when considering problems of cultural ancestry.

I began with the Ronquinan Saladoid peoples, who occupied the middle and lower Orinoco Valley during the second millennium B.C., hypothesizing that the Ronquinans who lived in the lower-middle part of the valley around 1000 B.C. developed a new Barrancoid series and carried it downstream to the head of the Orinoco Delta, pushing the Ronquinans of that area toward the coast. The displaced Ronquinans evidently moved down the Boca Grande, on the east side of the delta, and turned up the streams that flow toward the delta from northwestern Guyana and Venezuelan Guayana. I have suggested that the migrants developed the Cedrosan Saladoid subseries of cultures along these streams and carried it to the coast. They would then have expanded westward past the mouth of the delta to the island of Trinidad and turned northward through Tobago into the Lesser Antilles.

Their movement into Trinidad, Tobago, and the Antilles was not a wave engulfing all the islands in their path. Instead, the first Cedrosans colonized only the areas that offered the most favorable conditions. For example, they bypassed northern Trinidad and the Peninsula of Paria, which lacked extensive flood plains, and Barbados, which was too remote, and settled on the Atlantic coasts of high islands, like Martinique, Guadeloupe, and Antigua, because the trade winds that beat against the mountains there sustain luxuriant rain forests, to which they had been accustomed in their Guianan homeland.

When they reached the Leeward Islands, they split into two groups. Most of them proceeded along the Atlantic side of that archipelago, passing through St. Thomas to the northern coast of Puerto Rico and establishing a frontier with the Courian Casimiroids at the Mona Passage, which separates Puerto Rico from Hispaniola. A minority moved along the Caribbean side of the archipelago past St. Croix to Vieques Island and the eastern coast of Puerto Rico. The migrants along the Atlantic route diversified into a succession of Cedrosan Saladoid populations, culminating in the Hacienda Grande people on the frontier along the northern, western, and southern coasts of Puerto Rico. The migrants along the Caribbean route diverged into a La Hueca people on Vieques Island and the eastern coast of Puerto Rico proper. I have tentatively assigned the La Hueca people to a separate Huecan Saladoid subseries.

The repeopling of the Lesser Antilles and Puerto Rico took place during the second half of the first millennium B.C. In the first century or so A.D. the Hacienda Grande culture spread backward into the La Hueca area, and the Hacienda Grande people advanced across the Mona Passage, extending their frontier to the eastern tip of Hispaniola, where it remained until circa 600 A.D. On that frontier, the Hacienda Grande people evolved through the Cuevas into a new Ostionan Ostionoid subseries, which gradually expanded into the interior of Puerto Rico and resumed the previous advance into Hispaniola. Some of the Ostionans proceeded through Samaná Bay and the Cibao Valley in the northern part of the Dominican Republic to the coast of Haiti; thence they moved along the northeastern peninsula and across the Windward Passage to the eastern tip of Cuba, where they established a frontier with the Redondan Casimiroids. Other Ostionans moved along the southern coast of the Dominican Republic, through the southwestern peninsula of Haiti, and across the Jamaica Channel to the southern coast of Jamaica, which was apparently still virgin territory.

The frontier remained on the eastern tip of Cuba from about 600 to 900 A.D. During that time, the Ostionan peoples living behind it in the Cibao Valley of the northern Dominican Republic developed a new Meillacan subseries, which spread to the peoples on the frontier, who carried it into central Cuba and northern Jamaica. This expansion moved the frontier to the position it occupied in the time of Columbus. Meanwhile, Ostionans from the Windward Passage area, that is, from the northwestern peninsula of Haiti or the eastern part of Cuba, apparently moved into the southern Bahama Islands and there developed into a Palmetto people, who expanded into the rest of the Bahamian Archipelago.

The reasons for all these movements are poorly known. External pressure or internal population growth may have been a factor in some cases; the motive in other cases may have been to exploit resources not readily available in the homelands. The movement of Ronquinan Saladoid peoples from the lower Orinoco Valley into the Guianas and Trinidad is an example of external pressure; these peoples were apparently pushed through the Orinoco Delta by Barrancoid invaders from farther upstream. The late expansion of the Cedrosan Saladoids into the low islands of the Lesser Antilles may instead have been due to internal population growth. In contrast, the Cedrosan Saladoids may have originally been enticed to move into the Lesser Antilles by the wealth of forest resources and agricultural land, as in the case of the westward advance of Anglo-Americans in the United States.

At one time or another it has been claimed that each of the subseries and many of the individual peoples mentioned here migrated from the South American mainland. If my evaluation of the most plausible claims is correct, only the Cedrosan Saladoid peoples actually came from the mainland; all the others developed in the islands. This situation parallels that found elsewhere in the world. In the British Isles, for example, scholars assumed until recently that each new people and culture had migrated from the mainland; now local development is the preferred explanation (Renfrew 1973). Similarly, Thor Hyerdahl's theory that the Polynesians were the product of two successive migrations into the Central Pacific area, one from South America and the other from Asia, has been replaced by a hypothesis of evolution from a Lapita culture that was native to Melanesia (Rouse 1986: 19–42).

Today archeologists no longer think just of migration when attempting to explain the appearance of a new people and culture but consider all possible explanations, including divergence, acculturation, transculturation, and parallel development, as well as migration; and they weigh these processes against each other in accordance with the principle of multiple working hypotheses (Rouse 1986: 1–18). Most researchers have learned not to treat migration hypotheses as ruling theories, which can be "proved" by compiling data in their favor, because this kind of reasoning is circular.

Instead, they proceed by a process of elimination, considering the evidence for and against each alternative hypothesis, as I have done in this chapter.

They have also learned not to work directly in terms of peoples and their motives, for this, too, creates a ruling theory, which is unprovable. Instead, they base their conclusions on the distribution and development of the peoples' cultures, a procedure that enables them to weigh the evidence for and against population movement and its alternatives.

Long-distance trade was an important alternative during the early part of the repeopling process, or so it seems. The original Saladoid invaders evidently remained in contact with South America and continued to obtain luxury goods from there via ports of trade in Tobago, Montserrat, and Vieques islands. Contact was broken off after the Saladoids arrived in Puerto Rico, and the repeopling of the rest of the West Indies took place in isolation.

These conclusions derive from the study of the distribution and development of the Ronquinan, Cedrosan, and Huecan Saladoid subseries, which mark the advance of the Ceramic/Archaic-age frontier from the Orinoco Valley to Puerto Rico, and the Ostionan and Meillacan Ostionan subseries and Palmetto culture, which mark the expansion of the frontier through the rest of the West Indies. I have approached these cultural units in two ways. First, I have sought to determine the homeland of each and examine its genesis there. Then I have traced its movement from the homeland and studied the manner in which the expanding population modified its customs in adaptation to the differing natural and cultural conditions it encountered as it moved. We have seen that the Meillacan, Ostionoid, and Palmetto peoples, at the very end of the migration, evolved into the Western Tainos, who were the ethnic subgroup encountered by Columbus when he first reached the Americas. The rise of the Classic Tainos, who lived in the center of the West Indies, and of the Eastern Tainos, who occupied the Island-Carib frontier, closest to the source of the migration, remain to be considered.

THE EMERGENCE

OF THE TAINOS

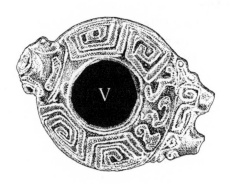

Unfortunately, the genesis of the Tainos, the most important theme of this book, has been too little studied to do it justice. West Indian archeologists assumed for many years that the Tainos had come from the mainland, in effect passing the problem of genesis to their mainland colleagues. The latter saw no reason to study it, so it was ignored.

My involvement with the problem began as a graduate student at Yale University in the late 1930s, when I had to reconcile the hypotheses of Gudmund Hatt (1924), a Danish archeologist who had excavated in the Virgin Islands, and Froelich G. Rainey (1940), a fellow graduate student who had dug in Puerto Rico before me. Both agreed that the cultures we now call Saladoid were the result of a population movement from South America. Hatt, however, concluded that the subsequent Ostionoid cultures had originated in Hispaniola and spread from there to the Virgin Islands, whereas Rainey thought that the bearers of the Ostionoid cultures had also come from South America. Because the Ostionoid peoples were ancestral to the Tainos, this meant that Hatt placed the Taino homeland in the Greater Antilles, whereas Rainey conformed to the prevailing belief that it was in South America.

To decide between the two conflicting hypotheses, I studied the changes in ceramics from level to level within the underlying Saladoid and the overlying Ostionoid strata excavated by Rainey in Puerto Rico. I found a trend from painted to plain pottery as I proceeded from the bottom to the top levels in his Saladoid strata and from plain to modeled-incised pottery as I proceeded from the bottom to the top levels in his Ostionoid strata. This led me to hypothesize a period of predominantly plain pottery between the times when painted and modeled-incised decoration were dominant.

While in Puerto Rico during the summers of 1936–38, I searched for and found assemblages dating from such a period. The pottery of these assemblages was transitional between the Saladoid and Ostionoid ceramics excavated by Rainey, hence it confirmed Hatt's theory of local development (Rouse 1952). The transitional pottery filled a gap in our previous knowledge of Puerto Rican chronology, which had arisen because the local collectors, upon whom we had relied for information about sites, were only interested in decorated potsherds. It now became clear that the ceramics had evolved through two phases of elaborate decoration, which were separated by a phase of plain pottery (Rouse 1986: 118–20).

From the ceramic trends observed in Rainey's Saladoid and Ostionoid strata I developed the chronological system shown in figure 26. It consists of four periods numbered I to IV, each divided into two parts. Periods Ia and Ib are preceramic. Period IIa is the time when painted pottery was dominant; and Period IIb, the time when it was going out of fashion. Period IIIa is that of the newly found plain pottery. The later modeled-incised ware began during Period IIIb and reached its climax in Period IVa. Period IVb is historic.

The earlier calendric dates for the eight periods are based on the radiocarbon measurements cited in the previous two chapters. The measurements from which the later dates are derived are too numerous to be given here (for a summary, see Rouse, Allaire, and Boomert 1985). Suffice it to say that these dates are well established for the central part of Ostionoid territory, including not only Puerto Rico but also the adjacent parts of Hispaniola to the west and the Virgin Islands to the east. We do not yet possess enough information to be able to determine with certainty whether the dates also apply to the frontier Ostionoids farther west, whom we considered in the last chapter, and to those farther east, who are discussed below.

The third column in the figure shows how the archeologically defined peoples and cultures fit into the chronological system. Period Ia, which lasted from circa 4000 to 2000 B.C., is the time when the Casimiroid Indians crossed the Yucatán Channel into Cuba and Hispaniola. During Period Ib, from circa 2000 to 300 B.C., the Ortoiroids expanded from South America into the Lesser Antilles, the Virgin Islands, and Puerto Rico, where they came into contact with the Casimiroids.

Cedrosan Saladoid peoples from South America replaced the Ortoiroids during Period IIa, from 300 B.C. to 400 A.D. The presumed divergence of the Huecan Saladoids and their reintegration into the Cedrosan subseries also took place at this time. The Cedrosans survived through Period IIb,

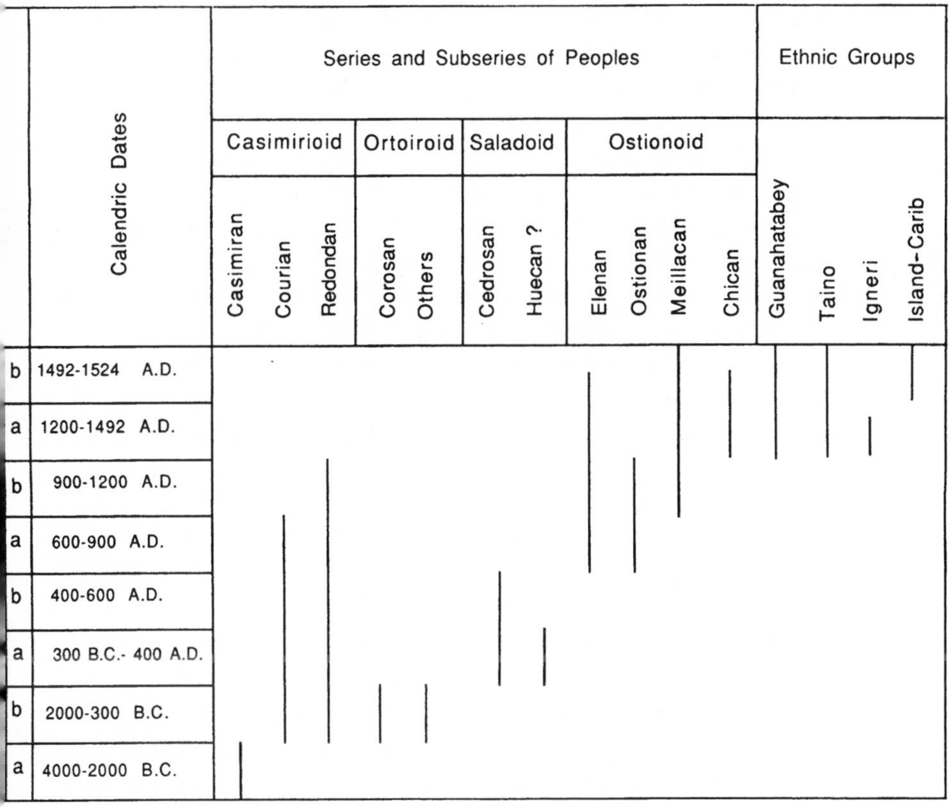

Fig. 26. Lithically or ceramically defined periods and their calendric dates. The culturally and the ethnically defined population groups are plotted against them.

from 400 to 600 A.D., after which they diverged into a pair of Ostionoid subseries: Elenan, extending from Guadeloupe to eastern Puerto Rico, and Ostionan, in western Puerto Rico and on the eastern tip of Hispaniola.

Period IIIa, from 600 to 900 A.D., was the time when the Ostionans expanded westward to southern Jamaica, eastern Cuba, and the central part of the Bahamian Archipelago. The Elenans and the Ostionans who remained behind in Puerto Rico persisted throughout Period IIIb, from 900 to 1200 A.D. The Ostionans of eastern Hispaniola evolved at this time into the Chicans; and the Ostionans of the north-central part of the island, into the Meillacans. The Ostionans in western Hispaniola, Jamaica, and Cuba adopted Meillacan culture, and the Bahamian Ostionans developed their own local way of life.

During Period IVa, from 1200 to 1492 A.D., Chican culture spread eastward through the Mona Passage area and westward through Hispaniola, except for its southwestern tip. Chican outposts were also established on St. Croix in the Virgin Islands and on the eastern tip of Cuba, and the Chicans influenced the development of pottery in the rest of the Virgin Islands, the northern Leewards, Jamaica, and central Cuba.

Period IVa is the earliest one in which we can make a definite correlation between these peoples and cultures, who are defined by their remains, and the ethnic groups of Columbus's time, who are defined by documentary evidence. The ethnic groups are also shown in figure 26. The Chicans of Period IVa may be identified as the Classic Tainos; the Meillacans who survived beyond the western limit of Chican expansion, as the Western Tainos; and the Elenans who persisted on the frontier beyond the eastern limit of the expansion, as the Eastern Tainos. The Guanahatabeys, Igneris, and Island-Caribs are also included in the figure to complete the picture of the distribution of aboriginal ethnic groups in the West Indies during protohistoric and historic time.

The set of periods defined in figure 26 parallels the sequence of Lithic, Archaic, and Ceramic ages, around which the discussion of the peopling and repeopling of the West Indies was organized. The two are distinct and contrasting systems. Ages express the level of a people's development. Because they occur at different times in different places, their distributions have to be plotted in the bodies of chronological charts, as in figures 8 and 9. Periods are measures of time and have the same values in all of the areas included in the body of a chart and hence may be placed along its sides. Ages are often called units of relative time, and periods, units of absolute time (Rouse 1972: 107–16).

Ages have proved useful in tracing population movements because both ages and population movements are defined by innovations. Periods, in contrast, provide a better framework within which to study the processes of social interaction and cultural evolution. They tell us which peoples were contemporaneous and hence capable of interacting with each other and developing in coordination; and they provide a scale along which we can follow the process of development.

Because this chapter focuses upon development, I have organized it by period. The system of ages plays only a secondary role: it is used to distinguish between the level of development of the central Ostionoids, who advanced into the Formative age by creating ball courts and other public works, and the frontier Ostionoids to their west and east, who remained in the Ceramic age. The central Ostionans evolved into the Classic Tainos; the other two populations became the Western and Eastern Tainos, respectively.

The developments on the western frontier have already been discussed in connection with the advance of the Ostionoids from eastern Hispaniola into the rest of the Greater Antilles and the Bahamian Archipelago (chap. 4). Here we are concerned with the evolution of the central Ostionoids into the Classic Tainos, the evolution of the Ostionoids who lived on the eastern frontier into the Eastern Tainos, and the appearance of the Island-Caribs in the Windward Islands, beyond the eastern frontier.

The Central Ostionoid Peoples, 600–1500

The Ostionans who expanded westward from the Mona Passage area at the beginning of Period IIIa developed Meillacan culture during Period IIIb in response to the new natural and cultural conditions they encountered. The Ostionans who remained behind in the Mona Passage area, not being exposed to these conditions, retained their original culture throughout Period IIIb.

The size of the two populations increased steadily during post-Saladoid time. Both groups expanded into the major mountain valleys in Period IIIa and fanned out into the rest of the interior in Period IIIb. By Period IVa, their center had shifted from the coast to the interior (Rouse 1952: 566–71). Their rise in population may have been facilitated by the development of mounded agricultural fields (conucos), a practice presumed to have arisen among the Meillacans in the Cibao Valley of north-central Hispaniola, whose broad alluvial plains are most favorable for it, and to have spread eastward from there to Puerto Rico. Alternatively, the population increase may have been touched off by the diffusion of Indian corn from South America (Shaun D. Sullivan, personal communication). This appears less likely, because the Tainos and their ancestors used corn as a vegetable rather than as a staple crop. We do not yet know when it reached the West Indies; its remnants have been found only in disturbed deposits.

The inhabitants of Puerto Rico also expanded at the time from the coastal plains to the beaches, apparently to more fully exploit the shellfish and other fish available there and in the sea, much as the Western Tainos did. The composition of the local populace appears to have remained unchanged. There is no evidence of the intrusion of peoples across either the western or the eastern frontier.

The pottery of the central area during Period IIIa consists of a number of local styles assigned to the Ostionan subseries (fig. 14). These styles share a single redware. The potters retained the Saladoid preference for open bowls with outsloping sides and still used red paint mainly to cover single elements of shape, such as the inwardly beveled rims of open bowls. Increasingly, however, they extended the paint over the entire vessel, converting it into an overall red slip. They also began to make more use of the tradition of simply modeled faces and geometric figures inherited from their terminal Saladoid ancestors (fig. 23*b,f*).

Toward the close of Period IIIa, the Anadel people, who made the Ostionan pottery on the Dominican side of the Mona Passage, began to produce unpainted pottery decorated with small appliqué heads and limbs comparable to those of the Meillac style in the Cibao Valley farther west. Manuel García Arévalo (personal communication) has called this kind of pottery Punta. It is not shown in figure 14 because it does not appear to be the full ceramic style of a separate people. Instead, it may be a secondary ware resulting from interaction between the Anadel and Meillac peoples.

During Period IIIb, the Anadel potters developed a new, Atajadizo style, which was the first in the Chican subseries: they abandoned their previous red and appliqué (Punta) wares, developed a preference for constricted-mouth bowls with shoulders curving inward, and decorated the rims or handles of their vessels with animal and human head lugs. The lugs continued to be modeled, as in the previous redware, or appliquéd, as in the Punta ware, and to have limbs attached to the bases (Veloz Maggiolo and others 1976: 28–72).

The Atajadizo potters also began to make curvilinearly incised designs, some of which contain lines ending in dots. They put them on the shoulders of constricted bowls or inside open bowls and alternated them with rectilinearly incised designs, which appear to have been borrowed from Meillac pottery. Overall, the Atajadizo style consists of a single ware, which may be termed modeled-incised to distinguish it from the previous Ostiones duality of red and appliqué (Punta) wares and from the single, rectilinearly incised ware in the contemporaneous Meillacan styles to the west. The excavators suggest that the new modeled-incised ware was derived from Barrancoid pottery in South America (Veloz Maggiolo and others 1976: 244). There is, however, a better source closer to home—the Cedrosan Saladoid pottery of Period IIa in the Mona Passage area. Its modes of modeling and incision, notably head lugs, ovoid motifs, and mazelike incisions, could have survived in woodcarving after their disappearance from Cedrosan Saladoid pottery in Period IIb and been transferred to Chican ceramics in Period IIIb. Alternatively, the local artisans could have copied the designs from finds in nearby archeological deposits. I found evidence that the inhabitants of several Puerto Rican sites picked up potsherds and kept them as curios.

The rise of the Atajadizo style during Period IIIb may be said to parallel the rise of the El Caimito style during Period IIa. If I am correct, both developments were inspired by Cedrosan Saladoid ceramics, yet they took place in different cultural contexts, within the Courian Casimiroid subseries in the case of El Caimito pottery and within the Chican Ostionoid subseries in the case of Atajadizo pottery. It is probably no accident that both events happened in the same area; the earlier one may indirectly have affected the later one, causing the reappearance of lines ending in dots (compare figs. 22 and 27).

The potters of Period IIIb on the Puerto Rican side of the Mona Passage were beyond the area of Meillac and El Caimito influence, so they retained their eponymous Ostiones style. Toward the end of Period IIIb, they began to experiment with incision and appliqué lugs like those of the Atajadizo style. Whereas the Atajadizo potters had put these modes of decoration on both the outer walls of constricted-mouth bowls and the inner walls of open bowls, the Ostiones potters preferred to place them on the inwardly beveled rims of open bowls, which they were still decorating with red paint. They had to broaden the beveling of their rims and simplify the incised designs in order to fit the two together (fig. 23a). In effect, the Ostiones potters of western Puerto Rico transferred incised and appliqué work from the modeled-incised ware of the Atajadizo style to their own redware. By so doing, they produced a modified form of Ostiones-style pottery. During Period IVa, the Atajadizo potters on the Dominican side of the passage developed a second Chican style, which is known as Guayabal (Veloz Maggiolo and others 1976: 73–176). Its surfaces were less highly polished; and its modeled-incised lugs and incised designs, more complex.

Boca Chica, another Chican style with more highly polished surfaces and better modeling-incision, developed farther west along the southern coast of the Dominican Republic. Its potters established a colony in the middle of the southern coast of Puerto Rico, settling at Santa Isabel, on the boundary between the local Ostionan and Elenan potters (Rouse 1986: 148–50). They introduced their own form of Chican pottery (fig. 27b) and influenced the two groups to develop theirs, Capá in Ostionan territory and Esperanza in Elenan territory. The former was thinner, more delicate, and more elaborately decorated than the latter (compare a and c in fig. 27).

Potsherds of both the intrusive Boca Chica and the local Capá and Esperanza styles have been found as trade ware throughout Puerto Rico, unlike in the previous periods, which show little evidence of trade. This increased interaction may be correlated with the rise of chiefdoms (Rouse and Alegría 1990: 68). In Period IVa, Chican pottery also spread westward from the Mona Passage area to the Meillacan peoples in the rest of Hispaniola, except for the outer half of its southwestern peninsula (Rouse and Moore 1985). Again, the pottery became simpler the farther it went.

The spread continued across the Windward Passage to the previously

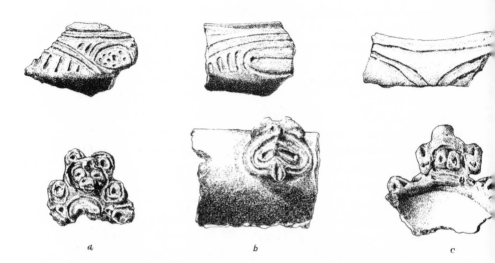

Fig. 27. Chican Ostionoid pottery: *a*, Capá style; *b*, Boca Chica style; *c*, Esperanza style. All are from Puerto Rico. They illustrate the effect of the colony of Boca Chica potters from the Dominican Republic on the native Ostionan (*a*) and Elenan (*c*) potters (after Rouse 1986, fig. 29).

Meillacan area on the eastern tip of Cuba (Rouse 1986: 164–66). The Tainos told the conquistadors that people from Hispaniola—presumably Chicans—had recently moved to this area (Lovén 1935: 69).

From ceramics let us turn to the rubber-ball game, which was widespread throughout the tropical Americas in the time of Columbus. It was mostly played on unstructured ball grounds (Stern 1949). Only the Mayas, their neighbors—including the Hohokam peoples in the southwestern United States—and the central Ostionoids built artificial courts for the purpose. Earlier, I raised the possibility that the unstructured ceremonial areas recently found in Saladoid and Ostionoid sites, at Maisabel in north-central Puerto Rico (Siegel 1990), for example, might also have been used for playing ball. It remains to be determined whether games were actually played there and, if so, whether the practice persisted without interruption until historic time, when it was observed by the conquistadors among the Western and presumably also the Eastern Tainos.

Archeologists have had more success in reconstructing the prehistory of the ball and dance courts described by the chroniclers. The earliest known occurrences of these structures are at the Elenan Ostionoid sites of Bronce and Tibes, near Ponce in south-central Puerto Rico, both of which date from Periods IIIa and IIIb. From there, the courts apparently spread eastward to St. Croix in the Virgin Islands and westward through Hispaniola to eastern Cuba, becoming associated with Chican pottery in the process.

It may be no accident that the earliest court sites date from Periods IIIa or IIIb, when the Ostionoids were moving into the interior of Puerto Rico. The foothills and mountains on the island are among the most rugged in the Greater Antilles and would have offered a strong incentive to level the ground and form embankments. The earliest known courts, at Bronce and Tibes, are, however, situated on relatively flat ground, which needed only slight leveling. They were lined with stone slabs, set on end or laid flat, and have yielded burials reminiscent of those in the ceremonial area at Maisabel. The subsequent Chican peoples lacked this practice; their burials occur in separate cemeteries (Morse 1990: 57).

The most elaborate and specialized complex of ball and dance courts has been found at the Caguana site (also known as Capá), in the mountains northwest of Bronce and Tibes. That site has yielded Ostionan and Chican pottery dating from Periods IIIb and IVa, respectively. Originally excavated by J. Alden Mason (1941), it has been restored by Ricardo E. Alegría (1983) for the Instituto de Cultura Puertorriqueña.

Central to the Caguana site is a large, rectangular dance court. Its sides are lined with vertically placed limestone slabs or granite boulders; its ends are closed with stone pavements. Many of the slabs and boulders are decorated with petroglyphs, which portray zemis. A smaller oval structure of uncertain function is attached to one side. It, too, is bounded by stones. Flanking the dance court is a longer and narrower structure lined with stones on all four sides, which has been identified as a ball court. It contains no petroglyphs. Seven similarly shaped courts of uncertain function surround the central structures. Some are open ended and others completely enclosed (fig. 28).

The Caguana Indians leveled their courts by digging out and terracing the uphill sides. Spectators are thought to have observed the dances and games from these terraces and from nearby mounds of earth, possibly constructed for the purpose. The excavators also encountered the floors and posts of several large, rectangular buildings, which may have been chiefs' houses or temples. Mason (1941: 264) has suggested that Caguana was the seat of Guarionex, an important cacique when the Spaniards arrived.

Other Puerto Rican sites of Periods IIIb and IVa contain roadlike structures lined with closely spaced, parallel earthen embankments, which bring to mind a roadway encountered by Columbus when he landed on the western end of the island during his second voyage (Rouse 1952: 484–89). The structures were presumably used for ceremonial purposes rather than for

Fig. 28. The Caguana dance and ball courts. *Top,* row of stone slabs lining the central dance court, the petroglyphs marked with chalk to show more clearly. The second one from the left portrays Atabey, the mother goddess. *Bottom,* aerial view of the site. The large, square central dance court is left of center; the central ball court, just beneath it (top photograph courtesy of José R. Oliver; bottom photograph courtesy of A. Gus Pantel).

transportation, which was done on foot and hence would have required only paths.

Many major Puerto Rican village sites, such as Hacienda Grande, lack artificial courts and roadways (for example, Rouse and Alegría 1990). Conversely, some courts are located in the countryside, perhaps because they were built on boundaries between chiefdoms for extramural games.

It is not uncommon to find fragments of "stone collars" and "elbow stones" in and around the Puerto Rican courts. The collars are complete rings shaped to fit around the human waist (fig. 31b). The elbow stones are partial rings that may have been completed by attaching cordage to their ends. Both appear to have had wooden prototypes. Analogies in Mesoamerican archeology suggest that the wooden and the lighter-stone collars and elbow stones were worn by ball players as belts with which to protect their bodies and to deflect the ball (Ekholm 1961). The more massive collars must have been purely ceremonial, as among the Mayas and their neighbors.

The public structures and their contents become simpler and less specialized as one travels eastward and westward from central Puerto Rico. The easternmost structure, at Salt River on St. Croix, consists of a single dance and ball court in the middle of a village site (Morse 1990). Behind the court is a cemetery and an area containing scattered human bones, which was probably where the Chicans worshiped the bones of their ancestors. Large three-pointed zemis and fragments of stone belts are surprisingly common at the Salt River site, considering that it is on the eastern edge of the distribution of the ball court.

The best evidence for westward diffusion from Puerto Rico has been obtained at Atajadizo and Guayabal, on the Hispaniolan side of the Mona Passage. The former site, dating from Period IIIb, lacks public structures. The latter site, dating from Period IVa, has two dance or ball courts, roads lined with stones, a residential area, and a separate cemetery containing burials. Fragments of stone belts were found in the courts (Veloz Maggiolo and others 1976).

The courts become larger in size but fewer in number as one moves westward through the Dominican Republic (Wilson 1990a: 24–26). The largest structure is the Corral de los Indios, a circular enclosure in the southwest that may have been the seat of Chief Caonabo. Single courts lined only with earthen embankments prevail in Haiti and Cuba (Alegría 1983). All these structures are accompanied by Chican pottery dating from Period IVa. Ball belts, however, do not extend farther west than central Hispaniola (Hatt 1932: 6).

Finally, Sullivan (1981: 135–203) has discovered a complex of public structures on Middle Caicos Island, north of Haiti. It consists of two small plazas or house sites and a roadway, all lined with piles of stones in the absence of slabs. The roadway leads from the site to a salt-collecting area, which is believed to be the source of the village's prosperity. The only Period IVa, Formative-age site that cannot be assigned to the Chican subseries, it yielded Palmetto pottery accompanied by a smaller quantity of modeled-incised ware, which could have been obtained from Hispaniola in exchange for locally produced salt or deposited by Chican overlords from Haiti.

We may conclude that West Indian dance and ball courts originated in the recently discovered Saladoid practice of clustering houses around ceremonial areas. The Puerto Rico Ostionoids began to construct dance and ball courts during Period IIIa or IIIb and to use ball belts of stone during Period IVa. Both these practices then spread to St. Croix and to the eastern and central parts of Hispaniola. The stone belts stopped there, but the courts continued through the rest of Hispaniola to eastern Cuba and the Turks and Caicos islands. Unstructured dance and ball grounds survived beyond the range of the courts.

Before the recent discoveries, it was reasonable to explain the resemblances between the Mesoamerican and West Indian ball courts and belts by postulating diffusion from the Mayas and their mainland neighbors, either via Yucatán or along the western and southern shores of the Caribbean Sea (Alegría 1983: 154–55). Now we must also consider the possibility of parallel development from an earlier form of the game played on unstructured grounds, which appears to have been widespread throughout tropical America. This possibility seems to me to better fit the available evidence.

The Saladoids of Period IIa placed considerable emphasis on burial, after which the practice declined in importance. A revival took place during Periods IIIb and IVa, when the graves were once again grouped in cemeteries, either within the settlements or in caves, and were furnished with grave goods. The latter practice testifies to increasing differences in status. Yet archeologists have found no traces of the more exotic forms of burial described by the conquistadors.

Three finds from Period IVa indicate intensification of the practice of worshiping ancestors. A cave in the Dominican Republic has yielded a statuette of cotton woven around a human skull resting on a large stone, which had been substituted for the bones of the torso (fig. 29e). Elsewhere, a clay and a wooden urn appear to have served as containers in which to keep the bones of ancestors. Both artifacts are highly decorated with human

Fig. 29. Ostionoid/Taino zemis: *a*, stone three-pointer, believed to represent the supreme deity, Yúcahu; *b*, stone head of Maquetaurie Guayaba, Lord of the Land of the Dead; *c*, shell carving of Opiyelguobirán, the dog deity, who watched over the spirits of the dead; *d*, wooden statuette of Baibrama, the zemi who helped cassava grow; *e*, cotton zemi of an ancestor, woven around a human skull and supporting stone; *f*, wooden statuette of a bird fishing. Figs. *a* and *e* are from the Dominican Republic; *b*, from Puerto Rico; *c*, from Antigua; *d* and *f*, from Jamaica (*a*, after Rouse 1986, fig. 27*c*; *b*, *c*, after Arrom 1989, pls. 29, 41; *d*–*f*, after Montas, Borrell, and Moya Pons 1983: 40, 38, 44).

figures that may portray ancestral zemis. (Arrom 1989, pl. 42, illustrates the second one.)

Many other kinds of religiously significant artifacts from Period IVa are also known. They may be divided into three groups: sculpted figures of zemis, paraphernalia used in worshiping the figures, and secular objects decorated with representations of zemis.

FIGURES OF ZEMIS

Archeologists and ethnohistorians approach the figures differently, archeologists treating them as artifacts, to be classified descriptively, and ethnohistorians identifying the deities portrayed by the figures, basing their conclusions primarily on Father Ramón Pané's report to Columbus on Taino religion. In discussing the identifications, I rely primarily upon research by my Yale colleague José J. Arrom (1989).

By Period IVa, the small, plain three-pointed stones of the Saladoid cultures had evolved into much larger and heavier objects, which bear relief carvings of humans or animals, often combined with geometric motifs like those on Chican pottery (fig. 29a). These specimens are limited to the Chicans of the Mona Passage area; they do not occur among the Meillacans on the western frontier or the Elenans in the east. Ethnohistorically they are Classic Taino.

Arrom (1989: 17–30) identifies the large carved three-pointers as the Tainos' supreme deity, Yúcahu. The name Yúcahu means spirit of cassava, he argues, and Pané mentions the use of three-pointers to increase the yield of cassava. Zemis were buried in the conucos for this purpose.

The late Ostionoid/Taino practice of worshiping or hiding figures of zemis in caves has preserved statuettes of wood, especially on Hispaniola and Jamaica. A lesser number of the statuettes are made of stone. About two feet high, they consist of standing, squatting, or reclining figures, most surmounted by circular platters upon which the worshipers placed the hallucinogenic snuff they took during rituals. Men, women, animals, birds, and fish are represented (fig. 29d,f). Many humans have prominent genitalia. Other anatomical features, such as ribs, are also portrayed with considerable fidelity. Disks and crosshatched pieces of shell were inlaid to represent the eyes and teeth. The chroniclers tell us that statuettes of zemis were also made from cotton. The figure woven around a human skull is the only known survivor, with the possible exception of an artifact from the conquest period (fig. 39a).

A few of the statuettes are female. Arrom (1989: 31–36) identifies them as Atabey, mother of Yúcahu. She was the goddess of human fertility, to whom women prayed for success in childbirth.

A number of the examples appear to represent a male zemi known as Baibrama. The Classic Tainos sought his assistance in growing cassava and in curing persons poisoned by its juice (Arrom 1989: 67–73). Baibrama is shown in a standing or squatting position with an erect penis, as if urinating to increase the growth of crops (fig. 29d). Several examples bear cassava stems or shoots. All are topped by solid wooden bowls, which take the place of the platters on other statuettes. They may have been intended to portray the bowls in which the women collected the cassava juice and boiled it to remove its poison.

Some statuettes of wood or stone have tears streaming down their cheeks. Arrom (1989: 37–45) identifies them as Boinayel, Son of the Gray Serpent, who was the Taino rain god. Pané reports that Boinayel figures could perspire as if they were producing rainwater. The stone zemis would have perspired if placed in damp caves, where water could condense on them. Boinayel is sometimes paired with a twin named Márohu (fig. 31f). Because the name means cloudless, Arrom (1989: 39) considers Márohu to be the deity of fair weather.

One statuette of wood, another of stone, and a carved shell portray Opiyelguobirán, the dog deity (fig. 29c). Pané reports that he watched over the spirits of the dead (Arrom 1989: 61–66). The Classic Tainos believed that the spirits of the dead lived in Coaybay, a remote island region, and were ruled by Maquetaurie Guayaba, Lord of the Land of the Dead. A group of large, cadaverous stone faces are thought by Arrom (1989: 52–56) to represent this deity (fig. 29b). Several of them are tenoned or attached to elbow stones. One is carved on a three-pointer—an exception to the pattern identifying three-pointers with Yúcahu.

Petroglyphs were another means of picturing zemis. They occur in caves, on natural outcrops of stone, and on the slabs lining dance courts. A petroglyph in the central court at Caguana, Puerto Rico, may have represented Atabey, the mother of Yúcahu.

RELIGIOUS PARAPHERNALIA

The Cedrosan and Huecan Saladoid worshipers had inhaled snuff from pottery vessels fitted out with small tubes, which they could insert in their nostrils (fig. 21e). The Ostionan Ostionoids continued this practice (Rouse and Alegría 1990), but the Chican Ostionoids put snuff on the platforms on the tops of their zemis and inhaled it through separate tubes of wood or bone (fig. 5d). Some of the surviving tubes are highly decorated with figures of zemis (fig. 30a).

A number of late Ostionoid assemblages have yielded spatulas of wood, bone, or shell, which appear to have been used to induce vomiting in the

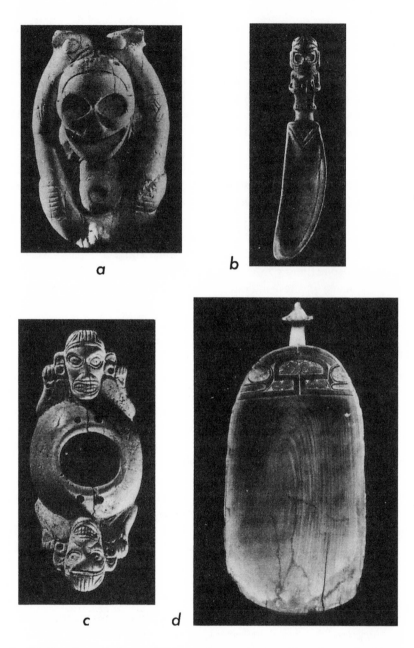

Fig. 30. Paraphernalia for worshiping zemis: *a*, pair of snuffing tubes made of bone; *b*, vomiting spatula of bone; *c*, bone vessel; *d*, wooden platter. Figs. *a–c* are from the Dominican Republic; *d*, from Cuba (*a*, *b*, after Montas, Borrell, and Moya Pons 1983: 85, 80; *c*, after Scott 1985, pl. 76; *d*, after Arrom 1989, pl. 66).

ritual of purification described by Pané. Most are decorated with figures of zemis (fig. 30b).

Finally, the wooden artifacts include a number of small tables and platters that may have seen service in rituals (fig. 30d). The more highly decorated vessels of wood, bone, and pottery could also have been used for this purpose (fig. 30c).

SECULAR ART

In chapter 1 we saw that the Classic Tainos decorated their household utensils and personal ornaments with figures of their zemis. Projecting this practice back into prehistory, I would suggest that the original Saladoid migrants introduced it in Period IIa, that it lost popularity in Periods IIb and IIIa, and that it was revived in Periods IIIb and IVa, especially among the Meillacan and Chican Ostionoid peoples. A renewed interest in zemism is indicated by the increasing popularity of human and animal adornos on the household pottery (fig. 27). In the final period these images were extended to stone pestles, axes, and other tools that the Saladoid artisans had left plain (fig. 31c,e).

A unique design in stone or clay—a pair of spirally arranged arms attached to a human body—is thought to symbolize the hurricane (fig. 31c). Arrom (1989: 46–51) identifies it as Guabancex, the Lady of the Winds. According to Pané, she had two assistants, Guataubá, a herald who produced the hurricane-force winds, and Coatrisquie, who caused the accompanying floodwaters.

The Saladoid potters of Period IIa had made effigy vessels and figurines in the form of zemis. The practice died out at the end of that period and was not revived until Period IVa (fig. 31h). Arrom (1989: 77–89) concludes that the Period IVa examples represent the Earth Goddess, Itiba Cahubasba.

Among the personal ornaments thought to portray zemis are tiny, flexed human figures carved of stone and pierced at the top for suspension (fig. 31d). Pané says that these were placed on the forehead. Animal and human amulets were also worn on the body (fig. 31a,f). Arrom (1989: 43–45) identifies many as Boinayel, the rain god. Small human masks carved of shell are also worth noting. They may be the signs of rank known to Columbus as guaíza (García Arévalo 1982: 26). Some could have portrayed ancestral zemis. Most of the Taino ornaments have not survived archeologically because they were made of perishable materials. A belt woven of cotton is a possible exception; it is discussed with the other Historic-age artifacts in the next chapter.

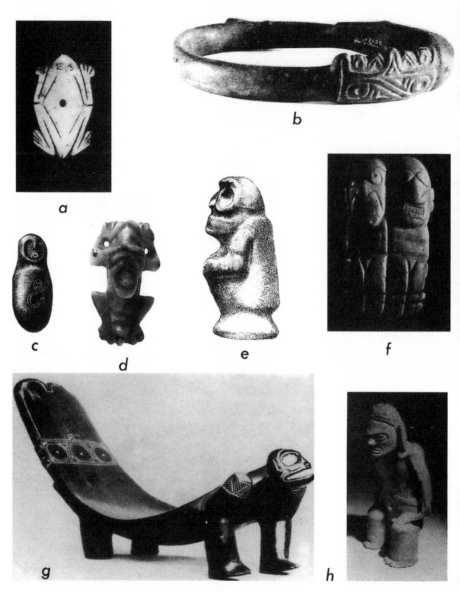

Fig. 31. Representations of zemis on secular artifacts: *a*, frog pendant of shell; *b*, ball belt (stone collar) of stone; *c*, celt-shaped stone engraved with a zemi, probably Guabancex, the goddess of the hurricane; *d*, tiny zemi worn by a warrior on his forehead; *e*, pestle carved in the form of a zemi; *f*, pendant of stone with twin zemis, possibly Guabancex's assistants; *g*, wooden stool (*duho*) inlaid with gold; *h*, turtle-backed effigy vessel. Fig. *a* is from Cuba; *b*, from Puerto Rico; *c, e–h*, from the Dominican Republic; *d*, from Haiti (*a–c, g, h* after Arrom 1989, pls. 28, 58, 62, 63, 56; *d*, Yale Peabody Museum specimen; *e*, after Rouse 1986, fig. 27*d*; *f*, after Montas, Borrell, and Moya Pons 1983: 96).

Several wooden rattles, used to accompany dances, bear figures of zemis. So also do the ball belts (stone collars and elbow stones; fig. 31*b*).

Finally, wooden stools (duho) are decorated with zemis. Because they were a sign of chiefly rank and their style places them in Period IVa, they testify to the existence of chiefdoms at that time. The presence of elaborate grave goods, which were also tokens of chiefly rank, confirm this dating. Most stools are carved, presumably with images of the chiefs' own zemis. Several are inlaid with gold leaf, which was another prerogative of the caciques (fig. 31*g*).

CONCLUSIONS

The religious and secular art of the Taino had its roots in the Saladoid cultures of Periods IIa and IIb. It began to develop during Period IIIa, between 600 and 900 A.D., and reached maturity in Period IVa, beginning circa 1200 A.D. All of the post-Saladoid peoples in the northern part of the West Indies appear to have contributed to its growth, exchanging ideas and beliefs while interacting with each other.

Archeologically speaking, the art is diagnostic of the latest Ostionoid peoples. It was most common among the Chican Ostionoids but also occurred among the Meillacans of Jamaica (fig. 29*f*) and Cuba (fig. 31*a*), the Palmetto people of the Bahamian Archipelago (Arrom 1989, pl. 22), and the later Elenans of the Leeward Islands (Arrom 1989, pl. 13). Ethnohistorically speaking, it reached its climax among the Classic Tainos—hence their name—and also flourished among the Western Tainos. Its distribution among the Eastern Tainos and the Island-Caribs is discussed below.

The Eastern Ostionoid Peoples, 600–1640

The Elenan Ostionoid peoples, who occupied the eastern frontier, originally extended from central Puerto Rico through the Virgin and Leeward islands to Guadeloupe. Their boundary in Puerto Rico is difficult to trace because Puerto Rican pottery was transitional. The zone of transition appears to have extended diagonally across the middle of the island from the southwest to the northeast.

The Elenans diverged from the Ostionans in Period IIIa. Their terminal date varies from place to place: in eastern Puerto Rico and on St. Croix, they succumbed to the Chican expansion that took place during Period IVa, and on Guadeloupe, they gave way to the Island-Caribs during Period IVa or IVb. Too little is known about the post-Saladoid archeology of the intervening islands to determine how long the Elenans lasted there. On the larger islands, they probably survived as Eastern Tainos until Period IVb, but the inhabitants of the smaller islands may have succumbed to raids by Island-Caribs based in Guadeloupe (Davis and Goodwin 1990: 45).

Like the Ostionans farther west, the Elenans became more numerous during Period IIIa. They look as though they underwent a population explosion because they were unable to expand into Archaic-age territory, as the Ostionans were doing, and hence had to absorb their growing population within their homeland. Some authors postulate a migration from the Windward Islands to explain their spurt in numbers, but the archeological evidence does not support this hypothesis. It is unclear whether the population continued to grow during Period IIIb. Island-Carib raids appear to have caused a decline during Period IVa.

The Elenans continued to inhabit the major sites settled by their Saladoid ancestors—for example, Hacienda Grande and Maisabel in Puerto Rico, Sorcé on Vieques Island, Salt River on St. Croix, and Indian Creek on Antigua—and expanded to the previously uninhabited land on beaches and in the interior of the larger islands, especially Puerto Rico. They supported the growth in population by improving agriculture, developing deep-sea fishing, and collecting more shellfish (Wing and Scudder 1980; Wing 1990).

A stable population is also indicated by the ceramic trends, best known for eastern Puerto Rico and the Virgin Islands in the north and Antigua, near the southern end of the Leeward chain (Rouse 1974, 1976, 1982a). During Period IIb, the pottery in both places lost decoration and became simpler in shape, as elsewhere in Ostionoid territory. Zic incision and modeled-incised designs died out, and white-on-red painted motifs became crude and rectilinear.

Period IIIa was a time of local variation. Strap handles survived in the north, and white-on-red painting gave way to red and smudged designs, like those among the neighboring Ostionan peoples (fig. 32d). Decoration became less common. Strap handles disappeared from Antigua in the south, but rectilinear white-on-red designs continued to be made there—along with curvilinearly incised designs, scratched pottery, and legged griddles, all of which show a southern influence.

Period IIIb is characterized by thick-walled hemispherical bowls. Many of them were topped off with coarse, cylindrical coils of clay, which often came apart when the vessels were discarded (fig. 32b,c). The rims of others were thickened by adding ridges (fig. 32a). The northern potters decorated their vessels with vestigial handles and vertical incised lines (fig. 32c). Southern potters retained their previous ornamentation except for white paint, which gradually disappeared.

During Period IVa, the Chican subseries, which had developed in the

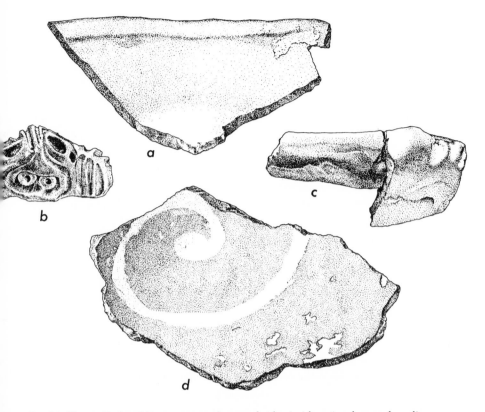

Fig. 32. Elenan Ostionoid pottery: *a*, undecorated ridge inside a rim; *b*, top of a cylindrical rim modeled and incised with a bat-head design; *c*, cylindrical rim bearing a vestigial handle flanked by deep vertical grooves; *d*, red-on-plain spiral, painted in the resist technique. Figs. *a–c* are from the Santa Elena culture; *d*, from the Monserrate culture (Yale Peabody Museum specimens).

Dominican Republic, spread to Puerto Rico and St. Croix, if not to the rest of the Virgin Islands, and strongly influenced the pottery of the northern Leewards. Bowls with incurving shoulders were now decorated with modeled-incised lugs and curvilinearly incised designs. They are a prominent feature of the late prehistoric pottery on Anguilla and Saba (Douglas 1991; Hofman and Hoogland 1991). Farther south, the pottery of this period is too poorly known to be characterized.

Settlement patterns became more complex during the course of the ceramic sequence. The inhabitants of the Maisabel site in Puerto Rico had already begun to deposit their refuse around a central plaza during Period IIa and to bury their dead in the plaza. There is reason to believe that they continued both practices during Periods IIb and IIIa. They could also have danced and played ball in the plaza, but evidence that they did has not survived (Siegel 1990).

Like Maisabel, the sites of Bronce and Tibes, along the southern coast of Puerto Rico, are on the Elenan frontier, adjoining the Ostionan peoples. Their pottery is transitional from Elenan to Ostionan, dating from Periods IIIa and IIIb. Because the sites contain the first public structures in the West Indies—the earliest structures identifiable as dance plazas and ball courts (Robinson, Lundberg, and Walker 1983–85; González Colón 1984)—they may be said to mark the beginning of the Formative age.

The Indian Creek site on Antigua contains a ring of middens situated alongside a small stream some distance inland (Rouse 1974, fig. 1). When the Cedrosans first settled that site during Period IIa, they deposited their refuse in heaps at the downstream end of the eventual ring and on the side adjacent to the stream. During Period IIb they began to fill in the rest of the ring, and their Elenan descendants completed the process during Period IIIa.

Because the aim of the research was chronological, the excavators did not explore the center of the ring to determine what activities took place there. Fred Olsen (1974: 213–14) thought he had found a ball court upstream from the ring, but the stone slabs upon which he based his conclusion are too irregularly distributed to be convincing. It is not impossible, however, that the refuse-free area within the ring served as a dance and ball ground even though it does not have the structure of a court. Such unstructured ground is also evident at the nearby site of Mamora Bay, dating from Period IIIb, and it is documented for the Eastern Tainos of Columbus's time.

The production of small, plain three-pointed zemis persisted from Period IIb into Period IIIa, providing another linkage between the Cedrosan and Elenan peoples. These objects increased in size during Period IIIb and began to be decorated, with complex carved figures in Puerto Rico and the Virgin Islands or with incised lines on Antigua. The carved figures were part of the more general development of stone sculpture among the central Ostionoids.

Other forms of late Ostionoid/Classic Taino art are relatively rare. Two shell carvings have already been mentioned—a figure of the dog deity, Opiyelguobirán, from Antigua and a geometrically incised conical object from Montserrat. It is not known whether these were made locally or were obtained by trade with the Greater Antilles.

The trading system established by the Saladoids had died out by the end of Period IIa. Only local exchange remained; Jay B. Haviser, Jr. (1990), has concluded, for example, that St. Martin and nearby Anguilla Island, in the northern Leewards, functioned as an interaction sphere during post-Saladoid time. Long-distance trade must have been revived during Period IVa, for the importation of copper-gold ornaments (guanín) from South America is mentioned by the conquistadors.

Beyond the Eastern Frontier, 600–1640

The Windward Islands are at the southern end of the Lesser Antilles, outside the territory of the Ostionoid/Taino peoples. Nevertheless, they deserve our attention because their inhabitants formed part of the Tainos' environment, and the two populations interacted.

The system of periods used in discussing the emergence of the Tainos is not applicable to the Windward Islands. More useful are the archeologically defined series of peoples and cultures, from Saladoid through Troumassoid to Suazoid, and the local succession of ethnic groups mentioned in the historical sources—the Igneris and the Island-Caribs (fig. 26). The archeological sequence is based on the old, single-level system of classifying peoples and cultures; the bi-level system used elsewhere in this book has not yet been extended to the Windward Islands.

Here I pay special attention to the island of Martinique, not only because of its relatively large size and central position but also because more archeology has been done there. Our best knowledge of the distribution of settlements comes from that island.

SALADOID SERIES

The pottery of the Windward Islands began to diverge from that in the rest of the West Indies about 300–400 A.D. with the spread of new modes of modeling-incision from Barrancoid potters on the mainland. In effect, the interaction sphere that had developed at the mouth of the Orinoco River expanded into the West Indies at this time. Bypassing Barbados, which was off the main line of travel and trade, it extended northward to Guadeloupe. The Saladoid pottery beyond that point was unaffected; it had the Greater Antillean trend toward plainware. To my knowledge, the Barrancoid influence was limited to pottery. The Saladoid people of Martinique continued to live in the moist northeastern part of that island, where they had originally settled during the middle of the first millennium B.C.

TROUMASSOID SERIES

If the radiocarbon measurements are correct, the Saladoid series in the Windward Islands evolved into the Troumassoid between 500 and 600 A.D., about the same time that the Saladoid peoples and cultures farther

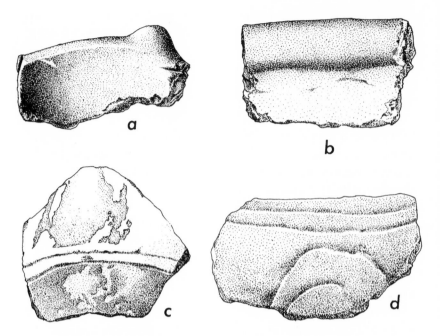

Fig. 33. Troumassoid pottery: *a*, wedge-shaped lug on a triangular rim; *b*, red-painted ridge inside a rim; *c*, white design on badly worn red slip; *d*, curvilinearly incised design. All are from the Troumassé B culture (Yale Peabody Museum specimens).

north were beginning to diverge into Ostionoid peoples and cultures. The Troumassoid series lasted until around 1000 (Rouse, Allaire, and Boomert 1985, table 4).

During this time, the inhabitants of Martinique expanded from the northeastern part of the island into the more arid southeastern sector. They apparently began to depend more on farming and fishing and less on gathering produce from the rain forests (Allaire 1977: 312–13; 1991).

Unlike the Ostionoid potters farther north, the Troumassoid potters continued to decorate their vessels with red, black, and white paint, often in zones outlined with curvilinearly incised lines (fig. 33*b,c*). Purely incised designs, composed of spirals and other curvilinear motifs, were also common (fig. 33*d*). The Barrancoid-inspired modeling-incision of late Saladoid time was abandoned, but the Saladoid practice of making wedge-shaped lugs continued (fig. 33*a*; Allaire 1977: 312–14).

In late Troumassoid time, the pottery became cruder and plainer. Painting was more often linear and was done only in red and black. Loop handles disappeared, as among the contemporaneous Leeward Islanders. Vessels were fitted with legs, pedestals, or annular bases; and griddles were made with legs attached, like those in Antigua, to the north (McKusick 1960, fig. 9 and pls. 1, 2; Allaire 1977: 315–17).

Clay spindle whorls first appeared in late Troumassoid time. Louis Allaire (1990) infers that there was increasing production of cotton, which grows well in the dry southeastern part of Martinique. He also calls attention to the possibility that the late Troumassoids in the southeast began to specialize in the production of salt, paralleling the situation in the Bahamian Archipelago. The finds from this period in southern Martinique and northern St. Lucia are so similar as to suggest that the two areas functioned as an interaction sphere.

SUAZOID SERIES

By the end of the first millennium A.D., when this series made its appearance, the Indians of Martinique had completely abandoned the northeastern part of the island and were concentrated in the southeastern quadrant (Allaire 1991). They remained there until 1450, when, to judge from the patterning of radiocarbon dates, they abruptly disappeared (Allaire 1977, 1991). To my knowledge, no European trade ware has been found at their sites, either in Martinique or on the other islands.

The late Troumassoid trend toward coarse plainware reached its climax in Suazoid time. Most vessels were thicker and more poorly made and were tempered with a greater variety of materials, including crushed shell and tiny pebbles (Bullen 1964, pl. 23). Surfaces were often scratched or scraped, and for a while rims were roughened by finger impression (fig. 34*b,c,e*). Legs and footed griddles retained their popularity (fig. 34*c*).

The emphasis upon coarse plainware parallels that in the Palmetto style of the Bahamian Archipelago. Like the Palmetto potters, the Suazoid peoples continued to produce a small minority of fine, decorated pottery that bore painted or incised designs (fig. 34*d*). The painting continued to be both areal and linear. The incision grew simpler but still included scrolls and circles. There are also local forms of lugs, including pegs (fig. 34*a*) and heads with flat faces, appliquéd noses and eyebrows, punctated or slashed mouths, nostrils, and eyes, and pierced ears.

Suazoid vessels and griddles are accompanied by an unusual variety of other types of clay artifacts, including pot stands, spindle whorls, stamps, figurines, and pierced cylinders known as loom weights. Stone grinders and pestles and shell celts, gouges, and scrapers are also diagnostic (Allaire 1977: 318–26).

The reappearance of head lugs and figurines, which had been absent since Saladoid time, suggests an intensification of the worship of zemis. This is also indicated by the presence of ritual objects of Chican Ostionoid/

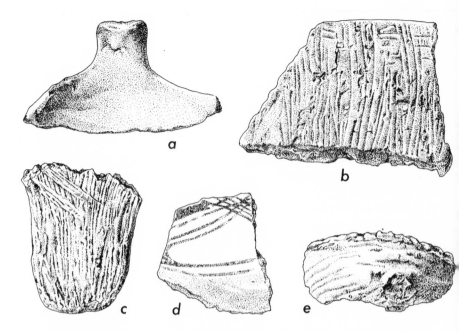

Fig. 34. Suazoid pottery: *a,* peg-shaped lug on the end of a bowl; *b,* scarified rim sherd; *c,* scarified griddle leg; *d,* vessel body that is red slipped and surmounted by a linear black design on a plain surface (this type of potsherd is called Caliviny Polychrome); *e,* simple hemispherical bowl with a finger-impressed rim (Yale Peabody Museum specimens).

Classic Taino types, which probably date from 1200, when the Chicans began to expand into the Virgin and Leeward islands, to 1450, when Suazoid culture apparently came to an end. Included are large three-pointers, a statuette topped with a snuffing platform, a tube that could have been used to inhale snuff (cohoba), a stool (duho), and human face masks (guaíza). With a few exceptions, all appear to have been made locally. According to Allaire (1990), "they are essentially imitations or reduced models, usually in clay, of ... pieces made of stone or wood" by the Chicans/Classic Tainos.

These specimens are decorated with typical Classic Taino images. Allaire has been able to identify Atabey, mother of the supreme deity, and Boinayel, the rain god. He also cites indirect evidence for the presence of the ball game. As in the Leeward Islands, it must have been played on open grounds rather than structured courts.

ISLAND-CARIBS

Just as the pioneers in Greater Antillean archeology ascribed all the remains they found to the Tainos, the initial collectors in the Windward

Islands assumed that all their finds were Island-Carib. When the Suazoid remains were discovered, they unhesitatingly attributed them to that source, especially because Suazoid pottery was so drab. The Island-Caribs would have made poor pottery, it was argued, because they were "savages" and cannibals.

As our understanding of Suazoid culture has improved, it has become clear that its people were more sophisticated than their pottery had led us to believe. They are now seen to be the climax of a continuous period of local development that began in Saladoid time. William G. Haag (1965: 242–45) was the first to reach this conclusion. It has since been documented in detail by Allaire (1977, 1990) and reaffirmed by David D. Davis and R. Christopher Goodwin (1990). Allaire notes that the Suazoids could hardly have adopted so many elements of Ostionoid iconography if the two series of peoples had not had a common Saladoid ancestry.

Allaire (1991) has also called attention to a sharp difference between the Suazoid and Island-Carib settlement patterns on the island of Martinique. As we have seen, the Suazoids were concentrated in the dry southeastern part of that island. The Island-Caribs, by contrast, lived in the moist northeast.

How are we to explain these continuities and disjunctions? The best way, it seems to me, is to correlate the Suazoid peoples and their cultures with the Igneris, that is, with the ethnic group that the Island-Caribs claimed to have conquered. I would suggest that the Suazoid series/Igneri ethnic group came into existence about 1000 and became extinct about 1450 when Caribs invaded from the mainland.

In making this suggestion, I am assuming the validity of the Island-Carib origin traditions as they are documented in the historical sources. Most archeologists accept these traditions (see Allaire 1980), but a few (like Davis and Goodwin 1990) argue against them. I prefer to accept the judgment of my colleagues in ethnohistory, who tell me that the documentation of the traditions is extensive and internally consistent. I am reminded that the linguist Douglas Taylor (1939) originally questioned my use of the Igneri-to-Island-Carib sequence, which I had taken from an ethnohistorian, Sven Lovén (1935: vi), but he changed his mind after discovering the sources from which Lovén had obtained the sequence. Indeed, many modern linguists prefer to apply the name Igneri to the language of the Island-Caribs, in the belief that the Island-Caribs retained the language of their predecessors.

In my opinion, the time has come for archeologists to join their ethnohistorical and linguistic colleagues in accepting the existence of a change in ethnic group from Igneri to Island-Carib, despite the survival of the Igneri language. The archeological and ethnohistorical evidence suggests that the change took place between 1450, when the Suazoid series came to an end, and 1493, when Columbus encountered Island-Caribs on Guadeloupe.

How and why did the change happen? There are three possibilities: it may have been a local development in the Windward Islands, as hypothesized by Davis and Goodwin (1990); it may have been the result of further population movement from South America, comparable to the previous Saladoid repeopling of the Windward Islands (Louis Allaire and Aad Boomert, personal communication); or it may have been the consequence of the assimilation of Island-Caribs into the local Igneri population after Island-Carib war parties from the mainland conquered them. The last alternative seems to me to best fit the available evidence (Rouse 1986: 154).

The Carib invaders presumably came from the rain forests of the Guianas or the Peninsula of Paria. They may have chosen to settle in the moist northeastern part of Martinique rather than the dry southeast, where the Suazoids/Igneris lived, because, like the Saladoids before them, they preferred the kind of environment they had experienced in their homeland. They could have used the rain forests of the northeast as a base from which to attack and destroy the Suazoid/Igneri settlements on the rest of the island. Their practice of bride capture would have led them to install the local women and children in separate family houses in their own villages.

In proposing this solution to the Carib problem, I do not mean to imply that the presumed invaders necessarily settled first on Martinique, although that island might have attracted them because it was large, centrally located, and relatively wealthy, to judge from the nature of the archeological remains. If the invaders came in war parties, they could have conquered the Suazoids/Igneris on various islands but would not have been numerous enough to replace them. Instead, they would have mixed with them and adopted their language.

Archeologists may be expected to play a major role in finally resolving the problem. They should look for assemblages that can be securely dated between 1450, when we lose sight of the Suazoid series, and the seventeenth century, when Europeans began to settle the Lesser Antilles. Northeastern Martinique would be a good place to start such a search. Why have no Island-Carib remains been found there? The reason may be that the fieldwork has been done primarily by collectors seeking decorated pottery, as in the early archeological research in Puerto Rico. Because the ethnohistorical evidence indicates that the seventeenth-century Island-Carib pottery on Martinique was plain, it would be well to look for sites with that kind of pottery.

Another good place to look would be on the island of St. Vincent, where

Boomert (1986) has distinguished a Cayo style, with both decorated and plain vessels. The chronological position and ethnic affiliation of this style are unknown, but Boomert suggests that its pottery might have been produced by fifteenth-century mainland-Carib invaders, who subsequently abandoned their decoration and restricted themselves to plainware like that made by the seventeenth-century Island-Caribs. This change might be part of the general trend toward plain pottery in other parts of the Caribbean during post-Columbian time (Rouse and Cruxent 1963: 138; Deagan 1987: 347). Chronological research is needed on both Martinique and St. Vincent to determine the sequence of ceramic styles on those islands from the fifteenth to the seventeenth century.

CONCLUSIONS

The inhabitants of the Windward Islands began to go their own way about 300 A.D. The late Saladoid peoples of those islands had been subjected to strong Barrancoid influence from the mainland. The subsequent Troumassoid peoples continued to emphasize painting and incision instead of participating in the late Saladoid and early Ostionoid trend toward plain pottery. The Suazoids/Igneris, who came next, did have plainer pottery, and they do show influences from the late Ostionoids/Tainos, especially in religion, but they did not construct dance plazas and ball courts—and thereby advance into the Formative age. In my opinion, mainland-Carib war parties modified the Suazoid/Igneri culture but were unable to replace it with their own culture or to impose their own language.

The Suazoid peoples/Igneri ethnic group must have functioned as intermediaries between the mainlanders and the Ostionoids/Tainos, passing copper-gold ornaments from the former to the latter. If I am right, the Island-Caribs took over this trade or interrupted it only decades before the arrival of Columbus.

Conclusions

Perhaps the greatest advance in West Indian archeology since I entered the field in the 1930s has been the discovery that the ancestors of the Tainos created two outstanding forms of art, Saladoid in Period IIa and Ostionoid in Periods IIIb and IVa. The two were separated by a "dark age" during Periods IIb and IIIa. Many cultural traits—such as the cultivation of cassava, the firing of clay griddles for making bread from its flour, and the production of three-pointers and equipment for taking snuff—persisted through this dark age. Other traits, such as bottles, effigy vessels, figurines, masks, modeled-incised lugs, and curvilinearly incised designs, died out at the end of Period IIa and were revived in modified form during Period IIIb or IVa. Long-distance trading between South America and the Greater Antilles was also resumed at that time. Such a revival is not uncommon in other parts of the world. For example, the Mochica culture of Peru subsequently reappeared as the Chimu, Minoan civilization as classic Greek, and Roman art as the Renaissance, in each case after a considerable lapse of time.

When comparing the two West Indian climaxes, we may say that Saladoid artifacts are relatively small, fine, and delicately ornamented, and Ostionoid specimens heavier, bolder, and more massive. Saladoid pottery combines painting, modeling, and incision; Ostionoid pottery emphasizes modeling and incision. Saladoid incised lines are narrower and more deeply incised, Ostionoid lines more broadly and shallowly engraved. (Meillacan incision is an exception.) Saladoid designs appear sophisticated, Ostionoid designs exuberant. In the terminology of Mesoamerican archeology, Saladoid art is classic, and Ostionoid art postclassic.

These differences are exemplified by the three-pointers and other artwork carved in stone. Saladoid three-pointers are tiny compared to the Ostionoid three-pointers, and they lack their decoration. Clearly, the Saladoid artisans could not make such large and complex stone artifacts as the Ostionoid statuettes, collars, and elbow stones, nor did they produce so great a range of specialized ceremonial equipment.

A third major form of art, Casimiroid, has recently been recognized in the Greater Antilles, where it preceded Ostionoid art. It resembles Ostionoid art in its massivity and boldness; and its artisans were also able to make and decorate large and complex stone artifacts, many of which appear to have had ritual significance. This art could have influenced the development from Saladoid to Ostionoid. Indeed, a number of Casimiroid types of artifacts were incorporated into Ostionoid cultures, including stone vessels, axes as opposed to celts, conical pestles, flint blades (in Hispaniola), shell gouges (in Cuba), and stone balls and pegs.

Ostionoid art may therefore be regarded as a blend of Saladoid and Casimiroid elements, tied together by local innovations. This should not surprise us. Schools of artists and their products are inherently open to outside influences, unlike species of plants and animals, which remain pure because they cannot interbreed (Rouse 1972: 195–211).

The population that remained behind in the Ostionan homeland in the Mona Passage area while the other members of the subseries were pushing the frontier of the Ceramic/Archaic age westward had the advantage of living in a central position, with access to a greater number of innovations. They synthesized them to form a new Chican subseries, which subsequently spread to the immediate neighbors, Meillacans to the west and Elenans to the east, and eventually became the ethnic subgroup that is known as Classic Taino.

Recent research has pinpointed the origin of several elements of Chican culture. The practice of mounding fields into conucos is believed on slender evidence to have originated in the Cibao Valley of north-central Hispaniola and diffused eastward into Puerto Rico and westward into Jamaica. Chican pottery occurs earliest on the eastern end of Hispaniola, whence it spread across the Mona Passage to Puerto Rico and St. Croix and through central and northeastern Hispaniola to the adjacent tip of Cuba, becoming simpler as it went. It also influenced the pottery of central Cuba and the northern Leeward Islands.

Dance enclosures, ball courts, and other public works followed still another trajectory. The earliest examples have been found in central Puerto Rico, on the boundary between the Ostionan and Elenan subseries, and they reached their greatest complexity there during Chican time. They spread eastward to St. Croix and westward through Hispaniola to eastern Cuba and Middle Caicos Island in the Bahamian Archipelago, becoming simpler along the way. Ball belts of stone, that is, collars and elbows, are limited to the eastern part of the distribution of the courts. Both the belts and the courts may have developed from the practice of playing ball on unstructured grounds, which could have been introduced by the Saladoids.

Elenan, the easternmost division of the Ostionoid series, appears to have evolved locally in eastern Puerto Rico, the Virgin Islands, and the Leewards. In Puerto Rico and St. Croix, it was assimilated into the Chican subseries, becoming Classic Taino. In the rest of the Virgin Islands and in the northern Leewards, where it survived, it shows strong Chican influence, which is one reason for identifying the protohistoric inhabitants of those islands as Eastern Tainos. I have extended that label to the inhabitants of the southern Leewards because, even though the pottery of those islands is transitional, the sites appear to contain dance and ball grounds (though not artificially constructed courts) and because three-pointers persisted throughout the local sequence.

The Windward Islands, still farther south, are much better known archeologically. The picture that has emerged there is one of local development. Alone among all the post-Saladoid series of peoples in the West Indies, the initial Troumassoids retained elaborately painted and curvilinearly incised pottery. As that pottery evolved into the Suazoid styles, it gradually became coarse and plain, although fine ware with painted and incised decoration did not entirely disappear. Both the typology and the iconography of the Suazoid artifacts indicate Ostionoid influence, to which the Suazoids may have been receptive because they shared a common Saladoid ancestry.

The evidence of local development and Ostionoid influence belies the widespread belief that the Suazoid peoples were the Island-Caribs. I have suggested that they were instead the Igneris, whom the Island-Caribs claimed to have conquered. Unfortunately, this hypothesis is not yet testable archeologically because assemblages of artifacts laid down by the Island-Caribs cannot be identified.

In this connection, I think it important to recognize that archeology and ethnohistory are separate subdisciplines, each with its own kind of data and a body of methods tailored to that kind. The results based on one type of data should not be employed in studying results based on the other. Instead, the researcher should draw separate conclusions from each kind of data, using the methods appropriate to each, and then compare the conclusions. If they agree, both may be considered valid. If not, the researcher must go back and separately redo the studies to determine what went wrong.

Biologists refer to this kind of research strategy as consilience, because the scientists who use it make independent studies of different lines of evidence in a search for conclusions that "jump together" (Gould 1989: 282). I relied on the principle of consilience in chapter 2 when I compared the results achieved by archeologists, linguists, and physical anthropologists in studying the ancestries of the Tainos and found that they mutually support each other and when I checked changes in ceramics against changes in other aspects of culture.

The strategy of consilience has been little used to date in investigating the origin of the Island-Caribs. Archeologists and ethnohistorians who work on this problem have tended to mix their respective kinds of evidence instead of studying each kind separately and comparing results. Specialists in the archeology of the Windward Islands need to work out a more detailed set of culturally defined periods, as I have done in the islands farther north, and to draw conclusions from it about the origin of the Island-Caribs. Ethnohistorians can best contribute to the common goal by making in-depth studies of the Island-Carib documentary evidence, which is more extensive than many archeologists realize. Solution of the Island-Carib problem must await the completion of these two tasks and comparison of their results.

If asked to weigh the relative importance of archeological and ethno-historical research in solving the problems of cultural and ethnic origin discussed in this chapter, I would have to give priority to archeology, because it is favored by a potentially larger body of data. The balance changes in the historic period, discussed in the next chapter. More documentary information is available there, and so researchers become more dependent on the results of ethnohistorical studies.

T H E   S E C O N D
R E P E O P L I N G

VI

We humans are ethnocentric, tending to overlook events in which neither we nor our ancestors participated. Columbus's career is a case in point. People of European descent honor the admiral for his discovery of the "New World" but give no credit to the Native Americans for having previously found it. From the standpoint of humanity as a whole, it would be more accurate to say that Columbus discovered a new route from Europe to the Americas.

Two other routes between the hemispheres had been found before Columbus's time. The ancestors of the American Indians had moved from Siberia into Alaska and the rest of the New World toward the end of the Ice ages, and the Norse had traveled from Iceland to Greenland and Newfoundland in the tenth century A.D.

It was the Casimiroid and Ortoiroid Indians who originally discovered and peopled the West Indies. They were the indigenous inhabitants and, as such, had the misfortune to be almost entirely exterminated by the Saladoid invaders and their descendants, the Ostionoids. The Ostionoids evolved into the Tainos, who eventually suffered the same fate that their ancestors had inflicted upon the Casimiroids and Ortoiroids. The Tainos, too, were replaced by foreign peoples, including not only colonists from Spain and other European countries but also the slaves whom the colonists imported from other parts of the Caribbean area and from sub-Saharan Africa. The present chapter is concerned with this second repeopling of the West Indies.

The extinctions that took place during the two repeoplings exemplify the process of genocide. Revisionist historians blame the conquistadors in general and Columbus in particular for causing the genocide of the

Tainos. Actually, this event resulted from circumstance: all the parties to the event had to adapt to the natural, cultural, and social conditions in which they lived.

In discussing the extinction of the Casimiroids and the Ortoiroids in chapter 4, I relied primarily upon archeological research. If I were to follow the same procedure here, I would base conclusions about the fall of the Tainos on the results of excavation in the sites they inhabited after the arrival of the Spaniards, that is, during Period IVb of the ceramically defined chronology (fig. 26). Unfortunately, the second repeopling happened so fast that Indian habitation sites dating from Period IVb are scarce and difficult to find. The archeologists who study that period have preferred to focus ethnocentrically on the remains of their own ancestors, that is, on the colonial settlers and, in recent years, their African slaves.

Research on the aboriginal sites inhabited during Period IVb is still in its infancy. No Guanahatabey or Island-Carib sites from that period have yet been identified, and few Taino sites have been systematically excavated (Deagan 1987, 1988). Conclusions about the repeopling have to be drawn almost entirely from the ethnohistorical research. Here I summarize the results of that research and note the relevant archeological evidence.

The ethnohistorical documents are written in terms of social units, that is, individuals and the societies to which they belonged. Ethnic groups, which are instead defined culturally, linguistically, or biologically, play only a secondary role in the historical record. Consequently, the deeds of individuals and the social groups to which they belonged, rather than the ethnic groups and their cultures, languages, and biologies, give shape to this chapter. It is divided into three parts. First, I review Columbus's arrival and his contacts with the Tainos and their neighbors as he explored the islands between 1492 and 1504. Then I look at Spain's conquest of the West Indies, from its start in 1494 during the admiral's second voyage. I carry the discussion to 1524, by which time the Taino population had broken down into small, isolated communities struggling to survive in a dominantly Spanish population, and append a summary of the decline of the Island-Caribs during the seventeenth and eighteenth centuries. Finally, I consider the subsequent survival of individuals of Taino descent, the persistence of some elements of their culture and language, and the recent revival of others.

The Voyages of Columbus, 1492–1504

Directly or indirectly, Columbus has supplied most of our ethnohistorical information about the Tainos; we need to know about him in order to be able to evaluate that information. He was well prepared by training and experience to explore the Americas. He had read the classical literature about the two ways of traveling east to China—the silk route through Central Asia and the maritime route across the Indian Ocean and around Southeast Asia—had studied Marco Polo's account of his journey along those routes, and had lived among the Portuguese navigators who were establishing a new maritime route around South Africa to the Spice Islands. Moreover, he had sailed on Portuguese voyages to the western limits of European colonization in his time, Iceland, in the North Atlantic, and West Africa, in the South Atlantic (Morison 1942, 1:26–106; Morison 1963: 11–25).

He knew that it should be possible to reach China and Indonesia by traveling west across the Atlantic Ocean and onward around the globe. Like his contemporaries, he greatly underestimated the distances westward from Portugal to China and from the islands off West Africa, where the Portuguese and the Spaniards had established colonies, to Indonesia. Wrongly believing that these two routes were shorter and easier than the corresponding routes to the east, he decided to search for them. When the Portuguese showed no interest, he turned to the king and queen of Spain, who backed him because he offered an opportunity to overcome the Portuguese lead in the race to exploit the riches of Asia.

Columbus undertook four voyages. During the first two, he searched for a short route to Japan and China. During the last two he sailed farther south in an attempt to travel to the Indies. He reached the Bahamian Archipelago and the Greater Antilles in the first voyage, the Lesser Antilles in the second, South America in the third, and Central America in the fourth (fig. 35). He discovered the Tainos during his first voyage and traced their limits during the second.

Exploration was not his only objective. He also sought gold and other kinds of wealth, to benefit himself—he insisted that he and his family be granted title to any land he colonized—and to indemnify the king and queen of Spain for the expenses they had incurred on his behalf.

FIRST VOYAGE

His original voyage is too poorly documented to determine its exact course. The only primary sources are an abstract of his daily journal, published by Father Bartolomé de Las Casas, a contemporary authority, and a letter in which he reported on his trip to the king and queen (Jane 1960; Dunn and Kelley 1989).

The voyage began in Palos, Spain, on August 3, 1492. Columbus sailed his flotilla of three small ships, the *Santa María, Pinta,* and *Niña,* to the Canary Islands, a Spanish possession off the coast of Morocco, where he

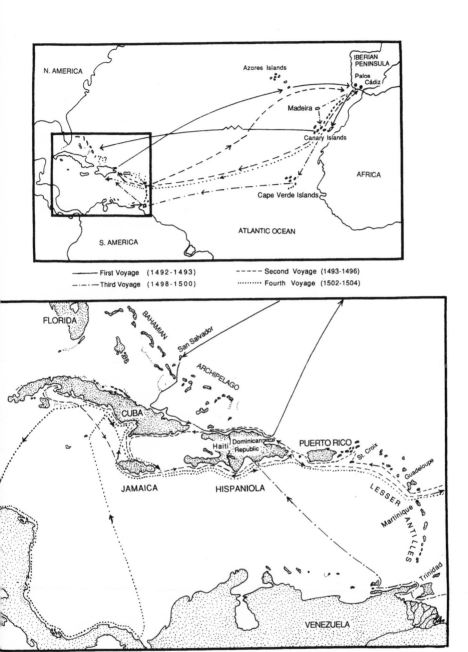

Fig. 35. The voyages of Columbus, 1492–1504. The return legs of the third and fourth voyages are not shown for lack of information.

took on supplies. Leaving the Canaries on September 5, he proceeded more or less directly westward into the uncharted waters of the Atlantic Ocean. He was able to maintain a steady course except in mid-passage, where his ships were buffeted by contrary winds. Twice thereafter, he observed birds flying toward the southwest. The second time he turned to follow them, assuming that they were heading for land. This change of course brought him to an island in the Bahamian Archipelago on October 12, 1492.

The Tainos called the island Guanahaní. Columbus took possession of it in the name of the king and queen of Spain and renamed it San Salvador. The inadequacy of his documentation and the consequent difficulty in plotting his course have made it impossible to determine exactly where he landed. Students of the subject have placed his landfall all the way from Turks Island, at the southern end of the Bahamian Archipelago, to Egg Island, at the entrance to New Providence Channel in the north (Gerace 1987). In the absence of a consensus, I have accepted the landfall identified by the late Samuel Eliot Morison, who made a thorough study of the documents and checked them by retracing Columbus's course in a sailing vessel (Morison 1942, 1:264–366; see also Wolper 1964 and Wilson 1990a: 35–73). He places it at centrally located Watling Island, which has consequently become known as San Salvador. Joseph Judge (1986) has recently argued that the landfall took place at Samaná Cay, the next island to the southeast. He bases his theory on a computer study of the figures in Columbus's journal. These figures, however, are too sparse and too vague to be conclusive.

The available archeological evidence supports Morison's hypothesis. Columbus first set foot on a beach in front of a Taino village. The remains of such a village have been found at Long Bay, on the beach where Morison concluded that the landing had taken place. Excavating there, Charles A. Hoffman (1987) has encountered refuse laid down by the Palmetto people, who occupied the Bahamas in late prehistoric time. Mixed in the refuse were a coin, thirty-four European potsherds, ten whole or fragmentary glass beads, and two brass buckles. The coin is of a type minted in Spain between 1471 and 1474. The other artifacts, which are contemporaneous in style, come from three places in Spain where such types were being manufactured at that time, as has been shown by laboratory analysis (Brill and others 1987). Opponents of Morison's hypothesis note that the Long Bay Tainos could have obtained these European artifacts through trade with natives who lived at one of the other potential landfalls. To my knowledge, no comparable finds have been made elsewhere.

Columbus took on board six Tainos, intending to teach them Spanish so that they could interpret for him and to carry them to Spain to show to his royal sponsors. They directed him through the inner Bahama Islands to Cuba, where he arrived on October 28. Morison (1942, 1:335–51) concludes that Columbus first went ashore at Bariay, near the present town of Gibara. From a nearby village, which has not been located, he sent emissaries inland to investigate a false report by his Indian guides that the local cacique possessed gold artifacts.

Morison thought that the cacique lived in the vicinity of the modern city of Holguín, and indeed, Cuban archeologists have found an extraordinary number of Spanish trade objects at the nearby Meillacan site of Yayal (Rouse 1942: 115–19). Most of them date from the conquest period, but several coins might have been laid down during Columbus's time. Other students of the first voyage disagree with Morison (Gerace 1987). They place Columbus's Cuban landfall and the trip inland farther west, among other Meillacan peoples, or farther east, among the Chican people who had occupied the eastern tip of Cuba during Period IVa. I am aware of no finds of contact-period trade goods in either place.

Columbus himself believed that he had reached Japan or a peninsula (perhaps Korea?) that would lead him westward to China. After turning briefly in that direction, he decided to investigate instead a report by his Indian guides that gold was available on Hispaniola to the east. As he set off toward that island, one of his ships, the *Pinta,* broke away from him and moved out into the Bahama Channel. Martín Alonzo Pinzón, its master, had become increasingly impatient with Columbus's reliance on the advice of his Indian passengers, who were accustomed to paddle along the shore making frequent stops. He decided to beat the admiral to the gold by sailing ahead through the open sea.

Columbus proceeded more slowly along the Cuban shore. Finding no gold there, he crossed the Windward Passage to Hispaniola, explored its northwestern peninsula, and ended up near Cap-Haïtien, now the principal port on the northern coast of Haiti. There he was well received by the local chief, Guacanagarí (fig. 36), and was pleased to observe the presence of gold ornaments (Sauer 1966: 23–29; Wilson 1990a: 60–73, fig. 2). He was unable to search for the source of the gold, however. His flagship, the *Santa María,* foundered on a reef the night before Christmas, forcing him to prepare for a return to Spain in the only other available ship, the *Niña.* He built a fort called La Navidad to house the men he was unable to crowd into the *Niña,* supplied them with provisions for a year's stay, and left them under the care of Chief Guacanagarí.

Archeologists have searched in vain for traces of the shipwrecked *Santa María.* William H. Hodge, head of a local mission hospital, believes that he has found the site of La Navidad at Caille Brûlée, on the shore near Cap-

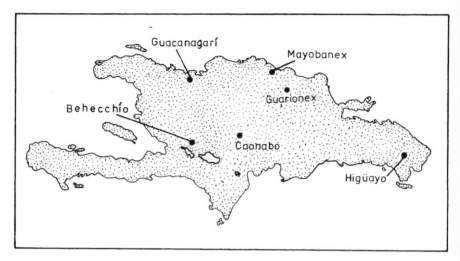

Fig. 36. Home villages of Hispaniolan chiefs in the time of Columbus.

Haïtien, and Kathleen Deagan and colleagues from the Florida Museum of Natural History have excavated the nearby Indian site of En Bas Saline, which may have been the residence of Chief Guacanagarí. It has yielded typically Chican artifacts and burials, dating from the final aboriginal occupation of the area, together with Spanish trade goods (Fuson 1987: 231–32; Deagan 1987, 1988).

Traveling eastward along the coast of Hispaniola in the *Niña,* Columbus soon encountered Martín Alonzo Pinzón, who was searching for him. Pinzón had sailed the *Pinta* north to the southernmost Bahamas, whence he had proceeded directly to the central part of the northern coast of Hispaniola. He sent a search party into the Cibao Valley to investigate a report that gold was being mined there. The report was verified: he succeeded where Columbus had failed.

The two ships continued past the scene of Pinzón's discovery to the mouth of Samaná Bay in northeastern Hispaniola. There they were threatened for the first time by Indians armed with bows and arrows, who are thought to have been Ciguayos, a variant group of Tainos. The local chief received them nonetheless hospitably and gave them gifts of gold and other materials (Morison 1942, 1:367–402).

On January 16, 1493, Columbus and Pinzón left Samaná Bay on the return trip to Spain. Although they became separated during a storm, both arrived back at Palos on the same day, March 15. Columbus reported to the king and queen that the people he encountered were not as civilized as the Japanese and Chinese, whom he had expected to find, but that they became

progressively more developed as he proceeded through Cuba into Hispaniola. Thus he recognized the distinction between Western and Classic
Tainos that is made in this volume.

His finds aroused great enthusiasm in Spain. He presented the six Taino
passengers to his royal sponsors, who had them baptized. The king, queen,
and infante acted as their godparents. One Indian remained at the court,
where he died two years later. The rest went back to the West Indies
with Columbus. One of them, who took the name of Diego Colón, served
as Columbus's interpreter throughout his second voyage (Morison 1942,
2:14).

SECOND VOYAGE

Columbus returned to Hispaniola in the fall of 1493. His objectives were
not only to rescue the sailors he had left at La Navidad and to complete the
exploration of the Greater Antilles cut short by the shipwreck of the *Santa
María* but also to found a colony on Hispaniola. The king and queen instructed him to establish gold mines, install settlers, develop trade with the
Tainos, and convert them to Christianity. They provided him with a fleet of
seventeen ships, abundant supplies, and about 1,500 men, including a doc-
tor, a map maker, and several clerics—among them Father Ramón Pané,
who was to make a study of the Taino religion. No women were on board.

The fleet left the port of Cádiz, Spain, on September 25, stopping again
in the Canary Islands to reprovision and to take on farm animals for the
new enterprise. From there Columbus sailed before the wind on a more
southerly route than before. Since his Taino passengers had told him that
the Lesser Antilles extend farther out into the Atlantic than the islands he
had previously explored, he expected to be able to make a shorter and
quicker passage; and thus he discovered the best route to the West Indies.

On November 3 he arrived off Dominica, at the northern end of the
Windward Islands. There he turned northwest, intending to proceed immediately to the relief of the Spaniards he had left at La Navidad, but was
delayed for six days in Guadeloupe, at the entry into the Leeward Islands,
when a landing party became lost in its forests. The layover gave him an
opportunity to investigate the reports about the Island-Caribs that he had
heard from the Tainos. The islanders fled from their villages as his men
approached, leaving behind partially dismembered human bodies, which
the crew took to be evidence that the Island-Caribs ate human flesh for
nourishment. They did not consider the alternative possibility—that the
pieces might have been intended for use in rituals.

The landing parties rescued women and children seized by the Island-
Caribs in Puerto Rico. Again viewing the situation from the standpoint of

their own culture, the sailors assumed that the women had been enslaved when in fact they were witnessing the result of bride capture (Morison 1963: 211–12, 234–37). They reported more accurately that the Island-Caribs were good farmers, skilled potters, and excellent weavers, like the ancestral Igneris.

Guided by his Taino passengers, Columbus proceeded northward along the Caribbean side of the Leeward Islands, naming each island as he went but exploring none of them, for he wanted to reach Hispaniola as soon as possible. He entered the Virgin Islands via St. Croix and stopped for fresh water at Salt River, on its northern shore. The inhabitants again fled, but the Europeans were able to intercept an incoming party of canoeists, which defended itself valiantly with bows and arrows before being captured (Morison 1963: 212, 237–38).

The admiral refers to the captives as "Caribs." This name creates a problem. There is but one habitation site at Salt River, and it has been intensively excavated (Booy 1919; Hatt 1924; Vescelius 1952; Morse 1990), yielding only Saladoid, Ostionoid, and French colonial remains. Suazoid pottery, which some experts have identified as Island-Carib, is nowhere in evidence. Instead, the latest prehistoric assemblages are typically Chican, indicating occupation by the Classic Tainos.

How are we to explain the discrepancy between the ethnohistorical and archeological evidence? Columbus and his native passengers, from whom he presumably obtained the Carib identification, may have been using that term to refer not to the specific ethnic group they had encountered in Guadeloupe but to any hostile Indians, especially those from the small eastern islands, as was the practice during the subsequent conquest period. If so, the term tells us nothing about the nature of the local inhabitants, and we shall have to identify them on the basis of the archeological rather than the ethnohistorical evidence.

From that standpoint, there are two possibilities. The Classic Tainos may have recently abandoned the site in the face of Island-Carib attacks, allowing the Island-Caribs to use it as a staging area from which to raid the Tainos in Puerto Rico. Alternatively, the people encountered by Columbus may have been a local variant on the Classic Tainos, like the Borinqueños of Puerto Rico and the Ciguayos of northeastern Hispaniola, whom they resemble in their warlike attitude and their use of the bow and arrow. My preference is for the second alternative. So far as I am aware, neither the St. Croix Indians, the Borinqueños, nor the Ciguayos are reported to have practiced cannibalism. The Indians encountered at Salt River did have bride capture, but this practice was not necessarily limited to the Island-Caribs (Sued Badillo 1978). In either case, Morison (1942, 2:82–88) has to be mistaken in assuming that the Island-Caribs inhabited the Virgin Islands. If they were there at all, they would have been visitors, like the Meillacans who went to Middle Caicos Island for salt. This is one instance in which archeological data override inadequate historical evidence, contrary to the general rule.

From St. Croix, the fleet made its way through the rest of the Virgin Islands to Vieques and the southern coast of Puerto Rico. Morison thinks that Columbus landed at Boquerón Bay, at the southern end of Puerto Rico's western coast, but others place the landing farther north. Archeology has been unable to contribute to the solution of this problem.

The rest of the trip to La Navidad, on the northern coast of Haiti, passed without incident. When Columbus arrived on November 28, 1493, he found the fort in ruins and his men dead. Chief Guacanagarí disclaimed responsibility, saying that the massacre had been ordered by Caonabo, head of the chiefdom of Maguana, across the central mountains in southern Hispaniola (fig. 36), because the Spaniards had mistreated subjects of his. This provocation is not surprising: Columbus had manned the *Santa María* with unprincipled adventurers rather than professional sailors.

Accepting Guacanagarí's explanation, Columbus proceeded with his plans for colonization. From January to April he built a town on the Dominican coast near the Cibao goldfield, naming it Isabela after the queen (fig. 37). He sent prospectors inland to search for nuggets in the river sands and built a fort, which he called Santo Tomás, to protect them. Thus began the first European gold rush in the Americas (Sauer 1966: 77–81).

The ruins of the town of Isabela, which still stand on the northern coast of the Dominican Republic, have been repeatedly excavated, most recently by archeologists from Venezuela and the Florida Museum of Natural History (José M. Cruxent and Kathleen Deagan, personal communication). Among the finds made there are Chican potsherds, which confirm the upper end of the ceramic chronology used in chapter 5. Dominican archeologists have also located Indian villages along the route from Isabela to Santo Tomás (Anderson-Córdova 1990: 68).

On April 24, 1494, Columbus resumed his previous exploration of the Greater Antilles. Leaving the administration of the newly established colony to a council headed by his brother Diego, he set out in the *Niña*, accompanied by two smaller vessels. He sailed across the Windward Passage to Cuba and began to explore the southern coast of that island, intending to pursue his belief that it was a peninsula attached to the mainland of China. Temporarily diverted to the northern coast of Jamaica by a report that its inhabitants had gold, he returned to the southern coast of Cuba when he was unable to find any and followed it all the way into Guanahatabey ter-

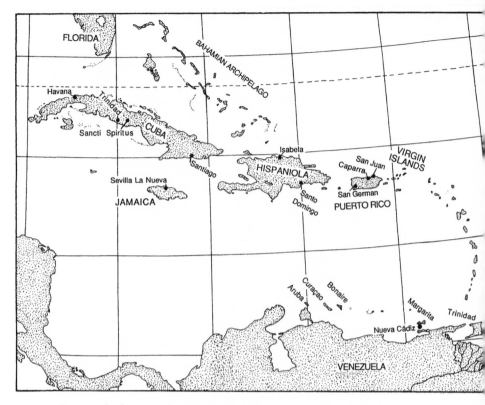

Fig. 37. The first Spanish settlements in the Caribbean, 1494–1515.

ritory—to judge by the failure of his Taino interpreter, Diego Colón, to understand the language at his last stop.

Columbus turned back before reaching the end of the island because by this time he had convinced himself that Cuba was a peninsula. He and his companions have left us little information about the customs of the peoples he encountered, nor have any of his landing places been identified archeologically, so far as I am aware (Morison 1942, 2:117–62). The admiral made his way back to Isabela via the southern coasts of Jamaica and Hispaniola. On Jamaica he was impressed by the finely decorated canoes and elaborate personal ornaments, among them a pendant of copper-gold alloy from South America, but was put off by the lack of native gold. He arrived back in Isabela on September 29, 1494, having circumnavigated all of the Greater Antilles except northern and western Cuba.

Around this time, he commissioned Father Ramón Pané's study of the native religion. Pané obtained his information from the Tainos who lived in the vicinity of Isabela and its goldfield. His work has been termed the first anthropological research in the New World (Bourne 1906); and his report, the first literature written there (Arrom 1988).

Many Spaniards were repelled by the Taino religion. They are said to have burned hundreds of cotton zemis, believing them to be representations of the devil (Montás, Borrell, and Moya Pons 1983: 38–39). They carried few Taino artifacts of any kind back to Spain, presumably because so many of them were decorated with zemis. As a result, Taino culture is poorly represented in Spanish museums.

Columbus now devoted most of his attention to the affairs of state in Hispaniola, which did not go well. The mines yielded less gold than he had expected, the seed crops brought from Spain proved to be unsuited to the tropics, and the accompanying livestock had to be consumed because the colonists were unable to grow sufficient food or to obtain enough from the Tainos. The king and queen were obliged to send additional supplies, for which they received little recompense.

In the spring of 1496, Columbus went back to Spain to answer complaints about his stewardship, leaving another brother, Bartolomé, in charge. He departed from Isabela on April 20, stopping in Guadeloupe for provisions and arriving in Cádiz on June 11. Contrary winds delayed him; he was not aware that by traveling north from Hispaniola he could have taken advantage of the trade winds that blow from west to east at higher latitudes.

THIRD VOYAGE

Columbus was unable to return to Hispaniola until May 1498. On this trip he divided his fleet, sending one half directly to Hispaniola and sailing the other half south to the Cape Verde Islands, a Portuguese colony, whence he crossed the Atlantic to the Guianas. During the next two weeks he explored the southern coast of Trinidad and the Peninsula of Paria, where he had the good fortune to see ornaments made from pearls as well as the copper-gold alloy. Then he sailed past Cubagua and Margarita islands and across the Caribbean Sea to Santo Domingo, a town on the southern coast of Hispaniola that his brother Bartolomé had established in his absence to take the place of Isabela, which had proved to be badly sited.

He spent the next two years attempting unsuccessfully to govern the colony from Santo Domingo. The mines still produced less gold than expected; and many colonists, unable to make a living from them, returned to Spain. Others rebelled against his rule. The king and queen were finally obliged to send an administrator to take over the government. That official was so provoked by what he found that he shipped Columbus and his two brothers back to Spain in chains during the fall of 1500, thereby terminating the crown's grant of the colony to Columbus and his family.

The admiral was thus unable to follow up his discovery of South America, as he had hoped to do. Other explorers traced the source of the pearls he had observed on the Peninsula of Paria to Cubagua Island, which he had bypassed, and established the town of Nueva Cádiz there to exploit the find (Rouse and Cruxent 1963: 134–38). For the first time the crown acquired an appreciable source of revenue in the New World. Columbus did not even have his name applied to his finds; that honor went to another navigator, Amerigo Vespucci, who demonstrated to the public that South America was a separate continent.

FOURTH VOYAGE

The king and queen soon released Columbus and his brothers from prison but prohibited them from returning to the colony in Hispaniola. Nevertheless, the admiral was allowed to make one more voyage of exploration. Leaving Cádiz in the spring of 1502, he sailed past Santo Domingo, where he was refused permission to land, and proceeded along the southern coasts of Jamaica and Cuba. He then crossed the Caribbean Sea to Central America and explored its coast from Honduras to Panama. Unfortunately, his ships became so infested with worms that two of them sank. On his return voyage he had to beach the other two at St. Ann's Bay in northern Jamaica. He was marooned there for a whole year, living in the stranded ships on food supplied by the local Indians. He was finally rescued in the fall of 1504 and went back to Spain. By this time he was seriously ill; he died two years later.

In preparation for the Columbus quincentenary, archeologists have unsuccessfully attempted to find the remains of Columbus's two ships in St. Ann's Bay, Jamaica. The Indian villages that supplied him with food have not yet been located, either.

Conquest, 1494–1797

Columbus was an excellent navigator and a talented explorer, but he lacked administrative ability. From the very beginning, when he staffed his flagship, the *Santa María*, with adventurers who caused their own demise at La Navidad, he failed to build a solid base in Hispaniola for the colonization of the rest of the Caribbean area. That task had to be done by his successors. By 1500, when he and his brothers were stripped of their right to govern Hispaniola and sent home in disgrace, they had been able to conquer only the northern coast of the island and a central corridor extending from the abandoned town of Isabela in the north to Santo Domingo on the southern coast. This corridor passed through the original goldfield in the Cibao Valley, which was then called the Vega Real, and a second field on the opposite side of the Cordillera Central. They built a string of forts along the corridor and removed the regional and district chiefs to prevent them from organizing resistance against colonial rule.

The accounts of these activities provide important insights into the nature of Taino culture (Wilson 1990a: 74–110). Columbus himself set up the first fort at Santo Tomás during March 1494, intending to use it to defend the northern goldfield against the threat of attack by Caonabo, ruler of a chiefdom south of the Cordillera Central, whom he believed to be responsible for the previous destruction of La Navidad. While he was away that summer exploring Cuba and Jamaica, the garrison of the fort began to exploit the local Indians, stealing their possessions and raping the women, just as the occupants of La Navidad seem to have done before. The Tainos retaliated by destroying their own villages and fields and retreating into the forests. Many of them suffered from hunger as a result.

When Columbus returned from his voyage of exploration in the fall of 1494, he sent an emissary, Alonzo de Ojeda, to visit Caonabo in an attempt to forestall a possible rebellion. Ojeda captured Caonabo by luring him out of his town with gifts and the offer of a horseback ride. Columbus then shipped him off to Spain; he died of unknown causes during the trip.

The revolt that Columbus had feared took place in March 1495. It was led by a coalition of local chiefs that included Caonabo's brothers and was put down with the help of Guacanagarí, the cacique who had blamed Caonabo for the destruction of La Navidad. The opposing chiefs were killed, and a number of their followers were captured.

Meanwhile, the mines were yielding little gold; and many colonists, dissatisfied with the fruits of their labors, had returned to Spain. When the crown complained about the lack of income from the colony, Columbus sent a shipload of captives to Spain to be sold as slaves in a desperate attempt to satisfy that complaint. The slaves proved to be poor workers, unable to resist European diseases, and the crown decided to free them for practical as well as humanitarian reasons. It ordered the surviving Indians to be shipped back to Hispaniola, and included for good measure those whom the returning colonists had brought to Spain to serve as their household servants.

The remaining rebels were distributed among the colonists and put to work in mining, ranching, or household service (fig. 38). Their ranks were

Fig. 38. Tainos panning gold for the Spaniards with native bowls of wood (after Oviedo y Valdés 1851–55, vol. 1, pl. 2).

thinned by poor working conditions and a famine in 1495–96, which the Spaniards may have brought on by failing to allow the laborers sufficient time for hunting, fishing, and farming.

Guarionex, head of the chiefdom of Magua, to the east of the goldfield, had not participated in the insurrection of 1495. Columbus built a new fort at Concepción de la Vega, close to his village, to keep him quiet and imposed a system of tribute upon all the surviving chiefs in the Cibao Valley. They were expected to make periodic payments of gold, cotton, or food to the colonial government, depending on their resources, but found it impossible to meet their quotas.

Bartolomé Columbus governed the colony while his brother was in Spain from 1496 to 1498. He developed the second goldfield in the south-central part of the island and moved the capital to Santo Domingo on the southern coast to be near it. In January 1497 he paid a state visit to Behecchío, head of the chiefdom of Xaraguá, in the southwestern corner of the island, and his sister Anacaona, widow of Caonabo, who may have inherited Caonabo's chiefdom after her husband died in captivity. Behecchío and Anacaona received Bartolomé with great ceremony and many gifts and agreed to his request that they submit to the system of tribute that Christopher Columbus had established north of the central mountains.

Later in 1497, Bartolomé ordered the abandonment of the previous capital at Isabela. Its mayor, Francisco Roldán, objected and marched against the fort at Concepción de la Vega, intending to capture it and take control of the northern goldfield. Unable to do so, he and his followers fled across the central mountains and took refuge in Xaraguá, in the southwestern corner of the island. Chief Behecchío and his sister Anacaona received them peaceably and granted them asylum, using their arrival as a pretext to abandon the system of tribute that had been imposed by the colonial government.

Shortly thereafter, a coalition of fourteen local chiefs, including Guarionex, decided to move against the fort at Concepción de la Vega. Bartolomé defeated the coalition in a surprise night attack and captured the chiefs, killing many of them. He released Guarionex and the other survivors when they promised to submit to Spanish rule, but many local Indians were subsequently pressed into service in the goldfield.

In the spring of 1498, just before Christopher Columbus returned from Spain, Guarionex and some companions took refuge among the Ciguayo Tainos, who lived in the mountains northeast of Cibao Valley (the Cordillera Septentrional). Bartolomé ordered their chief, Mayobanex, to return the refugees to him. When he refused, Bartolomé attacked the Indians, captured Guarionex and Mayobanex, and imprisoned them. Both died of natural causes while in Spanish custody. When Christopher Columbus returned to Hispaniola in the summer of 1498, he placated Roldán by authorizing him to seize Indians in the chiefdom of Xaraguá and divide them among his followers to use as forced laborers at the goldfields. This action has become known as *repartimiento* (Anderson-Córdova 1990: 68–76).

When Francisco de Bobadilla took over from the Columbus family in 1500, only three hundred Spaniards remained in the colony, living in Santo Domingo and a town in each of the goldfields. Bobadilla was instructed to increase the output of the mines and to free the Indians. Finding these two tasks incompatible, he chose to retain the repartimiento, though without adding to it. He increased productivity by offering a greater share of the profits to the Spaniards whose Indians labored in the goldfields (Sauer 1966: 102–6).

Nicolas de Ovando, who succeeded Bobadilla in 1502, brought along 2,500 colonists, including the first European families to arrive in the Americas. A thousand of the men are said to have died while prospecting for gold. Others established farms, devoting them primarily to livestock, for Spanish crops did not flourish.

Ovando felt it necessary to remove the threat to the new settlers that was posed by the surviving hierarchies of chiefs at either end of Hispaniola. He accomplished this task by eliminating the principal caciques, first in the southeastern chiefdom of Higüey and then in southwestern Xaraguá. Unlike the Columbus family, he proceeded forcefully and with great brutality. Soon after his arrival in 1502, the Higüey Indians rebelled to avenge the killing of one of their chiefs by a Spanish attack dog. Ovando rounded up six or seven hundred of them, put them in a chief's bohío, or house, and had them knifed to death. He then ordered their bodies to be dragged into the adjoining plaza and publicly counted.

In the fall of 1503, he paid another formal visit to Xaraguá, where he was well received by Chief Anacaona, whose brother Behecchío had died. She convened a meeting of some eighty district chiefs in her bohío, whereupon Ovando ordered his soldiers to block the door and burn them alive. Anacaona herself was hanged in deference to her rank. No reason was given for these actions, which destroyed the last independent chiefdoms in Hispaniola (Sauer 1966: 148–49; Wilson 1990a: 123, 133–34).

The crown had ordered Ovando to assemble the Indians near the goldfields so that they could more easily be put to work there, but he found it more practicable to refine and expand the practice of repartimiento, assigning whole Indian communities to individual Spanish settlers for use in the goldfields or on ranches. Each community had to spend six months at work and was then allowed to return to its own village for six months of recuperation. The time off was reduced to four months as the need for forced labor increased (Sauer 1966: 147–51; Anderson-Córdova 1990: 77–81).

Ovando named the new system after the *encomiendas* (estates) that he had previously administered in Spain. There was, however, a basic difference between the two. The encomiendas of Spain were grants of land; those of Hispaniola, rights to use the labor of Indian villages. In theory at least, each village continued to retain title to its land so long as it remained intact. The people were thus able to store cassava in the ground while away at work and to replant it during the rest period. The villagers continued to be led by their chief, who became in effect an overseer.

The advantage of the encomienda system was that it allowed the Indians to retain their own culture and language, to which they were able to revert during their rest periods. Unfortunately, it did not also ensure their health. They died in the goldfields, as had the Spaniards whom they replaced: they lived under unsanitary conditions, which caused them to contract fevers, and were overworked and undernourished. For example, they were not allowed enough free time to obtain meat and fish, whose protein they needed to supplement the starch provided by their cassava bread and sweet potatoes. Their population declined, and of the many hundreds of thousands who had lived during Columbus's time only sixty thousand were left by the end of Ovando's term as governor in 1509. All were members of encomiendas (Sauer 1966: 200–206).

The Spaniards adjusted to the tropics and prospered. Their population increased to about ten thousand, living in fifteen towns (*villas*) distributed throughout the island (Sauer 1966, fig. 20). Archeologists have located and excavated many of the towns and have documented their progress in adapting to local conditions (Deagan 1988).

Expansion into Puerto Rico took place shortly before the end of Ovando's tenure as governor. It was led by Juan Ponce de León, better known in the United States for his subsequent discovery of Florida. After participating in the Higüey massacre, he served as translator for a party that traveled across the Mona Passage, explored Puerto Rico, and discovered gold there. In 1508 the crown chose him to pursue those discoveries. He established Spanish settlements near the principal goldfields, at San Germán, in the southwestern part of the island, and at Caparra, in the northeast. Caparra was later moved to the islet of San Juan, where it became the capital.

Cowed by the Higüey massacre, the local Indians at first allowed themselves to be assigned to encomiendas for work in the mines and in ranches, but they soon rebelled under the leadership of a local cacique, Agüeybana. It is said that "Caribs" from the Virgin and Leeward islands joined them in the struggle. These were presumably Eastern Tainos; it is unlikely that the Classic Tainos of Puerto Rico would have been able to obtain help from their more remote enemies, the Island-Caribs. Once again, there is reason to believe that the term *Carib* was being loosely applied to all warlike Indians in the small eastern islands, regardless of their cultural affiliation.

The revolt was soon quelled, Agüeybana was put to death, and the local Indians who did not succeed in fleeing to Eastern Taino territory were returned to the encomiendas. Their allies from that territory, who did not fit into the encomienda system, were kept as slaves. They joined a small but growing number of Indians from other parts of the Caribbean area and Blacks from Africa in a separate social class, the members of which were wholly owned by their masters instead of being used as forced laborers. Most Indian slaves of this period came from the Bahamian Archipelago.

According to some reports, more than forty thousand Lucayan Tainos were removed from those islands between 1509 and 1513, causing a complete depopulation (Sauer 1966: 159–60).

By the time Ovando left office, he had established the policies through which Spain was to rule all its subsequent possessions in the Americas. His successor in administering these policies was Diego Columbus, son of the admiral, who had restored the family's fortunes in Spain. He was appointed viceroy of the Indies in 1509 and served in that capacity until 1524, presiding over the final stages in the decline of the Tainos.

One of his first actions was to conquer Jamaica, which attracted his attention despite its lack of gold because it was becoming a source of food and labor for the newly established Spanish colonies on the Central and South American mainland, including the pearl fisheries at Nueva Cádiz on Cubagua Island, now a dependency of Hispaniola. Diego Columbus entrusted the conquest of Jamaica to Juan de Esquivel, another participant in the Higüey massacre. He established a town of Sevilla La Nueva near Columbus's landing place on the northern coast of the island and assigned the local Indians to agricultural encomiendas, producing food and cotton. As usual, he ignored the crown's instructions to treat the Indians well and to Christianize them, and once again the population declined rapidly. Few Indians remained when Esquivel completed his term as governor in 1515 (Sauer 1966: 178–81).

In 1511, Diego Velázquez de Cuéllar undertook the conquest of Cuba. That official had participated in the Xaraguá massacre and had later subdued the southwestern peninsula of Hispaniola. He organized a pincer movement. He himself proceeded from his base on the southwestern peninsula to the eastern tip of Cuba, where he captured Hatuéy, a Hispaniolan chief who had fled there to escape Spanish rule. He burned him and his followers at the stake, thereby making Hatuéy a hero to modern Cubans, who equate his struggle against foreign oppression with their own fight against Spain and the United States.

Meanwhile, Pánfilo de Narváez, who had assisted Esquivel in the conquest of Jamaica, sailed from there to the southeastern coast of Cuba, then proceeded diagonally across the island to the vicinity of present-day Havana. He was accompanied by Bartolomé de Las Casas, an adventurer who later repented, joined the priesthood, and became known as the Protector of the Indians. Las Casas (1974: 53–57) has documented the atrocities committed against the Tainos during the passage across Cuba.

Velázquez and Narváez came together in Cienfuegos Bay, on the southern coast, and traveled northeast through the mountains, seeking gold. The finds they made attracted prospectors from other parts of the Caribbean area, and a pair of towns, Trinidad and Sancti Spiritus, were founded to service them. By 1515, six additional towns had been settled, including a capital at Santiago. Its position at the eastern end of the island reflects the Spanish view that Cuba was peripheral to Hispaniola, as it had been during Taino time. The capital was not moved to Havana, at the opposite end of the island, until its harbor became a port of call for the fleets that carried the wealth of the Aztecs and the Incas to Spain (Sauer 1966: 181–89).

It is worth noting that all the Spanish towns except those servicing the goldfields were situated in centers of Indian population—that is, in the best places for recruiting laborers. The residents of these towns obtained allotments of Indians and rented them to the prospectors, who took them to the mines.

Many Indians died in the goldfields. Las Casas (1951: 57) reports that only 10 percent of the members of three successive encomiendas originally totaling nine hundred survived after three months of service. There was a perpetual shortage of workers. In 1515, Velázquez sent raiders to the Bay Islands of Honduras to obtain an additional supply. Thus was the institution of slavery introduced into Cuba (Sauer 1966: 212–13).

The maltreatment of the Indians aroused much controversy. Other Spaniards joined Las Casas in denouncing it but with little success. The crown did attempt to restrict the practice of slavery by limiting it to "Caribs," that is, to the Indians who were supposed to be cannibals because they had shown hostility to the Spaniards. It ordered Rodrigo de Figueroa, a lawyer in Santo Domingo, to determine which islanders were Caribs and which were peaceful Indians (*guaitio*), not subject to slavery. After questioning the sailors who came to Santo Domingo over a period of two years, Figueroa came to the conclusion that only the natives of the Virgin Islands and the Lesser Antilles, Barbados excepted, were "Caribs." He specifically exempted the Indians of the Bahamian Archipelago, the Greater Antilles, and the small islands off the northern coast of South America. His decision came too late to save the Lucayan Tainos in the Bahamas from extinction, but it did furnish some protection to the inhabitants of Trinidad, Margarita, and the so-called Islas Gigantes (Aruba, Curaçao, and Bonaire) in northern South America. Contrary to a claim by Sauer (1966: 195), the term Carib tells us nothing about the ethnic composition of any of these islands.

The Hispaniolan goldfields became exhausted in the 1520s; the mines of Puerto Rico and Cuba, in the next decade. Thereafter, the encomiendas were devoted almost exclusively to animal husbandry and to the cultivation of sugar cane, which had been introduced from the Canary Islands in 1515.

The Spanish population declined markedly. Many towns were abandoned as their inhabitants left to seek their fortunes in Mexico in the 1520s and Peru in the 1530s. The West Indies became a backwater, whose main function was to supply food to the more developed parts of the Spanish empire and to service the fleets traveling to and from the mother country.

The number of Tainos in the encomiendas continued to fall. A census taken in 1514 recorded only 22,726 persons able to work. Some Indians, discouraged by their lot, committed suicide, hanging themselves or poisoning themselves with cassava juice. Many died in a smallpox epidemic of 1519. Others fled into uninhabited territory or took refuge among the Island-Caribs. In one instance, an encomienda led by a cacique named Enriquillo escaped to the interior of Hispaniola in 1519 and successfully maintained its independence until the crown finally pardoned it in 1533 (Vega 1987b: 157–65).

The number of Tainos in the encomiendas was reduced by outmarriage as well as by flight. There was a shortage of Spanish women in the colony, and unlike northern Europeans, the Spanish men had no prejudice against marrying into another ethnic group. According to the census of 1514, 40 percent of the Spanish men had Indian wives (Sauer 1966: 199). These women and their children were lost to the encomiendas (Rouse and Arrom 1991).

The Spaniards compensated for the decline of the encomiendas by increasing the importation of Indian slaves from other parts of the Caribbean area and Black slaves from Africa. By 1524, when Diego Columbus completed his term as viceroy, there were more slaves than Tainos; and by 1540, the former had almost completely replaced the latter (Anderson-Cordóva 1990: 218–76). The slaves introduced new customs; for example, the mainland Indians brought with them the processing of corn into flour, bread, and beer (Lovén 1935: 375).

Little research has been done on the archeology of the conquest-period Tainos. So far as I am aware, only one encomienda site has been definitely identified, Hacienda Grande, just east of San Juan in Puerto Rico. Its Indians were assigned to Ponce de León, who put them to work searching for gold in the Toa Valley, on the opposite side of the town of San Juan. Carib raiders attacked them while they were back in their home village during a rest period, killing their cacique, Luisa, and a Spanish official who had come to return them to the goldfield (Rouse and Alegría 1990: 5). The sites with Spanish colonial artifacts around the east Cuban city of Holguín may also have been occupied by encomienda Indians. No colonial artifacts that I know of have been found at Hacienda Grande. It is possible that the inhabitants reverted to their own culture when they returned to the site during their rest periods and, while there, used only native artifacts.

Hacienda Grande was subsequently inhabited by some of the first Black slaves imported from Africa. By that time, the local encomienda had died out and had been replaced by a Spanish farm that grew food for the townspeople of San Juan. Among the sites known to have been inhabited by Indian slaves is Nueva Cádiz on Cubagua Island (fig. 37). Excavation in its slave quarters has yielded potsherds presumably of the Palmetto style from the Bahamian Archipelago (Cruxent and Rouse 1958–59, 1:59).

Of the few Taino artifacts that found their way into European museums, the purely aboriginal ones have already been discussed. I know of only two that may combine Taino and foreign traits, and both are questionable because we do not know their proveniences. One, which could be the figure of a zemi, consists of a belt coiled into a cylinder and surmounted by a body, a head, and a possible snuffing platform (fig. 39b). The other is simply a belt (fig. 39a). Both are woven of cotton and overlaid with glass beads, mirrors, and, in the second case, iron hooks. Both are also decorated with human faces, which could either be representations of zemis or the signs of rank known as guaíza. However, the face of the full figure is made from rhinoceros horn, which could have come only from Africa, and its style of carving is reminiscent of that continent (Vega 1987b: 17–29; Vega 1989). Moreover, features of the simple belt are made of African shells (Rouse and Arrom 1991). The designs woven into both look African as well. If the artifacts did come from the Antilles, they would have to be considered syncretisms of Taino, European, and African traits.

The Island-Caribs in the Windward Islands—not to be confused with the "Caribs" of the Virgin and Leeward islands—were able to maintain their separate identity through the eighteenth century. The Spaniards left them alone, partially because their territory lacked gold and partially because the Island-Caribs, being expert raiders, were able to defend themselves against attack. Indeed, they, too, became slavers, preying upon the more peaceful Indians and selling to the English, French, and Dutch those they did not keep for themselves (Dreyfus 1983–84: 49).

Sharply increased demand for sugar in Europe led its nations to enter the West Indies and challenge Spanish control, beginning in 1625. They first moved into the islands that had been depopulated by the slavers. The British settled the Bahamian Archipelago, the French occupied the Virgin Islands (which were later taken over by the British followed by the Danes), and the British, French, and Dutch divided up the Leeward Islands. Spain also lost the two most thinly populated parts of the Greater Antilles, Jamaica to Britain and Haiti to France.

Britain and France used their new colonies both as centers of piracy directed against the remaining Spanish possessions and as bases from which to conquer the Island-Caribs in the Windward Islands (Dreyfus 1983–84:

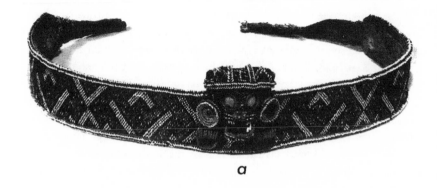

a

b

Fig. 39. Possible conquest-period Taino artifacts: *a*, woven cotton belt; *b*, cotton zemi (?). Proveniences unknown (after Montas, Borrell, and Moya Pons 1983: 91, 47).

47–50). Slowed by fierce resistance, they did not complete the latter project until 1797, when the British government finally deported the last independent group of Indians from St. Vincent to Central America. The deportees are known as Black-Caribs (Garifuna) because, while still in the Antilles, they intermarried with escaped African slaves from the British sugar plantations on Barbados (Taylor 1951: 15–27; Gonzalez 1988: 13–50). With their departure, the second repeopling of the West Indies may be said to have been completed.

Survival and Revival, 1524 On

Even though the Tainos themselves are extinct, persons claiming Taino ancestry have survived in all three of the Spanish-speaking countries: the Dominican Republic, Puerto Rico, and Cuba. The inhabitants of a reservation in the former British colony of Dominica still call themselves Caribs, too, although they no longer speak the native language and are culturally and biologically mixed. None of the modern West Indians who claim descent from either the Tainos or the Island-Caribs discriminate between their biological, linguistic, and cultural heritages. In fact, they have retained traits of all three kinds.

BIOLOGICAL TRAITS

Because few women came to the original Spanish colony during the first twelve years of its existence, when it was being governed by Christopher Columbus and Bobadilla, we may reasonably assume that the custom of intermarriage between Spaniards and Tainos began at that time. Intermarriage continued through the terms of Ovando and Diego Columbus; as we have seen, the census of 1514 found that 40 percent of the officially recognized wives of Spanish men were Indian. Consequently, a large proportion of the modern population of the Dominican Republic, Puerto Rico, and Cuba is able to claim partial descent from the Tainos.

A growing number of Spanish West Indians are stressing their native ancestry as a means of asserting their ethnic difference from the U.S. colossus to their north (García Arévalo 1988: 11–13; Vega 1987b: 117–18). Staunch native affiliation thrives in Puerto Rico, especially among the opponents of statehood, for whom it is a means of resisting assimilation with the United States. The people who claim Indian ancestry tend to assume that it was exclusively Taino, yet, as we have seen, increasing numbers of Indians were brought as slaves from other parts of the Caribbean area. These non-local Indians could easily have interbred with the Spaniards because many of them became household servants. The biological composition of the contemporary population has also been modified by intermarriage between Spaniards and Africans (Anderson-Córdova 1990: 218–76).

By contrast, there is relatively little Taino blood in the English-, Dutch-, and French-speaking parts of the West Indies, including the formerly Danish Virgin Islands, which now belong to the United States. All these islands were depopulated before they became European colonies, hence their present inhabitants can claim only European and African descent. The present inhabitants of the Windward Islands do have some Island-Carib blood, but it is largely limited to the French islands, where the Indians put into missions were assimilated. By contrast, the British had a policy of deporting the local Indians to other islands.

LINGUISTIC TRAITS

The contemporary Spanish-speaking people have inherited many linguistic as well as biological traits from the Tainos. These include not only social and cultural terms but also a large number of place names. The meanings of some terms have changed; for example, *batey* now means the land around a sugar factory or a country mansion rather than a ball or dance court. Small rural houses are now called bohíos, after the rectangular houses of the Tainos.

The English-, French-, and Dutch-speaking populations of the West Indies have acquired relatively few Taino words because they lacked direct contact with Tainos. They did not have the opportunity to learn Taino words from Indian mothers, as did the Spanish West Indians, and as a result, their use of native words is no greater than that among the English, French, and Dutch speakers elsewhere, who acquired Taino words through the Columbian exchange (see the Epilogue).

CULTURAL TRAITS

Fernando Ortiz (1947), a Cuban anthropologist who has written extensively on the survival of Taino cultural traits in his country, expresses the prevailing belief among the Spanish West Indians that they possess a plural culture, consisting of customs from three different sources—Spanish, Taino, and African. There can be no doubt, of course, that Spanish customs are dominant in the mix, just as Casimiroid customs prevailed over Saladoid in the culture known as El Caimito and just as the language of the Igneris, if not their culture, was dominant among the Island-Caribs.

The Taino part of the mix distinguishes the contemporary Spanish-speaking people of the West Indies from their English-, French-, and Dutch-speaking neighbors. This point was brought home to me at a conference on conservation in the British and American Virgin Islands. The conference broke down because the participating officials stated that they preferred to spend their limited financial resources in educating the local population rather than conserving its natural and cultural resources.

The anthropologists in attendance tried to revive the discussion by organizing a debate about the kind of education that should be given in the local schools. The social anthropologists in attendance, who specialized in African survivals, recommended that the students in local schools be taught about their African roots while the archeologists argued that they should instead be taught how the successive inhabitants of each island adapted to its environmental conditions. The social anthropologists won the argument. If the participants in the conference had been from Cuba, the Dominican Republic, or Puerto Rico, it would instead have been agreed that both African and Taino studies belong in the curriculum because both are part of the cultural heritage of the Spanish West Indies.

The British West Indian lack of affinity with the Native Americans extends also to the islands that were inhabited by Island-Caribs. There, it has been reinforced by the practice of segregating the few surviving Indians. The situation has been analyzed by my Yale colleague Michael G. Smith (1965: 162–75). He notes the existence in the present-day British West Indies of a plural society consisting of persons of white, Black, and mixed descent. The three groups share two cultural heritages, European and African, the second of which has become more important since the islands gained independence.

Conditions are similar in the former French colony of Haiti. The French who settled in the Windward Islands did, on the contrary, have an opportunity to interact with the Island-Caribs, and as a result, they acquired a triple cultural heritage, Indian as well as European and African. French traits continue to dominate, if only because the islands are organized into departments that are considered to be parts of metropolitan France.

The Spanish-speaking people of Puerto Rico are currently in a state of flux. It remains to be seen whether they will go the way of the French possessions by opting for statehood within the United States and, if that happens, whether and to what extent Anglo-American culture will become dominant over their Spanish, Taino, and African heritages.

REVIVAL

Just as a number of the art forms introduced by the Saladoid peoples during the first repeopling of the West Indies died out at the beginning of the Christian era, only to reappear a thousand years later, so too is Taino art now being revived, four centuries after the completion of the second repeopling. Bernardo Vega (1987a) calls this development Neo-Taino art; it could also be termed Post–Classic Taino.

There are several reasons for the revival. One is the need for business enterprises to develop new and attractive designs. Classic Taino motifs have proved apt and evocative (Pérez de Silva and Hostos 1939; García Arévalo 1988: 34–36).

The Spanish West Indians have also been attracted to Taino art as a means of strengthening their feelings of cultural identity vis-à-vis the United States. For example, when Puerto Rico chose commonwealth status to acquire a measure of political independence while retaining its economic union with the United States, Luis Muñoz Marín, the architect of that status, chose to reinforce it by promoting cultural independence. He asked a Puerto Rican anthropologist, Ricardo E. Alegría, to organize an Instituto de Cultura Puertorriqueña through which to strengthen the blend of Spanish, Taino, and African traits that characterizes Puerto Rican culture. Alegría organized museums, parks, and programs of research and instruction devoted to all three parts of the mix. The museums and parks are oriented toward Puerto Ricans rather than tourists. They are small and intimate to appeal to the local people and scattered around the island for ease of access. Alegría's reconstruction of the dance and ball courts at Caguana is an outstanding example (fig. 28). When the pro-statehood party defeated the commonwealth party in a recent election, it attempted to counter the influence of the Instituto de Cultura Puertorriqueña by promoting "universal" art.

The final reason for the revival of Taino art is that tourists have discovered it, particularly in the Dominican Republic, Puerto Rico, and Haiti— and have created a market for falsifications and reproductions. Some specimens are crudely done, but the best are equal in quality to the aboriginal artifacts (fig. 40). They differ in one or more ways: use of modern materials or techniques, modification of Taino shapes or motifs, and new combinations of modes of material, shape, and decoration.

The inhabitants of the other parts of the West Indies have not participated in the Neo-Taino development. They focus instead on their own ancestral forms of art.

Conclusions

The periods of discovery, conquest, and survival and revival were each marked by a contradiction. During the period of discovery, Columbus had difficulty reconciling his roles as explorer and administrator. He did succeed in exploring the Taino homeland during his first and second voyages

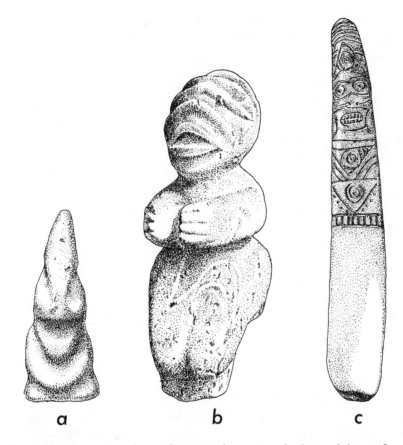

Fig. 40. Neo-Taino art: *a*, abstract figure carved on a piece of stalactite; *b*, human figure carved from coral limestone; *c*, design engraved on bone. All are from the Dominican Republic (*a*, Yale Peabody Museum specimen; *b*, *c*, Paul F. Burke collection).

and in discovering South and Central America during his third and fourth voyages but was prevented by his duties as governor from realizing the full potential of his finds. He performed poorly as an administrator: not only was he unable to keep peace among the Spanish settlers but he also contributed to the decline of the Tainos by failing to protect them.

The conquest period was plagued by a conflict between the crown's ideal of converting the Indians to Christianity and assimilating them into Spanish culture and the colonists' belief that they had to exploit the Indians in order to make a decent living. The colonists' belief prevailed, hastening the decline of the Tainos, but the seeds of survival and revival were sown. Spanish men married Taino women, and their descendants adopted Taino words and customs. The colonists from all the European countries imported many slaves, including Indians from other parts of the Caribbean area and Blacks from Africa—both of whom contributed to the ensuing biological, linguistic, and cultural mix.

In the current period of survival and revival the Spanish West Indians are able to claim partial descent from the Tainos, but the Dutch, English, and French speakers cannot do so because they arrived on the scene after the Tainos had become extinct. It is probably no accident that the Spanish West Indians favor calling their ancestors Taino, a word obtained from a language of their forebears, whereas the British West Indians prefer Arawak, the name of a tribe that their ancestors discovered in South America.

My discussion of the three periods has been hampered by another conflict of terms, between Carib, used for hostile Indians, and Island-Carib, referring to the inhabitants of the Windward Islands. Carib is a popular name, which the Classic Tainos of Hispaniola and Puerto Rico applied to their warlike neighbors to the east and south, including the Eastern Tainos of the Virgin and Leeward islands, and which the Spaniards adopted for the same purpose. Island-Carib is a scientific name, coined by anthropologists to distinguish the ethnic group that occupied the Windward Islands in the time of Columbus from the Tainos to their north and the Arawaks to their south.

Scientific names are adjectives, whose meanings depend upon the nouns to which they are attached (Rouse 1986: 197). When the adjective *Taino* modifies the phrase *ethnic group,* it refers to the local population that greeted Columbus upon his arrival in the West Indies. When it is combined with *people,* it specifies the bearers of the Taino culture. When coupled with *speech-community,* it indicates the speakers of the Taino language. Attached to *race,* it designates the persons who shared the Taino biology.

The four nouns can be used as synonyms when investigating the Tainos per se, because all members of that ethnic group had the same culture and language, if not the same biology. The nouns must, however, be treated separately when discussing the ancestries of the Tainos, because of the possibility that the group obtained its cultural, linguistic, and biological heritages from different sources (chap. 2).

In my subtitle, I refer to the Tainos as a people in order to signal my intention of focusing on their cultural heritage. I discuss their ethnic traits and their linguistic and biological heritages only as parts of the setting in which the Taino people lived.

Postgraduate students of mine from Germany and Japan have questioned my usage of the term *people* because their compatriots misused it during World War II: they failed to recognize that cultural, linguistic, and biological heritages need to be treated separately and that peoples are simply the bearers of cultural heritages (Rouse 1965). When so defined, the term *people* becomes scientifically acceptable.

People is sometimes used as a verb rather than a noun, in which case it refers to population movements into virgin territory, not previously inhabited by human beings. Peoplers were able to retain their cultures intact because they did not have to contend with previous peoples and cultures. I have applied the verb *repeople* to movements into already inhabited areas, during the course of which the migrants replaced or assimilated their predecessors and borrowed traits from their cultures.

The Saladoids and Ostionoids, who first repeopled the West Indies, differed in the way they traveled from the the Europeans and Africans, who carried out the second repeopling. The first repeoplers paddled canoes instead of sailing ships and lacked a knowledge of overseas navigation; they had to hop from island to island instead of venturing directly across open seas, as the second repeoplers did (compare chaps. 4 and 6). The contrasting behavior of Christopher Columbus and Martín Pinzón, the captain who accompanied him on his first voyage, illustrates this difference. Upon the advice of his Taino pilots, Columbus sailed along the coast of Cuba. Dissatisfied with his slow pace, Pinzón put out to sea and sailed ahead to Hispaniola. His navigational skills enabled him to discover the Cibao goldfield before Columbus could reach it.

Some of the archeologists who have studied the first repeopling of the West Indies have ascribed to the Indians the European ability to travel long distances overseas. Their assumption has led them to conclude that the El Caimito people proceeded directly from Colombia to Hispaniola without the benefit of sails. This improbable hypothesis is ethnocentric.

The role of peoples and cultures in the study of peopling and repeopling is self-evident. Not so easily recognized is the need to take both kinds of units into consideration when studying cultural change. As we saw in chapter 2, many Caribbeanists approach the process of change only in terms of cultural traits, divorced from the peoples who possessed them. They depict the rise and decline of Taino culture as a seamless fabric of individual traits. I have instead traced the traits from one people to another and have studied their integrations into each people's culture.

Use of this approach has made it possible for me to examine peoples' motives, needs, and activities and to infer the kinds of societies into which they organized themselves. It has also enabled me to correct an imbalance in the study of cultural change. Most authorities look only at the deeds of men and of women acting in men's roles. By viewing ethnic change from the perspective of whole peoples, I have been able to take the women and children into account and thereby to reach unorthodox conclusions about the genesis of the Island-Caribs and the "genocide" of the Tainos.

Finally, my focus on peoples has permitted me to distinguish cultural centers, to delimit frontiers in space and time, and to draw conclusions about cultural contact. The last subject is discussed further in the Epilogue.

E P I L O G U E

T H E   T A I N O S '   R O L E   I N

T H E   C O L U M B I A N   E X C H A N G E

The Taino people emerged during the latter part of the first millennium A.D. and reached maturity about 1200. They were still evolving when Columbus arrived, but soon succumbed to the effects of overwork, malnutrition, epidemics of introduced diseases, rebellion, emigration, and outmarriage. By 1524 they had ceased to exist as a separate population group. Parts of their biological, cultural, and linguistic heritages have nevertheless survived in the former Spanish colonies or have been revived there during the present century.

Before departing from the scene, they transmitted a number of biological, cultural, and linguistic traits to the Spaniards, who in turn passed them on to their neighbors, whence they spread throughout the Eastern Hemisphere. The historian Alfred W. Crosby, Jr., has termed this process the Columbian exchange.

Biological Traits

Thanks to the failure of the few attempts to import Tainos into Spain, the flow of human genes was almost entirely one way, from the Eastern to the Western Hemisphere. Crosby (1972: 35–63, 122–64), however, was able to include diseases in his discussion of the exchange. The Spaniards unwittingly hastened the decline of the Tainos by introducing new illnesses to which the Indians had not had an opportunity to develop immunity. In return, the Tainos may have given the invaders syphilis. Their myths describe its symptoms, and lesions on their skeletons could have been syphilis induced. An epidemic of the disease broke out in the Mediterranean Basin immediately after Columbus returned from his first voyage, but there is reason to believe that syphilis had existed there before then (Sauer 1966: 86). The Tainos may have contributed only a new and more virulent form of the disease.

Cultural Traits

The Tainos played a greater role in the exchange of foods, especially to tropical peoples of the Eastern Hemisphere (Crosby 1972: 165–207). Slave traders carried their principal crop, cassava (Taino casabe), to sub-Saharan Africa. It was widely adopted there because of its high yield, ability to survive for a long time in storage, and adaptability to savanna areas too dry for the local crops. In effect, it touched off an agricultural revolution and an accompanying population explosion. Cassava was slower to reach India and Southeast Asia but eventually became a staple food there in areas unsuitable for local crops like rice. Because Indian corn (maiz) grows well under temperate, not just tropical, conditions, the Spaniards were able to introduce it into their own country, whence it spread to the rest of the Mediterranean Basin and to central Europe. It serves mainly as cattle feed, a use to which it was presumably adapted on the cattle ranches established by the conquistadors in Hispaniola.

The Taino techniques for cultivating and processing cassava and corn went east with the plants. It should be noted, however, that the brewing of beer from either plant and the grinding of corn kernels into flour from which to bake bread were not transmitted. The Tainos lacked both procedures, which eventually spread from the American mainland to the tropical parts of the Eastern Hemisphere, where corn became a staple crop, preferred by many peoples to cassava.

We are indebted to the Tainos for a number of other food crops, including the sweet potato, bean, squash, and peanut, and for fruits like the guava, mamey, and pineapple. The Tainos were not, however, involved in the spread of the ordinary potato or the tomato. The Spaniards encountered these crops after they reached Middle and South America.

The Tainos also contributed rubber and tobacco to the Columbian exchange. Peoples throughout the world have emulated the Tainos in developing rubber-ball games and courts on which to play them. Cubans have been leaders in the production of cigars (tabaco) since pre-Columbian time.

The Spaniards admired the quality and artistry of the Tainos' canoes (canoa) and their weaving of cotton into hammocks (hamaca). They added both these items to their own cultural inventory, then transmitted them to other parts of the world.

Linguistic Traits

The Taino words for many of their foods and crafts accompanied the products themselves, as is indicated by the terms in parentheses above. Among the other English terms that originated among the Tainos are *barbecue, cannibal, hurricane,* and *savanna* (García Arévalo 1982: 30). The first is a later acquisition; it appears to have been carried to the United States by French speakers after they replaced the Tainos in Haiti (José J. Arrom, personal communication). Most etymologists trace the English word *cacique* back through Spanish to the Taino language.

The ideas expressed by the Taino loan words must have had an effect on social and intellectual thought in the Old World. It is probable, for example, that the distinction the Tainos made between themselves and the Caribs played a role in debates about the nobility of savages, and that the concept of cacique influenced European theorizing about social evolution.

Europeans were fascinated by the apparent simplicity of life among the Lucayans, the first Tainos encountered by Columbus. Peter Martyr thought that it confirmed the classical belief in an initial golden age, in which humans retained their original innocence, had not yet developed private property and social controls, and consequently lived in a state of complete happiness (Gerbi 1986: 53–54).

Conclusions

The Spaniards were not the first European people to come into sustained contact with Native Americans. The Norse had reached North America five hundred years earlier, advancing along a circumpolar route. Erik the Red colonized the southern part of Greenland, and several of his followers, among them his son Leif, briefly voyaged to the northern tip of Newfoundland, where they encountered Indians or Eskimos (Ingstad 1969). During the thirteenth century, Eskimos from northern Greenland settled alongside the Norse farms in the southern part of the island. The two peoples lived side by side until the time of Columbus, when the Norse perished during a "little ice age" that destroyed their pastures. The Eskimos survived, thanks to their reliance on hunting and fishing (Hatt 1953: 90–99).

The Norse and Eskimo remains show only a minimal exchange of traits, even though they coexisted as independent peoples three times as long as the Tainos and the Spaniards did. The two populations kept to themselves. Moreover, they were too remote and too peripheral to have affected the centers of development in Europe and the Americas (Rouse 1986: 59–62). The Tainos and the Spaniards, on the contrary, happened to live on the most direct route across the Atlantic Ocean at a time when advances in navigation opened up the possibility of round-trip voyages. The two groups interacted so strongly that they merged to form a new mestizo people. Even though Taino race, culture, and language became extinct in the process, individual Taino traits have survived, differentiating the Spanish West Indians from the British, Dutch, and French West Indians.

G L O S S A R Y

Only a primary meaning is given for each term except where conflicting usages might confuse the reader.

ABSOLUTE TIME. Measurement of time by calendric units, which retain their value throughout the region under study.

ACCULTURATION. Transmission of a culture to a neighboring people through interaction rather than population movement.

AFRICAN GEOGRAPHICAL RACE. Biologically defined population group in sub-Saharan Africa, from which slaves were brought to the West Indies during the Historic age.

AGE. Time-space unit defined by its level of technological development.

AGRO-CERAMIC AGE. Ceramic age.

AMAZONID LINEAGE. Biologically defined population group supposed to have inhabited the Amazon Basin and the eastern half of the Caribbean area during their Ceramic and Formative ages.

AMERICAN GEOGRAPHIC RACE. Biologically defined population group to which the American Indians belong.

ANADEL. Ostionan style in eastern Hispaniola at the beginning of the local Ceramic age.

ARAUQUINOID. Series in the Guiana Highlands and the adjacent lowlands during the latter part of the Ceramic age.

ARAWAK. (1) Ethnic group in the northern part of the Guianas, which formerly extended onto the high land around the Orinoco Delta; (2) Taino.

ARAWAKAN. Family of languages widely distributed through the Amazon Basin, the Guianas, the Orinoco Valley, and the eastern half of the Caribbean area in Columbus's time.

ARCHAIC AGE. Those local periods in the Americas during which stone grinding first appeared.

ARCHEOLOGICAL ANTHROPOLOGY. Subdiscipline that draws conclusions from the study of the remains of past peoples and their societies.

ARCHEOLOGY. (1) Curation of human remains; (2) use of human remains to solve problems of another discipline, such as anthropology or art history.

AREITO. Taino ceremony celebrating the deeds of ancestors.

ARROYO DEL PALO. Ostionan style in eastern Cuba at the beginning of the local Ceramic age.

173

ASSEMBLAGE. Artifacts and other remains found together in a site-unit—for example, in a single component or in one section and level.

ASSIMILATION. Absorption of immigrants into a population group or society.

AZTEC. Civilization in central Mexico during Columbus's time.

BALL BELT. Wooden or stone belt worn by the Tainos while playing ball.

BALL COURT. Structurally enclosed field for playing ball.

BALL GROUND. Unstructured field for playing ball.

BAND. A small, independent, and usually seminomadic settlement.

BANWAROID. Ortoiroid.

BARRANCOID. Series of styles thought to have originated in the lower middle part of the Orinoco Valley midway through the local Ceramic age. It subsequently spread to the high ground around the Orinoco Delta and may have continued into north-central Venezuela but not farther west, where its place was taken by a Malamboid series, which is characterized by a different kind of modeled-incised ware.

BARRERA-MORDÁN. Culture in the Dominican Republic during the local Lithic age.

BARREROID. Casimiroid.

BASIC VOCABULARY. Words that, because they express ideas common to all humans, are more likely to have been inherited than borrowed from neighboring speech-communities.

BATATA. Taino word for sweet potato.

BATEY. (1) Taino word for the ball game and for the court or ground on which it was played; (2) Spanish word for the land around a sugar factory or a country mansion.

BIOLOGICAL ANTHROPOLOGY. Physical anthropology.

BIOLOGICAL HERITAGE. Set of biological traits inherited by a local race from its ancestors; the core of that race's biology.

BIOLOGY. (1) Discipline that studies life on earth; (2) sum total of a race's biological traits. See also Plural biology.

BLACK-CARIB. Ethnic group that evolved among the Island-Caribs after the British moved them from St. Vincent to Central America.

BLADE. Stone tool struck off a prismatic core.

BOCA CHICA. Chican culture on the southeastern coast of Hispaniola during Period IVa.

BOHÍO. (1) Rectangular house inhabited by Tainos; (2) Spanish West Indian word for a small country dwelling.

BOHUTI. Taino medicine man or shaman.

BORINQUEN. Taino name for Puerto Rico and its inhabitants.

BOUTBOIS. Culture of Martinique during the local Archaic age.

BRONZE AGE. Those local periods in Eurasia and Africa during which bronze casting was first practiced.

BUREN. Taino name for the griddle used to bake cassava bread.

CABARET. Culture of Haiti during the local Lithic age.

CACIQUE. Taino word for chief, which has spread to both the Spanish and English languages.

CANEY. Taino word for round houses.

CANOA. Taino word for canoe.

CAPÁ. (1) Chican culture in western Puerto Rico during Period IVa; (2) alternative name for the Caguana site in Puerto Rico.

CARIB. (1) Ethnic group in the Guianas and around the Orinoco Delta during the Historic age; (2) popular name for the warlike Indians who inhabited the small islands east and south of Puerto Rico in Columbus's time. *See also* Black-Carib; Island-Carib.

CARIBAN. Family of languages widespread in the Guiana Highlands and the eastern and central parts of the Caribbean area during Columbus's time.

CASABE. Taino word for cassava. See also *Yuca*.

CASIMIRAN. Subseries of Casimiroid cultures in Cuba and Hispaniola during the local Lithic age.

CASIMIROID. Series in Cuba and Hispaniola during the local Lithic and Archaic ages; it appears to have survived in western Cuba until the arrival of Columbus.

CAYO. Style of pottery on St. Vincent Island, of uncertain age and ethnic affiliation.

CAYO REDONDO. Culture that succeeded Guayabo Blanco in western Cuba during the local Archaic age.

CEDROS. Cedrosan culture in Trinidad at the start of the local Ceramic age.

CEDROSAN. Saladoid subseries that marks the beginning of the Ceramic age along the northeastern coast of South America from Suriname to Margarita Island and in the West Indies from the Lesser Antilles to eastern Hispaniola.

CELT. Petaloid-shaped ax blade of stone or shell.

CERAMIC AGE. Those local periods in the Americas during which pottery making was first practiced.

CERAMIC STYLE (COMPLEX). (1) Sum total of a people's wares and modes—a site-unit; (2) cluster of a people's ceramic traits that has spread to neighboring peoples or has survived among subsequent peoples—a trait-unit.

CHICAN. Subseries of Ostionoid cultures in Puerto Rico and Hispaniola (except for the southwestern tip) during the local Formative age. It had outposts on St. Croix and in eastern Cuba.

CHIEFDOM. Taino polity governed by a hierarchy of village, district, and regional chiefs.

CHIMU. Civilization in Peru marked by the revival of Mochica traits.

CHOPPER. Cutting tool made by chipping one edge of a pebble.

CHRONOLOGICAL CHART. Diagram of the distribution of site- or trait-units in the dimensions of time and space.

CIBONEY. (1) Local group of Tainos in the central part of Cuba; (2) Guanahatabey.

CIGUAYO. (1) Regional chiefdom in northeastern Hispaniola, ruled by Mayo-banex; (2) variant group of Tainos in that chiefdom, or possibly a separate ethnic group.

CIRCUM-CARIBBEAN. Formative-age level of cultural development, which distinguishes the Classic Tainos from the Eastern and Western Tainos.

CLASSIC TAINOS. Inhabitants of the Taino heartland, that is, Hispaniola and Puerto Rico; they also had outposts on St. Croix, Middle Caicos Island, and the eastern tip of Cuba.

COA. Digging stick used by Taino farmers.

COAYBAY. Taino name for the land of the dead, said to be situated on a remote group of islands.

COGNATES. Words in different languages that have evolved from a common ancestor.

COHOBA. Hallucinogenic snuff taken by the Tainos while worshiping zemis.

COLONIZATION. (1) Establishment of a colonial government—a social process; (2) replacement of the people in one part of a local area by a foreign people—a cultural process.

COLUMBIAN EXCHANGE. Interchange of biological, cultural, and linguistic traits between peoples of the Eastern and Western hemispheres, resulting from Columbus's discovery of the most direct route between the two.

COMPLEX. See Ceramic style; Cultural complex; Trait-complex.

COMPONENT. Site or part of a site occupied by a single people and culture.

CONSILIENCE. The procedure of testing hypotheses by independently studying different lines of evidence in a search for conclusions that support each other.

CONUCO. Taino word for a field mounded to improve the production of cassava and sweet potatoes.

CORE. Stone from which flakes or blades have been struck.

COROSAN. Archaic-age subseries in the Virgin Islands and Puerto Rico, including the Krum Bay and Coroso cultures.

COROSO. Culture of Puerto Rico during the local Archaic age.

COURI. Culture of Haiti during the local Archaic age.

COURIAN. Subseries of Casimiroid cultures in Hispaniola during the local Archaic age.

CRANIAL DEFORMATION. Practice of exerting pressure on a child's skull in order to deform it.

CUEVAS. Final Cedrosan culture in the Vieques Sound and Mona Passage areas.

CULTURAL ANTHROPOLOGY. Study of peoples and their cultures, whether by archeologists, ethnohistorians, or ethnologists.

CULTURAL ARCHEOLOGY. Use of archeological remains to draw conclusions about peoples and their cultures.

CULTURAL COMPLEX. (1) Traits diagnostic of a people and culture—a site-unit; (2) trait-complex—a trait-unit.

CULTURAL ECOLOGY. Study of the adaptation of societies to their environment.

CULTURAL HERITAGE. Set of cultural traits inherited by a local people from its ancestors; the core of that people's culture.

CULTURAL HISTORY. (1) Study of the development of peoples' cultures; (2) study of the origins of cultural traits.

CULTURE. Sum total of a people's cultural traits.

DANCE COURT. Oval plaza or roadway delimited by earthworks and/or stone slabs.

DANCE GROUND. Unstructured plaza or roadway used for dancing and other public ceremonies.

DIAGNOSTIC TRADITION. Modes, wares, or other traits that are shared by all of the members of a series or subseries and can therefore be used to identify it.

DIFFUSION. Spread of biological, cultural, or linguistic traits from one person, society, or population group to another.

DIMENSION. A step in the procedure of stone chipping or pottery making, where the artisan could often choose among a number of alternative or optional modes.

DIVERGENCE. Division of a local race and its biology, a local people and its culture, or a local speech-community and its language into new units of the same kind, which happens when members of such a unit become separated from the rest and are no longer able to interbreed, interact, or intercommunicate closely with them.

DUAL BIOLOGY. *See* Plural biology.

DUAL CULTURE. *See* Plural culture.

DUAL LANGUAGE. *See* Plural language.

DUAL STYLE. *See* Plural style.

DUHO. Stool used by Taino chiefs as a sign of rank.

EASTERN TAINO. Name applied by professional taxonomists to all the historic inhabitants of the Virgin and Leeward islands, with the exception of a Classic Taino outpost in the north on St. Croix and Island-Carib outposts in the south on Guadeloupe and nearby islands. *Eastern Taino* should not be confused with *Carib,* the name popularly applied to all inhabitants of the Virgin Islands and the Lesser Antilles, regardless of their ethnic affiliation.

EDGE GRINDER. Pebble with grinding facets on its edges rather than its sides.

ELBOW STONE. Abbreviated stone belt worn by the Tainos while playing ball; believed to have been filled out with cordage.

EL CAIMITO. Courian culture in the eastern part of Hispaniola at the beginning of the local Ceramic age.

ELENAN. Ostionoid subseries that diverged from Cedrosan in the Leeward Islands and the Virgin Passage area circa 600 A.D. and eventually became the culture of the Eastern Tainos.

EL MAYAL. Cedrosan style in the Carúpano area of eastern Venezuela at the beginning of the local Ceramic age.

EL PALITO. Barrancoid style on the central coast of Venezuela midway through the local Ceramic age.

EL PORVENIR. Archaic-age culture in the Dominican Republic.

EMIGRATION. Movement of individuals out of an area in such small numbers that the local population is not affected.

ENCOMIENDA. System of forced labor whereby entire Taino villages were assigned to Spaniards under the direction of their chiefs; they worked for six to eight months, then returned to their own homes and tended their crops for the rest of the year.

ESPERANZA. Chican culture in eastern Puerto Rico during Period IVa.

ETHNIC GROUP. Historic-age population group characterized by a distinct biology, culture, and/or language.

ETHNOCENTRISM. Practice of looking at other peoples' cultures from the standpoint of one's own culture.

ETHNOHISTORICAL ANTHROPOLOGY (ETHNOHISTORY). Subdiscipline that draws conclusions from the study of documentary evidence.

ETHNOLOGICAL ANTHROPOLOGY (ETHNOLOGY). Subdiscipline that draws conclusions from the study of contemporary peoples and their societies.

FAMILY. Speech-communities and languages that are known to have descended from a common ancestor.

FAMILY TREE. A phylogenetic diagram showing the development of speech-communities and languages from their common ancestor.

FAN-SHAPED STONE. Artifact made by the Casimiran and Redondan peoples, presumably for ceremonial purposes.

FLAKE. Piece of stone struck off a more or less oval core.

FOREIGN TRAIT. Biological, cultural, or linguistic trait that has diffused from one people to another.

FORMATIVE AGE. Those local periods in the Americas during which public works were first constructed. *See also* Circum-Caribbean.

FOUNDERS' EFFECT. The simplification of a biology, culture, or language that takes place when a few of its bearers move from one area to another, carrying only part of its traits.

FRONTIER. Land on the spatial or temporal boundary between two cultures.

GARIFUNA. Black-Carib.

GENE FLOW. *See* Diffusion.

GENERAL PERIOD. Local areas and periods that share the same general trends and may therefore be assumed to have had similar calendric values.

GENOCIDE. Extinction of an ethnic group.

GEOGRAPHICAL RACE. Local races within regions the size of a continent that have been grouped together because they appear to be descended from a common ancestor.

GIOIA. Herb swallowed by Taino worshipers to induce vomiting.

GLOTTOCHRONOLOGY. Procedure of estimating the time since two languages diverged by studying the degree of difference in their basic vocabulary.

GRIDDLE. Flat disk of clay (now iron) used to bake cassava bread.

GUAÍZA. Pendant in the form of a human face worn by the Tainos as a sign of rank.

GUANAHATABEY. Ethnic group at the western end of Cuba.

GUANÍN. Copper-gold ornament traded to the Tainos from South America.

GUAPOID SERIES. Huecan subseries.

GUAITIAO. Taino name for peaceful Indians.

GUAYABAL. Chican culture in eastern Hispaniola during Period IVa.

GUAYABITOID. Series of styles in Trinidad and on the eastern coast of Venezuela at the close of the Ceramic age.

GUAYABO BLANCO. Original Archaic-age culture in western Cuba.

GUÁYIGA. Cycad whose roots were eaten by the Tainos and their predecessors.

HACIENDA GRANDE. Cedrosan culture on the northern, western, and eastern coasts of Puerto Rico at the beginning of the local Ceramic age.

HAITI. Taino name for Hispaniola and its inhabitants.

HAMACA. Taino word for hammock.

HIGÜEY. Regional chiefdom in the southeastern part of Hispaniola, ruled by Higüayo.

HISTORIC AGE. Time since the introduction of writing into each part of the Caribbean area.

HOHOKAM. Series of peoples in the southwestern United States at the beginning of the Christian era.

HORIZON. Segment of a tradition that can be used to indicate contemporaneity because it was distributed across several local areas for only a brief period of time.

HUECAN. Possible subseries of styles that may have developed independently at the northern and western ends of the distribution of the Saladoid series.

IGNERI (IERI, EYERI). Ethnic group that preceded the Island-Caribs in the Windward Islands.

IMMIGRATION. Movement of individuals into a new area in such small numbers that they are absorbed by the local population.

INCENSE BURNER. Taino vessel shaped like an inverted flower pot, possibly used to collect smoke with which to drive insects away.

INHALER. See Snuffing tube; Snuffing vessel.

INHERITED TRAIT. Biological, cultural, or linguistic trait that has been handed down from one style or culture to another.

INTERACTION SPHERE. Local periods whose inhabitants interacted so strongly that they mutually influenced each other.

IRON AGE. Those local periods in Eurasia and Africa during which iron working was first practiced.

ISLAND-CARIB. Ethnic group that inhabited the Windward Islands.

ISTHMID LINEAGE. Biologically defined group supposed to have extended from the Andes through Middle America during protohistoric time.

JOLLY BEACH. Archaic-age culture on Antigua Island.

KALINA. Island-Carib.

KRUM BAY. Archaic-age culture in the Virgin Islands.

LA CALETA. Outpost of the Hacienda Grande culture at the eastern end of Hispaniola.

LA HUECA. Saladoid culture in the Vieques Sound area of Puerto Rico at the beginning of the local Ceramic age.

LANGUAGE. Sum total of the linguistic traits of a speech-community.

LEXICOGRAPHY. *See* Glottochronology.

LINEAGE. Division of a geographical race, consisting of local races descended from a common ancestor.

LINGUISTIC ANTHROPOLOGY (LINGUISTICS). Subdiscipline that draws conclusions from the study of human languages.

LINGUISTIC FAMILY. *See* Family.

LINGUISTIC HERITAGE. Set of linguistic traits inherited by a local speech community from its ancestors; the core of that community's language.

LITHIC AGE. Those local periods in the Americas during which stone chipping was first practiced.

LITTLE RIVER. Ostionan style in southern Jamaica at the beginning of the local Ceramic age.

LOAN WORD. *See* Foreign trait.

LOCAL AREA. Unit of space small enough to be used to delimit a local people and its culture. *See also* Local period.

LOCAL PERIOD. Unit of time small enough to be used to delimit a local people and its culture. *See also* Local area.

LOCAL RACE. The inhabitants of a biologically homogeneous area and period.

LOKONO. ARAWAK (1).

LUCAYO. Taino name for the Bahamian Archipelago and its inhabitants.

MACRO-CHIBCHAN. Superfamily of languages in Colombia and Central America at the time of European contact.

MAGUÁ. Regional chiefdom in the lower Cibao Valley, Hispaniola, ruled by Guarionex.

MAGUANA. Regional chiefdom in south-central Hispaniola, ruled by Caonabo.

MAIPURAN. Subfamily of Arawakan languages, including Arawak, Island-Carib, and Taino.

MAIZ. Taino word for Indian corn.

MALAMBOID. Series in the lower Magdalena Valley midway through the local Ceramic age.

MANO AND METATE. Hand stone and underlying stone slab used to grind vegetable foods.

MARITIME SALADOID. Cedrosan Saladoid.

MAYA. Civilization in Yucatán during Columbus's time.

MEILLAC. Meillacan culture in the Cibao Valley and northern Haiti. It appears to have evolved from Anadel, an Ostionan culture, midway through the local Ceramic age.

MEILLACAN. Ostionoid subseries that arose in the Cibao Valley midway through the local Ceramic age and spread westward to Jamaica and central Cuba, where it became the culture of the Western Tainos.

MESOAMERICA. Culture area that extended from the northern part of Central America into Mexico during protohistoric time.

MESO-INDIAN AGE. Archaic age.

METATE. See Mano and metate.

MIDDEN. Deposit of food remains, discarded artifacts, and other refuse.

MIDDLE PALEOLITHIC AGE. Those local periods in Europe and the Middle East during which stone flaking was first practiced.

MOCHICA. Early Peruvian civilization, traits of which were subsequently revived in the Chimu civilization.

MODE. A type of artifactual feature, as opposed to a type of artifact or a type of potsherd.

MODELED-INCISED WARE. Tradition shared by the Barrancoid and Chican Ostionoid peoples; a parallel development from the ceramics of their Saladoid ancestors.

MOEITY. Division of a society into two halves.

MORDANOID. Casimiroid.

MULTIPLE-COMPONENT SITE. Place containing the remains of successive peoples and their cultures.

MULTIPLE-WARE STYLE. See Plural style.

NABORIA. Taino lower class.

NAGUA. Apron worn by Taino women.

NEO-INDIAN AGE. Ceramic age.

NEO-TAINO ART. Current revival of Classic Taino art.

NITAÍNO. Taino upper class.

ORTOIRE. Archaic-age culture of Trinidad.

ORTOIROID. Series extending from the high ground around the Orinoco Delta through the Lesser Antilles into Puerto Rico during the local Archaic age.

OSTIONAN. Initial Ostionoid subseries in the Mona Passage area, whose peoples introduced the Ceramic age into the rest of Hispaniola, Jamaica, eastern Cuba, and the southern Bahamas.

OSTIONES. Initial Ostionan culture, which evolved from the final Cedrosan culture, Cuevas, in the Mona Passage area midway through the Ceramic age.

OSTIONOID. Series that marks the westward spread of the Ceramic age from the Mona Passage area to central Cuba and the Bahamian Archipelago.

PAINTED WARE. White-on-red ware, a diagnostic of the Saladoid series.

PALEO-INDIAN AGE. Lithic age.

PALMETTO. People and culture that arose in the Bahamian Archipelago during the local Ceramic age.

PALMETTO WARE. Name frequently applied to the pottery of the Palmetto style, the only ware present in that style.

PASSAGE AREA. Culture area that includes the land on either side of a channel.

PEARLS. Cedrosan style in Grenada at the beginning of the local Ceramic age.

PEOPLE. The inhabitants of a local area and period, who by definition must have had a separate culture.

PEOPLE AND CULTURE. Two sides of a coin, one consisting of a local population group and the other of the cultural traits that define the group. *See also* Race and biology; Speech-community and language.

PEOPLING. Movement of a people into a previously uninhabited area.

PHASE. (1) Ceramic style; (2) culture.

PHYLOGENY. Family tree.

PHYSICAL ANTHROPOLOGY. Subdiscipline that draws conclusions from the study of human biologies.

PLAINWARE. Undecorated pottery in an assemblage. It can include plain sherds from the undecorated parts of vessels and plain vessels from different wares.

PLURAL BIOLOGY. Combination of two or more biologies in which one dominates the others.

PLURAL CULTURE. Combination of two or more cultures in which one dominates the others.

PLURAL LANGUAGE. Combination of two or more languages in which one dominates the others.

PLURAL STYLE. Combination of two or more wares in which one dominates the others.

POLYCHROME PAINTING. Use of three or more colors to decorate pottery.

POPULAR CLASSIFICATION. A people's way of classifying itself or aspects of its environment.

POPULATION GROUP. Human beings who originally lived within the same geographical and temporal limits, interbred, interacted, or intercommunicated, and consequently developed a single race, culture, or language.

POPULATION MOVEMENT. *See* Colonization (2); Peopling; Repeopling.

POST-CLASSIC TAINO ART. Neo-Taino art.

POST MOLD. Discoloration of the soil caused by the decay of a wooden post.

POTTERY TYPE. (1) Trait-unit formed by classifying potsherds; (2) trait-unit formed by classifying vessels and sherds into kinds of whole artifacts.

PROSPERITY. Cedrosan culture in the Virgin Islands at the beginning of the local Ceramic age.

PROTO-ARAWAKAN. Original language of the Arawakan family, believed to have been spoken on the central Amazon.

PROTO-LANGUAGE. Common ancestor of a group of languages.

PROTO-MAIPURAN. Original language in the Maipuran subfamily.

PROTO-NORTHERN. Language ancestral to Arawak, Island-Carib, and Taino.

PUEBLO. Series of peoples in the southwestern United States during the latter part of the local Ceramic age.

PUNTA. Unpainted minority ware within the Anadel style, characterized by small appliqué heads and limbs.

RACE AND BIOLOGY. Two sides of a coin, one consisting of a local population group and the other of the biological traits that define the group. *See also* People and culture; Speech-community and language.

RADIOCARBON DATING. Procedure of estimating the lapse of time since the death of an organism by measuring its loss of radioactive carbon.

RADIOMETRIC ANALYSIS. Measurement of the loss of any kind of radioactivity.

RECHIPPING. Trimming the edges of stone cores, flakes, or blades.

RECTILINEARLY INCISED WARE. Sole ware in the Meillacan subseries, a fusion of Ostionan and Casimiran traits.

REDONDAN. Casimiroid subseries in Cuba during the local Archaic age.

REDWARE. Name applied to the pottery of the Ostionan subseries because many of its sherds are painted red. It is the only ware present in most of the styles of that subseries.

RELATIVE TIME. Expression of time in terms of ages, which occur at different times in different places.

REPARTIMIENTO. Distribution of Tainos among the Spaniards for use as forced laborers.

REPEOPLING. Movement in which a foreign people replaces the previous inhabitants of an area.

RIDGED FIELD. Artificial levees made by heaping up rows of parallel ridges on which to grow crops.

RÍO GUAPO. Purely zic-ware style on the east-central coast of Venezuela at the beginning of the local Ceramic age.

RONQUINAN. The initial Saladoid subseries, which developed in the Orinoco Valley during the third and second millennia B.C.

SALADOID. Series marking the start of the Ceramic age in the Orinoco Valley and the eastern part of the Caribbean area during the first two millennia B.C. and the first centuries A.D.

SALADOID-BARRANCOID. (1) Cedrosan pottery of the Windward Islands and Guadeloupe between 250 and 600 A.D., which shows Barrancoid influence; (2) superseries that includes both the Saladoid series and its Barrancoid offshoot.

SCIENTIFIC CLASSIFICATION. Systematic classification of a people or aspects of its environment by specialists in taxonomy.

SEBORUCO. Culture of Cuba during the local Lithic age.

SERIATION. Procedure of dating assemblages of cultural remains by arranging them in the order of their development or in the order of changes in the popularity of key traits.

SERIES. (1) Cultural complexes or ceramic styles, together with the peoples and cultures they define, that are known to have descended from a common ancestor—a site-unit; (2) pottery types that are known to have descended from a common ancestor—a trait-unit.

SHELL GOUGE. Chopping tool made by beveling the cutting edge of a triangular segment of the outer whorl of a conch shell; it was presumably hafted transversely in a wooden handle.

SHRINE CAVE. Cave used to worship zemis or bury ancestors.

SINGLE-COMPONENT SITE. Place containing the remains of only one people and its culture.

SINGLE-WARE STYLE. Ceramic style consisting of only one ware.

SITE-UNIT. Unit formed by classifying archeological assemblages.

SLASH AND BURN. Agricultural technique used by the Tainos to make temporary clearings in the forest within which to grow corn and other lesser crops; contrasts with the use of permanently mounded fields (conucos) to grow cassava and sweet potatoes.

SNUFFING TUBE. Forked tube used by the Tainos to inhale cohoba.

SNUFFING VESSEL. Bowl with a pair of tubes at one end for use in inhaling cohoba.

SOCIAL ANTHROPOLOGY. Study of societies and their subcultures, whether by archeologists, ethnologists, or ethnohistorians.

SOCIAL ARCHEOLOGY. Use of archeological remains to draw conclusions about societies and their behavior.

SOCIETY. Group organized by a people to perform one or more of its activities.

SPEECH-COMMUNITY. Inhabitants of a linguistically homogeneous area and period.

SPEECH-COMMUNITY AND LANGUAGE. Two sides of a coin, one consisting of a local population group and the other of the linguistic traits that define the group. *See also* People and culture; Race and biology.

STONE AGE. Those local periods in Eurasia and Africa during which stone working was first practiced.

STONE COLLAR. Ball belt.

STRATIGRAPHY. Study of the layering and the vertical and horizontal distribution of archeological remains.

STYLE. *See* Ceramic style.

SUAZOID. Series of cultures in the Windward Islands toward the close of the local Ceramic age; it appears to be correlated with the Igneris rather than the Island-Caribs.

SUBCULTURE. Sum total of the cultural traits of a society.

SUBFAMILY. Division of a family whose members share a common ancestor.

SUBSERIES. Division of a series consisting of styles or cultures that share a common ancestor.

SUPERFAMILY. Families believed to have descended from a common ancestor.

SUPERSERIES. Series that have been grouped together in the belief that they are descended from a common ancestor.

TABACO. Taino word for cigar.

TAINO. Ethnic group that inhabited the Bahamian Archipelago, most of the Greater Antilles, and the northern part of the Lesser Antilles in the time of Columbus.

THREE-POINTER. Elongated, hollow-based, conical object of stone, clay, coral, or shell, which the Tainos used as a zemi to improve their production of cassava.

TOPIA. Baked clay cylinder used by flood-plain peoples to prop up the griddles on which they baked their cassava bread because no stones were available for the purpose.

TRADE WARE. Pottery in an assemblage that appears to have been obtained from neighboring peoples.

TRADITION. (1) Trait or cluster of traits that persists from one culture to another— a trait-unit; (2) series of peoples and cultures—a site-unit.

TRAIT-COMPLEX. Cluster of biological, cultural, and/or linguistic traits that diffuses or persists from one local population to another—a trait-unit. Trait-complex should not be confused with CULTURAL COMPLEX (1), which is a site-unit.

TRAIT-UNIT. Unit formed by classifying individual specimens.

TRANSCULTURATION. Exchange of cultural traits among neighboring peoples.

TRANT. Cedrosan culture on Montserrat Island at the beginning of the local Ceramic age.

TROPICAL FOREST. Ceramic-age level of cultural development, which was shared by the Western and Eastern Tainos.

TROUMASSOID. Series that developed in the Windward Islands midway through the local Ceramic age.

TYPE OF POTTERY. *See* Pottery type.

VIVÉ. Cedrosan culture in Martinique soon after the beginning of the local Ceramic age.

VOMITING SPATULA. Object that the Tainos thrust down their throats to induce vomiting as a means of purifying themselves before worshiping zemis.

WARAO. Ethnic group that still lives in the Orinoco Delta.

WARE. All or part of a ceramic style. Like a style, it includes not only modes of decoration, after which it is usually named, but also modes in all the other dimensions of ceramic analysis. If a ware extends from one style to another, it may be considered a horizon or tradition. *See also* Plural style; Single-ware style.

WESTERN TAINO. Name applied by professional taxonomists to the historic inhabitants of Jamaica, central Cuba, and the Bahamian Archipelago, with the possible exception of a Classic Taino outpost on Middle Caicos Island.

WHITE-ON-RED WARE. Tradition diagnostic of the Saladoid series. It is the only ware present in the Ronquinan subseries, the dominant ware in the Cedrosan subseries, and a vestigial feature of the Huecan(?) subseries.

WONOTOBO FALLS. Cedrosan culture in Suriname at the beginning of the local Ceramic age.

XARAGUÁ. Regional chiefdom in the southwestern part of Hispaniola, ruled by Behecchío.

YUCA. Taino name for the cassava plant. See also *Casabe*.

ZEMI. Taino deity or the figure of a deity.

ZIC WARE. Zoned-incised crosshatched pottery. It occurs as a secondary ware in the styles of the Cedrosan subseries and as the sole ware in the styles of the Huecan(?) subseries.

R E F E R E N C E S

Alegría, Ricardo E. 1978. *Apuntes en torno a la mitología de los Indios Taínos de las Antillas Mayores y sus orígenes Suramericanos.* San Juan: Centro de Estudios Avanzados de Puerto Rico y el Caribe.

—. 1981. *El uso de la terminología etno-histórica para designar las culturas aborígenes de las Antillas.* Cuadernos Prehispánicas. Valladolid: Seminario de Historia de América, University of Valladolid.

—. 1983. *Ball Courts and Ceremonial Plazas in the West Indies.* Yale University Publications in Anthropology, no. 79. New Haven.

Allaire, Louis. 1977. *Later Prehistory in Martinique and the Island Caribs: Problems in Ethnic Identification.* Ann Arbor, Mich.: University Microfilms International.

—. 1980. On the Historicity of Carib Migrations in the Lesser Antilles. *American Antiquity* 45(2): 238–45.

—. 1984. A Reconstruction of Early Historical Island Carib Pottery. *Southeastern Archaeology* 3(2): 121–33.

—. 1985a. The Archaeology of the Caribbean. In *The World Atlas of Archaeology,* ed. Christine Flon, pp. 370–71. Boston: G. K. Hall.

—. 1985b. Some Comments on the Ethnic Identity of the Taino-Carib Frontier. Paper presented at the Eighteenth Annual Chacmool Conference, Department of Archaeology, University of Calgary, November 7–10, 1985.

—. 1989. Volcanic Chronology and the Early Saladoid Occupation of Martinique. In *Early Ceramic Population Lifeways and Adaptive Strategies in the Caribbean,* ed. Peter E. Siegel, pp. 147–87. BAR International Series 506. Oxford, Eng.

—. 1990. Prehistoric Taino Interaction with the Lesser Antilles: The View from Martinique, F.W.I. Paper presented at the fifty-fifth annual meeting of the Society for American Archaeology, Las Vegas, Nev., April 18–22, 1990.

—. 1991. Understanding Suazey. In *Proceedings of the Thirteenth International Congress for Caribbean Archaeology, Held in Willemstad, Curaçao, on July 24–29, 1989,* pp. 715–28. Willemstad: Archaeological-Anthropological Institute of the Netherlands Antilles.

Allaire, Louis, and Mario Mattioni. 1983. Boutbois et le Goudinot: Deux gisements acéramiques de la Martinique. In *Proceedings of the Ninth International Congress for the Study of Pre-Columbian Cultures of the Lesser Antilles, Held in the Dominican Republic, August 2–8, 1981,* pp. 27–38. Montreal: Centre de Recherches Caraïbes, University of Montreal.

Anderson-Córdova, Karen. 1990. *Hispaniola and Puerto Rico: Indian Acculturation and Heterogeneity, 1492–1550.* Ann Arbor, Mich.: University Microfilms International.

Arens, W. 1979. *The Man Eating Myth: Anthropology and Anthropophagy.* New York: Oxford University Press.

Arrom, José J. 1988. *Fray Ramón Pané: Relación acerca de las antegüedades de los Indios (el primer tratado escrito en América).* 8th ed., rev. Mexico City: Siglo Veintiuno Editores.

———. 1989. *Mitología y artes prehispánicas de las Antillas.* Rev. ed. Mexico City: Siglo Veintiuno Editores.

Barrau, Jacques, and Christian Montbrun. 1978. La mangrove et l'insertion humaine dans las écosystèmes insulaires des Petites Antilles: Le cas de la Martinique et de la Guadeloupe. *Social Science Information* 17(6): 897–919. Beverly Hills: Sage Publications.

Binford, Lewis R. 1973. Interassemblage Variability: The Mousterian and the "Functional Argument." In *The Explanation of Cultural Change: Models in Prehistory,* ed. Colin Renfrew, pp. 227–54. London: Gerald Duckworth.

Bloomfield, Leonard. 1933. *Language.* New York: Holt, Rinehart, and Winston.

Boomert, Aad. 1978. Prehistoric Habitation Mounds in the Canje River Area? *Journal of the Walter Roth Museum of Archaeology and Anthropology* 1(1): 44–51. Georgetown: Department of Culture, Ministry of Education, Social Development, and Culture, Government of Guyana.

———. 1983. The Saladoid Occupation of Wonotobo Falls, Western Surinam. In *Proceedings of the Ninth International Congress for the Study of Pre-Columbian Cultures of the Lesser Antilles, Held in the Dominican Republic, August 2–8, 1981,* pp. 97–120. Montreal: Centre de Recherches Caraïbes, University of Montreal.

———. 1984. The Arawak Indians of Trinidad and Coastal Guiana, ca. 1500–1650. *Journal of Caribbean History* (Port of Spain) 19(2): 123–88.

———. 1986. The Cayo Complex of St. Vincent: Ethnohistorical and Archaeological Aspects of the Island-Carib Problem. *Antropológica* (Caracas) 66:3–68.

Booy, Theodoor de. 1919. *Archaeology of the Virgin Islands.* Indian Notes and Monographs, vol. 1, no. 1. New York: National Museum of the American Indian.

Bourne, Edward Gaylord. 1906. Columbus, Ramon Pane and the Beginning of American Anthropology. *Proceedings of the American Antiquarian Society,* n.s. 17:310–48.

Breton, R. P. Raymond. 1892. *Dictionaire Français-Caraïbe.* Rpt. Leipzig: B. G. Teubner.

Brill, Robert H., I. Lynus Barnes, Stephen S. C. Tong, Emile C. Joel, and Martin J. Murtaugh. 1987. Laboratory Studies of Some European Artifacts Excavated on San Salvador Island. In *Proceedings, First San Salvador Conference: Columbus and His World,* comp. Donald T. Gerace, pp. 247–92. San Salvador Island, Bahamas: College Center of the Finger Lakes, Bahamian Field Station.

Brinton, Daniel Garrison. 1871. The Arawack Language of Guiana in Its Linguistic and Ethnological Relations. *Transactions of the American Philosophical Society,* n.s. 14 (art. 4): 427–44.

Budinoff, Linda C. 1991. An Osteological Analysis of the Human Burials Recovered from an Early Site Located on the North Coast of Puerto Rico. In *Proceedings of the Twelfth International Congress of Caribbean Archaeology, Cayenne, French Guiana,* pp. 45–51. Martinique: International Association for Caribbean Archaeology.

Bullen, Ripley B. 1964. *The Archaeology of Grenada, West Indies.* Contributions of the Florida State Museum, Social Sciences, no. 11. Gainesville.

Burgess, George H., and Richard Franz. 1989. Zoogeography of the Antillean Freshwater Fish Fauna. In *Biogeography of the West Indies: Past, Present, and Future,* ed. Charles A. Woods, pp. 263–304. Gainesville, Fla.: Sandhill Crane Press.

Callaghan, Richard T. 1990. Mainland Origins of the Preceramic Cultures of the Greater Antilles. Ph.D. diss., University of Calgary.

Chanlatte Baik, Luis A. 1981. *La Hueca y Sorcé (Vieques, Puerto Rico): Primeras migraciones agroalfareras Antillanas—Nuevo esquema para los procesos culturales de la arqueología Antillana.* Santo Domingo: privately printed.

———. 1983. *Catálogo arqueología de Vieques: Exposición del 13 del Marzo al 22 de Abril de 1983.* Río Piedras: Museo de Antropología, Historia y Arte, University of Puerto Rico.

Cody, Annie K. 1991. From the Site of Pearls, Grenada: Exotic Lithics and Radiocarbon Dates. In *Proceedings of the Thirteenth International Congress for Caribbean Archaeology, Held in Willemstad, Curaçao, on July 24–29, 1989,* pp. 589–604. Willemstad: Archaeological-Anthropological Institute of the Netherlands Antilles.

Cosculluela, J. A. 1946. Prehistoric Cultures of Cuba. *American Antiquity* 12(1): 10–18.

Crosby, Alfred W., Jr. 1972. *The Columbian Exchange: Biological and Cultural Consequences of 1492.* Contributions in American Studies, ed. Robert H. Walker, no. 2. Westport, Conn.: Greenwood Press.

Cruxent, José M., and Irving Rouse. 1958–59. *An Archeological Chronology of Venezuela.* 2 vols. Social Science Monographs, no. 6. Washington, D.C.: Pan American Union.

———. 1969. Early Man in the West Indies. *Scientific American* 221(5): 42–52.

Davis, Dave D. 1974. Some Notes Concerning the Archaic Occupation of Antigua. In *Proceedings of the Fifth International Congress for the Study of Pre-Columbian Cultures of the Lesser Antilles, Antigua, July 22–28, 1973,* pp. 65–71. St. Johns: Antigua Archaeological Society.

———. 1982. Archaic Settlement and Resource Exploitation in the Lesser Antilles: Preliminary Information from Antigua. *Caribbean Journal of Science* (San Juan, P.R.) 17(1–4): 107–22.

Davis, Dave D., and R. Christopher Goodwin. 1990. Island Carib Origins: Evidence and Nonevidence. *American Antiquity* 55(1): 37–48.

Deagan, Kathleen. 1987. Initial Encounters: Arawak Responses to European Contact at the En Bas Saline Site, Haiti. In *Proceedings, First San Salvador Conference: Columbus and His World,* ed. Donald T. Gerace, pp. 341–59. San Salvador Island, Bahamas: College Center of the Finger Lakes, Bahamian Field Station.

———. 1988. The Archaeology of the Spanish Contact Period in the Caribbean. *Journal of World Prehistory* 2(2): 187–225.

Douglas, Nik. 1991. Recent Amerindian Finds on Anguilla. In *Proceedings of the Thirteenth International Congress for Caribbean Archaeology, Held in Willemstad, Curaçao, on July 24–29, 1989,* pp. 576–88. Willemstad: Archaeological-Anthropological Institute of the Netherlands Antilles.

Drewett, Peter L. 1989. Prehistoric Ceramic Population Lifeways and Adaptive Strategies on Barbados, Lesser Antilles. In *Early Ceramic Population Lifeways and Adaptive Strategies in the Caribbean,* ed. Peter E. Siegel, pp. 79–118. BAR International Series 506. Oxford, Eng.

Dreyfus, Simone. 1983–84. Historical and Political Anthropological Inter-Connections: The Multilinguistic Indigenous Polity of the "Carib" Islands and Mainland Coast from the Sixteenth to the Eighteenth Century. In "Themes in Political Organization: The Caribs and Their Neighbors," ed. Audrey Butt Colson and H. Dieter Heinen. *Antropológica* (Caracas) 59–62:39–55.

Dunn, Oliver, and James E. Kelley, Jr. 1989. *The* Diario *of Christopher Columbus's First Voyage to America, Abstracted by Fray Bartolomé de Las Casas.* Norman: University of Oklahoma Press.

Durand, Jean-François, and Henri Petitjean Roget. 1991. A propos d'un collier funeraire, Morel, Guadeloupe, les Huecoids sont-ils un mythe. In *Proceedings of the Twelfth International Congress for Caribbean Archaeology, Cayenne, French Guiana,* pp. 53–72. Martinique: International Association for Caribbean Archaeology.

Ekholm, Gordon F. 1961. Puerto Rican Stone "Collars" as Ball-Game Belts. In *Essays in Pre-Columbian Art and Archaeology,* by Samuel K. Lathrop and others, pp. 356–71. Cambridge: Harvard University Press.

Fewkes, Jesse Walter. 1907. The Aborigines of Porto Rico and the Neighboring Islands. In *Annual Report of the Bureau of American Ethnology for 1903–04,* no. 25, pp. 1–220. Washington, D.C.: Smithsonian Institution.

———. 1914. Relations of Aboriginal Culture and Environment in the Lesser Antilles. *Bulletin of the American Geographical Society* 46(9): 662–78.

Ford, James A. 1969. *A Comparison of Formative Cultures in the Americas: Diffusion or the Psychic Unity of Man.* Smithsonian Contributions to Anthropology, vol. 11. Washington, D.C.

Fuson, Robert E. 1987. *The Log of Christopher Columbus.* Camden, Me.: International Marine Publishing Co.

García Arévalo, Manuel. 1982. *Museo arqueológico regional, Altos de Chavón/ Regional Museum of Archeology, Altos de Chavón* (in English and Spanish). English translation by Michele Seminatore. La Romana, Dom.: Ediciones Museo Arqueológico Regional de Altos de Chavón.

————. 1988. *Indigenismo, arqueología, e identidad nacional.* Santo Domingo: Museo del Hombre Dominicano and Fundación García Arévalo.

Garn, Stanley M. 1965. *Human Races.* 2d ed. Springfield, Ill.: Charles C. Thomas.

Gerace, Donald T., comp. 1987. *Proceedings, First San Salvador Conference: Columbus and His World.* San Salvador Island, Bahamas: College Center of the Finger Lakes, Bahamian Field Station.

Gerbi, Antonello. 1986. *Nature in the New World: From Christopher Columbus to Gonzalo Fernández de Oviedo.* Trans. Jeremy Moyle. Pittsburgh: University of Pittsburgh Press.

Glazier, Stephen D. 1991. Impressions of Aboriginal Technology: The Case of the Caribbean Canoe. In *Proceedings of the Thirteenth International Congress for Caribbean Archaeology, Held in Willemstad, Curaçao, on July 24–29, 1989,* pp. 149–61. Willemstad: Archaeological-Anthropological Institute of the Netherlands Antilles.

Goeje, C. H. de. 1939. Nouvel examen des langues des Antilles avec notes sur les langues Arawak-Maipur et Caribe et vocabulaires Shebayo et Guayanna (Guayane). *Journal de la Société des Américanistes de Paris* 31:1–120.

Gonzalez, Nancie L. 1988. *Sojourners of the Caribbean: Ethnogenesis and Ethnohistory of the Garifuna.* Urbana: University of Illinois Press.

González Colón, Juan. 1984. Tibes: Un centro ceremonial indígena. M.A. thesis, Centro de Estudios Avanzados de Puerto Rico y el Caribe, San Juan, P.R.

Goodwin, R. Christopher. 1978. The History and Development of Osteology in the Caribbean Area. *Revista/Review Interamericana* (San Juan, P.R.) 8(3): 463–94.

————. 1979. The Prehistoric Cultural Ecology of St. Kitts, West Indies: A Case Study in Island Archeology. Ph.D. diss., Arizona State University, Tempe.

Gould, Stephen J. 1989. *Wonderful Life: The Burgess Shale and the Nature of History.* New York: W. W. Norton.

Gower, Charlotte. 1927. *The Northern and Southern Affiliations of Antillean Culture.* Memoirs of the American Anthropological Association, no. 35. Menasha, Wis.

Granberry, Julian H. 1980. West Indian Languages: A Review and Commentary. *Journal of the Virgin Islands Archaeological Society* 10:51–56.

————. 1987. Antillean Languages and the Aboriginal Settlement of the Bahamas: A Working Hypothesis. In *Proceedings of the Bahamas 1492 Conference, Freeport, Bahamas, November 1987,* ed. Charles A. Hoffman. Forthcoming.

Greenberg, Joseph H. 1960. The General Classification of Central and South American Languages. In *Selected Papers of the Fifth International Congress of Anthropological and Ethnological Sciences, Philadelphia, September 1–9, 1956,* ed. Anthony F. C. Wallace, pp. 791–94. Philadelphia: University of Pennsylvania Press.

————. 1987. *Language in the Americas.* Stanford: Stanford University Press.

Haag, William G. 1965. Pottery Typology in Certain Lesser Antilles. *American Antiquity* 31(2): 242–45.

Hahn, Paul G. 1960. The Cayo Redondo Culture and Its Chronology. Ph.D. diss., Yale University, New Haven.

Harrington, M. R. 1921. *Cuba before Columbus.* Indian Notes and Monographs, pts. 1, 2. New York: National Museum of the American Indian.

———. 1924. A West Indian Gem Center. *Indian Notes* (National Museum of the American Indian) 1(4): 184–89.

Hatt, Gudmund. 1924. Archaeology of the Virgin Islands. In *Proceedings of the Twenty-first International Congress of Americanists,* pt. 1, pp. 29–42. The Hague.

———. 1932. Notes on the Archaeology of Santo Domingo. *Geografisk Tidschrift* (Copenhagen) 35(1–2): 1–8.

———. 1953. Early Intrusion of Agriculture in the North Atlantic Subarctic Region. *Anthropological Papers of the University of Alaska* (Fairbanks) 2(1): 51–108.

Haviser, Jay B., Jr. 1987. Amerindian Cultural Geography on Curaçao. Ph.D. diss., Rijks Universiteit Leiden.

———. 1990. Geographic, Economic and Demographic Aspects of Amerindian Interaction between Anguilla and St. Martin–St. Maarten. Paper presented at the fifty-fifth annual meeting of the Society for American Archaeology, Las Vegas, Nev., April 18–22, 1990.

———. 1991. Preliminary Results from Test Excavations at the Hope Estate Site (SM-026), St. Martin. In *Proceedings of the Thirteenth International Congress for Caribbean Archaeology, Held in Willemstad, Curaçao, on July 24–29, 1989,* pp. 647–66. Willemstad: Archaeological-Anthropological Institute of the Netherlands Antilles.

Hock, Hans Henrich. 1986. *Principles of Historical Linguistics.* Berlin: Mouton de Gruyter.

Hoffman, Charles A. 1987. Archaeological Investigations at the Long Bay Site, San Salvador, Bahamas. In *Proceedings, First San Salvador Conference: Columbus and His World,* comp. Donald T. Gerace, pp. 247–92. San Salvador Island, Bahamas: College Center of the Finger Lakes, Bahamian Field Station.

Hofman, C. L., and M. L. P. Hoogland. 1991. The Later Prehistory of Saba, N.A.: The Settlement Site of Kelbey's Ridge (1300–1450 A.D.). In *Proceedings of the Thirteenth International Congress for Caribbean Archaeology, Held in Willemstad, Curaçao, on July 24–29, 1989,* pp. 477–92. Willemstad: Archaeological-Anthropological Institute of the Netherlands Antilles.

Hostos, Adolfo de. 1941. Notes on West Indian Hydrography in Its Relation to Prehistoric Migrations. In *Anthropological Papers: Papers Based Principally on Studies of the Prehistoric Archaeology and Ethnology of the Greater Antilles,* pp. 30–53. San Juan: Office of the Historian, Government of Puerto Rico.

Howells, William. 1954. *Back of History.* New York: Doubleday.

Imbelloni, José. 1938. Tabla classificatoria de los indios: Regiones biológicas y grupos raciales humanos de América. *Physis: Revista de la Sociedad Argentina de Ciencias Naturales* (Buenos Aires), year 4, vol. 12, pp. 229–49.

Ingstad, Helge. 1969. *Westward to Vineland: The Discovery of the Pre-Columbian Norse House-Sites in North America*. Trans. Erik J. Friis. New York: St. Martin's Press.

Jane, Cecil, trans. 1960. *The Journal of Christopher Columbus*. New York: Clarkson N. Potter.

Josselin de Jong, J. P. B. de. 1924. A Natural Prototype of Certain Three-Pointed Stones. In *Proceedings of the Twenty-first International Congress of Americanists*, pt. 1, pp. 43–55. The Hague.

Judge, Joseph. 1986. Where Columbus Found the New World. *National Geographic* 170(11): 566–99.

Keegan, William F. 1985. *Dynamic Horticulturalists: Population Expansion in the Prehistoric Bahamas*. Ann Arbor, Mich.: University Microfilms International.

———. 1989. Creating the Guanahatabey (Ciboney): The Modern Genesis of an Extinct Culture. *Antiquity* 63(239): 373–79.

Keegan, William F., and Morgan D. Maclachlan. 1989. The Evolution of Avunculocal Chiefdoms: A Reconstruction of Taino Kinship and Politics. *American Anthropologist* 91(3): 613–30.

Kidder, Alfred, II. 1944. *Archaeology of Northwestern Venezuela*. Papers of the Peabody Museum of American Archaeology and Ethnology, Harvard University, vol. 26, no. 1. Cambridge.

Kozłowski, Janusz K. 1974. *Preceramic Cultures in the Caribbean*. Zeszyty Naukowe, Uniwerstytetu Jagiellońskiego, vol. 386, Prace Archeologiczne, Zezyt 20. Kraków.

———. 1980. In Search of the Evolutionary Patterns of the Preceramic Cultures of the Caribbean. *Boletín del Museo del Hombre Dominicano* 9(13): 61–79.

Las Casas, Bartolomé de. 1951. *Historia de las Indias*. Edición de Agustín Millares Carlo. 3 vols. Biblioteca Americana, nos. 15–17. Mexico City: Fondo de Cultura Americana.

———. 1974. *The Devastation of the Indies: A Brief Account*. Trans. Herma Briffault New York: Seabury Press.

Lathrap, Donald W. 1970. *The Upper Amazon*. Ancient Peoples and Places, vol. 70. New York: Praeger Publishers.

Lehmann, Winifred D. 1962. *Historical Linguistics: An Introduction*. New York: Holt, Rinehart, and Winston.

Loukotka, Čestmír. 1968. *Classification of South American Indian Languages*. UCLA Latin American Center, Reference Series, vol. 7. University of California, Los Angeles.

Lovén, Sven. 1935. *Origin of the Tainan Culture, West Indies*. Göteborg: Elanders Bokfryckeri Äkfiebolag.

Lumbreras, Luis G. 1974. *The Peoples and Cultures of Ancient Peru*. Trans. Betty J. Meggers. Washington, D.C.: Smithsonian Institution Press.

Lundberg, Emily R. 1989. Preceramic Procurement Patterns at Krum Bay, Virgin Islands. Ph.D. diss., University of Illinois, Urbana.

———. 1991. Interrelationships among Preceramic Complexes of Puerto Rico and the Virgin Islands. In *Proceedings of the Thirteenth International Congress for Caribbean Archaeology, Held in Willemstad, Curaçao, on July 24–29, 1989*, pp. 73–85. Willemstad: Archaeological-Anthropological Institute of the Netherlands Antilles.

McKusick, Marshall. 1960. Distribution of Ceramic Styles in the Lesser Antilles, West Indies. Ph.D. diss., Yale University, New Haven.

————. 1970. Aboriginal Canoes in the West Indies. In *Papers in Caribbean Anthropology*, comp. Sidney W. Mintz. Yale University Publications in Anthropology, no. 63. New Haven.

MacNeish, Richard S., and Antoinette Nelken-Turner. 1983. *Final Annual Report of the Belize Archaic Archaeological Reconnaissance*. Boston: Center for Archaeological Studies, Boston University.

Mason, J. Alden. 1941. *A Large Archaeological Site at Capá, Utuado, with Notes on Other Puerto Rican Sites Visited in 1914–15*. Scientific Survey of Puerto Rico and the Virgin Islands, vol. 18, pt. 2. New York: New York Academy of Sciences.

Mattioni, M., and M. Nicolas. 1972. *Art précolombien de la Martinique*. Fort-de-France: Musée Départemental de la Martinique.

Meggers, Betty J., and Clifford Evans. 1957. *Archeological Investigations at the Mouth of the Amazon*. Bureau of American Ethnology, Bulletin 167. Washington, D.C.: Smithsonian Institution.

————. 1983. Lowland South America and the Antilles. In *Ancient South Americans*, ed. Jesse D. Jennings, pp. 287–335. San Francisco: W. H. Freeman.

Meyer, Jean. 1987. *Un flibustier français dans la mer de Antilles en 1618/1620: Manuscrit inédit du début du XVIIe siècle*. Paris: Editions Jean-Pierre Moreau.

Montas, Onorio, Pedro José Borrell, and Frank Moya Pons. 1983. *Arte Taíno*. Santo Domingo: Banco Central de la República Dominicana.

Moore, Clark. 1982. Investigation of Preceramic Sites on Ile à Vache, Haiti. *Florida Anthropologist* 35(4): 186–99.

————. 1991. Cabaret: Lithic Workshop Sites in Haiti. In *Proceedings of the Thirteenth International Congress for Caribbean Archaeology, Held in Willemstad, Curaçao, on July 24–29, 1989*, pp. 92–104. Willemstad: Archaeological-Anthropological Institute of the Netherlands Antilles.

Morison, Samuel Eliot. 1942. *Admiral of the Ocean Sea: A Life of Christopher Columbus*. 2 vols. Boston: Little, Brown.

————, trans. and ed. 1963. *Journals and Other Documents on the Life and Voyages of Christopher Columbus*. New York: Heritage Press.

Morse, Birgit F. 1990. The Pre-Columbian Ball and Dance Court at Salt River, St. Croix. *Folk: Journal of the Danish Ethnographical Society* (Copenhagen) 32:45–60.

Narganes Storde, Yvonne M. 1991. Secuencia cronológica de dos sitios arqueológicos de Puerto Rico (Sorcé, Vieques y Tecla, Guayanilla). In *Proceedings of the Thirteenth International Congress for Caribbean Archaeology, Held in Willemstad, Curaçao, on July 24–29, 1989*, pp. 628–46. Willemstad: Archaeological-Anthropological Institute of the Netherlands Antilles.

Newman, Marshall T. 1951. The Sequence of Indian Physical Types in South America. In *Papers on the Physical Anthropology of the American Indian,* ed. William S. Laughlin, pp. 69–97. New York: Viking Fund.

Noble, G. Kingsley. 1965. *Proto-Arawakan and Its Descendants.* Indiana University Publications in Anthropology and Linguistics, no. 38. Bloomington.

Núñez Jiménez, Antonio. 1975. *Cuba: Dibujos rupestres.* Havana: Editorial de Ciencias Sociales.

Oliver, José R. 1980. A Cultural Interpretation of the Iconographic Art Style of Caguanas Ceremonial Center, Puerto Rico. M.A. thesis, University of Illinois, Urbana.

———. 1989. The Archaeological, Linguistic, and Ethnohistorical Evidence for the Expansion of Arawakan into Northwestern Venezuela and Northeastern Colombia. Ph.D. diss., University of Illinois, Urbana.

Olsen, Fred. 1974. *On the Trail of the Arawaks.* The Civilization of the American Indian Series, vol. 129. Norman: University of Oklahoma Press.

Ortiz, Fernando. 1947. *Cuban Counterpoint: Tobacco and Sugar.* Trans. Harriet de Onís. New York: Alfred A. Knopf.

Oviedo y Valdés, Gonzalo Fernández de. 1851–55. *Historia general y natural de las indias.* 4 vols. Madrid: Imprenta de la Real Academia de la Historia.

———. 1959. *Natural History of the West Indies.* Trans. and ed. Sterling A. Stoudemire. University of North Carolina Studies in the Romance Languages and Literatures, no. 32. Chapel Hill: University of North Carolina Press.

Pantel, A. Gus. 1988. Precolumbian Flaked Stone Assemblages in the West Indies. Ph.D. diss., University of Tennessee, Knoxville.

Pérez de Silva, Matilde, and Adolfo de Hostos. 1939. *Industrial Applications of Indian Decorative Motifs of Puerto Rico.* Trans. Ida M. de Gallardo. Philadelphia: John C. Winston.

Pinchon, Robert. 1952. Introduction à l'archéologie Martiniquaise. *Journal de la Société des Américanistes* (Paris) 41(2): 305–52.

Plowman, Timothy. 1984. The Origin, Evolution, and Diffusion of Coca, *Erythroxylum* spp., in South and Central America. In *Pre-Columbian Plant Migrations,* ed. Doris Stone, pp. 125–63. Papers of the Peabody Museum of Archaeology and Ethnology, Harvard University, vol. 76. Cambridge.

Rainey, Froelich G. 1940. *Porto Rican Archaelogy.* Scientific Survey of Porto Rico and the Virgin Islands, vol. 18, pt. 1. New York: New York Academy of Sciences.

———. 1941. *Excavations in the Ft. Liberté Region, Haiti.* Yale University Publications in Anthropology, no. 23. New Haven.

Reichel-Dolmatoff, Gerardo. 1985. *Monsú: Un sitio arqueológico.* Bogotá: Biblioteca Banco Popular, Textos Universitarios.

Renfrew, Colin. 1973. *Before Civilization: The Radiocarbon Revolution and Prehistoric Europe.* New York: Alfred A. Knopf.

Ricketson, Oliver G., Jr. 1940. An Outline of the Basic Physical Factors Affecting Middle America. In *The Maya and Their Neighbors,* ed. Clarence L. Hay,

Ralph L. Linton, Samuel K. Lothrop, Harry L. Shapiro, and George C. Vaillant, pp. 10–31. New York: D. Appleton-Century.

Robinson, Linda S., Emily R. Lundberg, and Jeffrey B. Walker. 1983–85. *Archaeological Data Recovery at El Bronce, Puerto Rico: Final Report, Phases 1 and 2.* Christiansted, St. Croix: Archaeological Services, Daran.

Rodríguez, Miguel. 1991. Arqueología de Punta Candelero, Puerto Rico. In *Proceedings of the Thirteenth International Congress for Caribbean Archaeology, Held in Willemstad, Curaçao, on July 24–29, 1989*, pp. 605–27. Willemstad: Archaeological-Anthropological Institute of the Netherlands Antilles.

Roe, Peter G. 1989. A Grammatical Analysis of Cedrosan Saladoid Vessel Form Categories and Surface Decoration: Aesthetic and Technological Styles in Early Antillean Ceramics. In *Early Ceramic Population Lifeways and Adaptive Strategies in the Caribbean*, ed. Peter E. Siegel, pp. 267–382. BAR International Series 506. Oxford, Eng.

———. 1991. The Best Enemy Is a Defunct, Drilled and Decorative Enemy: Human Corporeal Art (Frontal Bone Pectorals) in Pre-Columbian Puerto Rico. In *Proceedings of the Thirteenth International Congress for Caribbean Archaeology, Held in Willemstad, Curaçao, on July 24–29, 1989*, pp. 854–73. Willemstad: Archaeological-Anthropological Institute of the Netherlands Antilles.

Roe, Peter G., A. Gus Pantel, Margaret E. Hamilton, and Terence Vidal. 1986. Montserrate Restudied: The 1978 C.E.A.P.R.C. Field Season at Luquillo Beach: Excavation Overview, Lithic, Malacological and Physical Anthropological Remains. MS in the Department of Anthropology, University of Delaware, Newark.

Roosevelt, Anna C. 1980. *Parmana: Prehistoric Maize and Manioc Subsistence along the Amazon and Orinoco.* New York: Academic Press.

———. 1989. Lost Civilizations of the Lower Amazon. *Natural History* 89(2): 74–83.

Roth, Henry Ling. 1887. The Aborigines of Hispaniola. *Journal of the Royal Anthropological Institute of Great Britain and Ireland* 16:247–86.

Roumain, Jacques. 1943. L'outillage lithique des Ciboney d'Haiti. *Bulletin du Bureau d'Ethnologie, République d'Haiti* 2:22–27.

Rouse, Irving. 1941. *Culture of the Ft. Liberté Region, Haiti.* Yale University Publications in Anthropology, no. 24. New Haven.

———. 1942. *Archeology of the Maniabón Hills, Cuba.* Yale University Publications in Anthropology, no. 26. New Haven.

———. 1948. The Arawak. In *Handbook of South American Indians*, ed. Julian H. Steward, vol. 4, pp. 507–46. Bulletin of the Bureau of American Ethnology, no. 143. Washington, D.C.

———. 1952. *Porto Rican Prehistory.* Scientific Survey of Porto Rico and the Virgin Islands, vol. 18, pts. 3–4. New York: New York Academy of Sciences.

———. 1953a. The Circum-Caribbean Theory, an Archaeological Test. *American Anthropologist* 55(2): 188–200.

———. 1953b. Indian Sites in Trinidad. In *On the Excavation of a Shell Mound at Palo Seco Trinidad, B.W.I.,* by J. A. Bullbrook, pp. 94–111. Yale University Publications in Anthropology, no. 50. New Haven.

————. 1960. The Entry of Man into the West Indies. In *Papers in Caribbean Anthropology,* comp. Sidney W. Mintz. Yale University Publications in Anthropology, nos. 57–64, no. 61. New Haven.

————. 1964. Prehistory of the West Indies. *Science* 144(3618): 499–513.

————. 1965. The Place of "Peoples" in Prehistoric Research. *Journal of the Royal Anthropological Institute* 95(1): 1–15.

————. 1972. *Introduction to Prehistory: A Systematic Approach.* New York: McGraw-Hill.

————. 1974. The Indian Creek Excavations. In *Proceedings of the Fifth International Congress for the Study of Pre-Columbian Cultures of the Lesser Antilles, Antigua, July 22–28, 1973,* ed. Ripley P. Bullen, pp. 166–76. Gainesville: Florida State Museum.

————. 1976. The Saladoid Sequence on Antigua and Its Aftermath. In *Proceedings of the Sixth International Congress for the Study of Pre-Columbian Cultures of the Lesser Antilles, Pointe-à-Pitre, Guadeloupe, July 6–12, 1975,* ed. Ripley P. Bullen, pp. 35–41. Gainesville: Florida State Museum.

————. 1978. The La Gruta Sequence and Its Implications. In *Unidad y variedad: Ensayos antropológicos en homenaje a José M. Cruxent,* ed. Erika Wagner and Alberta Zucchi, pp. 203–29. Caracas: Ediciones CEA-IVIC.

————. 1982a. Ceramic and Religious Development in the Greater Antilles. *Journal of New World Archaeology* 5(2): 45–55. Los Angeles: Institute of Archaeology, University of California.

————. 1982b. The Olsen Collection from Ile à Vache, Haiti. *Florida Anthropologist* 35(4): 169–85.

————. 1983. Diffusion and Interaction in the Orinoco Valley and on the Coast. In *Proceedings of the Ninth International Congress for the Study of Pre-Columbian Cultures of the Lesser Antilles, Held in the Dominican Republic, August 2–8, 1981,* pp. 1–11. Montreal: Centre de Recherches Caraïbes, University of Montreal.

————. 1986. *Migrations in Prehistory: Inferring Population Movement from Cultural Remains.* New Haven: Yale University Press.

————. 1987. Whom Did Columbus Discover in the West Indies? In "On the Trail of Columbus," ed. Charles A. Hoffman. *American Archaeologist* (Ridgefield, Conn.) 6(2): 83–87.

————. 1989a. Peoples and Cultures of the Saladoid Frontier in the Greater Antilles. In *Early Ceramic Population Lifeways and Adaptive Strategies in the Caribbean,* ed. Peter E. Siegel, pp. 383–403. BAR International Series 506. Oxford, Eng.

————. 1989b. Peopling and Repeopling of the West Indies. In *Biogeography of the West Indies,* ed. Charles A. Woods, pp. 119–35. Gainesville, Fla.: Sandhill Crane Press.

————. 1990. Social, Linguistic, and Stylistic Plurality in the West Indies. In *Proceedings of the Eleventh International Congress for Caribbean Archaeology, Held in San Juan, Puerto Rico, July and August, 1985*, pp. 56–63. San Juan: Fundación Arqueológica, Antropológica, e Histórica de Puerto Rico and others.

————. 1991. Ancestries of the Tainos: Amazonian or Circum-Caribbean? In *Proceedings of the Thirteenth International Congress for Caribbean Archaeology, Held in Willemstad, Curaçao, on July 24–29, 1989*, pp. 682–702. Willemstad: Archaeological-Anthropological Institute of the Netherlands Antilles.

Rouse, Irving, and Ricardo E. Alegría. 1990. *Excavations at María de la Cruz Cave and Hacienda Grande Village Site, Loiza, Puerto Rico*. Yale University Publications in Anthropology, no. 80. New Haven.

Rouse, Irving, Louis Allaire, and Aad Boomert. 1985. Eastern Venezuela, the Guianas, and the West Indies. MS prepared for an unpublished volume, "Chronologies in South American Archaeology," comp. Clement W. Meighan. Department of Anthropology, Yale University, New Haven.

Rouse, Irving, and José J. Arrom. 1991. The Taínos: Principal Inhabitants of Columbus' Indies. In *Circa 1492: Art in the Age of Exploration*, ed. Jay A. Levenson, pp. 509–13. New Haven: Yale University Press, 1991.

Rouse, Irving, and José M. Cruxent. 1963. *Venezuelan Archaeology*. New Haven: Yale University Press.

Rouse, Irving, and Clark Moore. 1985. Cultural Sequence in Southwestern Haiti. In *Proceedings of the Tenth International Congress for the Study of Pre-Columbian Cultures of the Lesser Antilles, Held in Fort-de-France, Martinique, 25–30 July 1983*, pp. 1–21. Montreal: Centre de Recherches Caraïbes, University of Montreal.

Sanoja, Mario, and Iraida Vargas. 1983. New Light on the Prehistory of Eastern Venezuela. *Advances in World Archaeology* 2:205–44. New York: Academic Press.

Sauer, Carl Ortwin. 1966. *The Early Spanish Main*. Berkeley: University of California Press.

Schultes, Richard Evans. 1984. Amazonian Cultigens and Their Northward and Westward Migration in Pre-Columbian Times. In *Pre-Columbian Plant Migrations*, ed. Doris Stone, pp. 19–37. Papers of the Peabody Museum of Archaeology and Ethnology, Harvard University, vol. 76. Cambridge.

Scott, John F. 1985. *The Art of the Taino from the Dominican Republic*. Gainesville: University Gallery, College of Fine Arts, University of Florida.

Sears, William H., and Shaun D. Sullivan. 1978. Bahamas Prehistory. *American Antiquity* 43(1): 3–25.

Siegel, Peter E. 1989. Site Structure, Demography, and Social Complexity in the Early Ceramic Age of the Caribbean. In *Early Ceramic Population Lifeways and Adaptive Strategies in the Caribbean*, ed. Siegel, pp. 193–245. BAR International Series 506. Oxford, Eng.

————. 1990. Occupational History of the Maisabel Site: A Progress Report. Centro de Investigaciones Indígenas de Puerto Rico, San Juan.

Smith, Michael G. 1965. *The Plural Society in the British West Indies*. Berkeley: University of California Press.

Stern, Theodore. 1949. *The Rubber-Ball Games of the Americas*. Monographs of the American Ethnological Society, no. 17. New York.

Stevens-Arroyo, Antonio M. 1988. *Cave of the Jagua: The Mythological World of the Tainos*. Albuquerque: University of New Mexico Press.

Steward, Julian H., ed. 1946–59. *Handbook of South American Indians*. 7 vols. Bureau of American Ethnology, Bulletin 143. Washington, D.C.: Smithsonian Institution.

———. 1947. American Culture History in the Light of South America. *Southwestern Journal of Anthropology* (Albuquerque) 3(2): 85–107.

Sturtevant, William C. 1961. Taino Agriculture. In *The Evolution of Horticultural Systems in Native America: Causes and Consequences*, ed. Johannes Wilbert, pp. 69–82. Caracas: Sociedad de Ciencias Naturales La Salle.

———. 1969. History and Ethnography of Some West Indian Starches. In *The Domestication of Plants and Animals*, ed. Peter J. Ucko and G. W. Dimbleby, pp. 177–99. London: Gerald Duckworth.

Sued Badillo, Jalil. 1978. *Los Caribes, realidad o fabula: Ensayos de rectificación histórica*. Río Piedras, P.R.: Editorial Antillana.

Sullivan, Shaun D. 1981. Prehistoric Patterns of Exploitation and Colonization in the Turks and Caicos Islands. Ph.D. diss., University of Illinois, Urbana.

Tacoma, Jouke. 1991. Precolumbian Human Skeletal Remains from Curaçao, Aruba, and Bonaire. In *Proceedings of the Thirteenth International Congress for Caribbean Archaeology, Held in Willemstad, Curaçao, on July 24–29, 1989*, pp. 802–12. Willemstad: Archaeological-Anthropological Institute of the Netherlands Antilles.

Taylor, Douglas. 1949. The Interpretation of Some Documentary Evidence on Carib Culture. *Southwestern Journal of Anthropology* (Albuquerque) 5(4): 379–92.

———. 1951. *The Black Carib of British Honduras*. Viking Fund Publications in Anthropology, no. 17. New York.

———. 1977a. *Languages of the West Indies*. Baltimore: Johns Hopkins University Press.

———. 1977b. A Note on Palikur and Northern Arawakan. *International Journal of American Linguistics* 43:58–60.

Taylor, Douglas, and Berend J. Hoff. 1980. The Linguistic Repertory of the Island-Carib in the Seventeenth Century: The Men's Language—a Carib Pidgin? *International Journal of American Linguistics* 46(4): 301–12.

Turner, Christy G., II. 1976. Dental Evidence on the Origins of the Ainu and Japanese. *Science* 193(4265): 911–13.

———. 1983. Dental Evidence for the Peopling of the Americas. In *Early Man in the New World*, ed. Richard Shutler, pp. 147–57. Beverly Hills, Calif.: Sage Publications.

Vega, Bernardo. 1979. *Los metales y los aborígenes de Hispaniola*. Santo Domingo: Museo del Hombre Dominicano.

——. 1987a. *Arte neotaíno*. Santo Domingo: Fundación Cultural Dominicana.

——. 1987b. *Santos, shamanes, y zemíes*. Santo Domingo: Fundación Cultural Dominicana.

——. 1989. Nuevas revelaciones sobre el zemí taíno del Museo Pignorini de Roma. *Isla Abierta*, supplement to *Hoy* (Santo Domingo), December 9, 1989, pp. 8–9.

Veloz Maggiolo, Marcio. 1976. *Medioambiente y adaptación humana en la prehistoria de Santo Domingo*, vol. 1. Santo Domingo: Editorial de la Universidad Autónoma de Santo Domingo.

——. 1980. *Las sociedades arcaicas de Santo Domingo*. Museo del Hombre Dominicano, Serie Investigaciones Antropológicas, no. 16; Fundación García Arévalo, Serie Investigaciones, no. 12. Santo Domingo.

Veloz Maggiolo, Marcio, and Carlos Angulo Valdés. 1981. La aparición de un ídolo de tres puntas en la tradición Malambo (Colombia). *Boletín del Museo del Hombre Dominicano* 10(17): 15–20.

Veloz Maggiolo, Marcio, and Elpidio Ortega. 1976. The Preceramic of the Dominican Republic: Some New Finds and Their Possible Relationships. In *Proceedings of the First Puerto Rican Symposium on Archaeology*, ed. Linda S. Robinson, pp. 147–201. San Juan: Fundación Arqueológica, Antropológica e Histórica de Puerto Rico.

Veloz Maggiolo, Marcio, Elpidio Ortega, and Angel Caba Fuentes. 1981. *Los modos de vida Meillacoides y sus posibles orígenes: Un estudio interpretativo*. Santo Domingo: Museo del Hombre Dominicano.

Veloz Maggiolo, Marcio, Elpidio Ortega, and Plinio Pina P. 1974. *El Caimito: Un antiguo complejo ceramista de las Antillas Mayores*. Museo del Hombre Dominicano, Serie Monográfica, no. 30. Santo Domingo: Ediciones Fundación García Arévalo.

Veloz Maggiolo, Marcio, Iraida Vargas, Mario Sanoja, and Fernando Luna Calderón. 1976. *Arqueología de Yuma (Dominican Republic)*. Santo Domingo: Taller.

Veloz Maggiolo, Marcio, and Bernardo Vega. 1982. The Antillean Preceramic: A New Approximation. *Journal of New World Archaeology* (University of California at Los Angeles) 5(2): 33–44.

Versteeg, Aad H. 1989. The Internal Organization of a Pioneer Settlement in the Lesser Antilles: The Saladoid Golden Rock Settlement on St. Eustatius, Netherlands Antilles. In *Early Ceramic Population Lifeways and Adaptive Strategies in the Caribbean*, ed. Peter E. Siegel, pp. 171–92. BAR International Series 506. Oxford, Eng.

——. 1991. Three Preceramic Sites in Aruba. In *Proceedings of the Thirteenth International Congress for Caribbean Archaeology, Held in Willemstad, Curaçao, on July 24–29, 1989*, pp. 105–26. Willemstad: Archaeological-Anthropological Institute of the Netherlands Antilles.

Vescelius, Gary S. 1952. The Cultural Chronology of St. Croix. B.A. thesis, Yale University, New Haven.

————. 1980. A Cultural Taxonomy for West Indian Archaeology. *Journal of the Virgin Islands Archaeological Society* 10:36–39.

Vescelius, Gary S., and Linda S. Robinson. 1979. Exotic Items in Archaeological Collections from St. Croix: Prehistoric Imports and Their Implications. Paper presented at the Eighth International Congress for the Study of Pre-Columbian Cultures of the Lesser Antilles, St. Kitts, July 30–August 4, 1979.

Watters, David R. 1980. Transect Surveying and Prehistoric Site Locations on Barbuda and Montserrat, Leeward Islands, West Indies. Ph.D. diss., University of Pittsburgh.

Watters, David R., and Irving Rouse. 1989. Environmental Diversity and Maritime Adaptations in the Caribbean Area. In *Early Ceramic Population Lifeways and Adaptive Strategies in the Caribbean*, ed. Peter E. Siegel, pp. 129–44. BAR International Series 506. Oxford, Eng.

Wilbert, Johannes, and Miguel Layrisse, eds. 1980. *Demographic and Biological Studies of the Warao Indians*. UCLA Latin American Studies, no. 45. Los Angeles.

Willey, Gordon R., Charles C. DiPeso, William A. Ritchie, Irving Rouse, John H. Rowe, and Donald Lathrap. 1956. An Archaeological Classification of Culture Contact Situations. In *Seminars in Archaeology: 1955*, ed. Robert Wauchope, pp. 1–30. Memoirs of the Society for American Archaeology, no. 11. Salt Lake City.

Wilson, Samuel N. 1990a. *Hispaniola: Caribbean Chiefdoms in the Age of Columbus*. Tuscaloosa: University of Alabama Press.

————. 1990b. Taino Elite Integration and Societal Complexity on Hispaniola. In *Proceedings of the Eleventh International Congress for Caribbean Archaeology in San Juan, Puerto Rico, July and August 1985*, pp. 517–21. San Juan: Fundación Arqueológica, Antropológica e Histórica de Puerto Rico and others.

Wing, Elizabeth S. 1980. Animal Remains from the Hacienda Grande Site. In *Excavations at María de la Cruz Cave and Hacienda Grande Village Site*, by Rouse and Alegría, pp. 87–101.

Wing, Elizabeth S., and Sylvia J. Scudder. 1980. Use of Animals by the Prehistoric Inhabitants of St. Kitts, West Indies. In *Proceedings of the Eighth International Congress for the Study of Pre-Columbian Cultures of the Lesser Antilles, St. Kitts, 30 July–4 August 1979*, pp. 237–45. Anthropological Research Papers, no. 22. Tempe: Arizona State University.

Wolper, Ruth G. Durlacher. 1964. *A New Theory Identifying the Locale of Columbus's Light, Landfall, and Landing*. Smithsonian Miscellaneous Collections, vol. 148, no. 1. Washington, D.C.

Woods, Charles A., and John F. Eisenberg. 1989. The Land Mammals of Madagascar and the Greater Antilles: Comparison and Analysis. In *Biogeography of the West Indies*, ed. Woods, pp. 799–862. Gainesville, Fla.: Sandhill Crane Press.

I N D E X

Absolute time, 108. *See also* Relative time
Acculturation, 72, 98–99, 103, 111–12
Adaptation, 30, 48, 104, 109, 163
Adzes, 84, 94
African geographical race, 43
Ages, 49–50, 74
Agriculture: Taino, 12, 18, 19; slash-and-burn, 12, 18, 75; Island-Carib, 23, 146; Saladoid, 34, 75, 76, 78, 84; Ostionoid, 88, 99, 109, 118, 124; Troumassoid, 128–29; Suazoid, 129; in the Columbian exchange, 170. *See also* Animal husbandry; Fields
Agüeybana (Puerto Rican chief), 155
Amazonian model, 30–31, 39
Amazonid lineage, 27, 45
American geographical race, 43
Amulets, 121
Anacaona (wife of Caonabo), 152–53, 154
Anadel people/culture, 110
Ancestor worship, 13, 15, 115, 116–18, 121
Animal husbandry, 154, 157
Anthropology, 26
Arauquinoid series, 72
Arawakan: family, 21, 27, 37; family tree, 39–40
Arawak language, 37, 38, 40–41, 42;
Arawaks (Lokonos), 5, 21, 24; origin of the name, 5, 166. *See also* Tainos
Archaic: level of cultural development, 20; age, 33
Archeology, 26, 118, 136–37
Areito (ceremonies), 14–15
Arroyo del Palo style, 95
Assemblages, 43, 49–50, 51
Assimilation, 88, 97–98, 132, 136
Atabey (female supreme deity), 13, 118, 119, 130
Atajadizo people/culture, 110–11, 115

Axes, 58, 59, 91
Aztecs, 157

Bahamian archipelago, 3
Baibrama (god of cassava), 119
Balance poles, 16
Ball: grounds, 15, 34, 80, 112–13, 115–16, 126, 130; game, 15–16, 18, 22, 170; courts (*batey*), 15–16, 112–13, 115–16, 126; belts, 115, 116 (*see also* Elbow stones; Stone: collars)
Balls: rubber, 15, 170; stone, 58, 60, 134
Bands (groups), 20, 24, 58; as level of social development, 33
Banwaroid series. *See* Ortoiroid series
Barbecue, 171
Barrancoid series: origin and expansion, 72, 75, 77, 80, 101, 103; trading, 84–85, 87; ceramics, 87, 110, 127, 128, 133
Barrera-Mordán people/culture, 51, 54–55
Barreroid series. *See* Casimiroid series
Basic vocabulary, 38
Baskets, 9, 12
Batata (sweet potato), 12, 170
Batey (ball courts), 15–16, 112–13, 115–16, 126. *See also* Tainos: survival of traits
Beans, 12, 170
Beer, 12, 158
Behecchio (chief of Xaragua), 152–53, 154
Belize series, 56
Belts: ball, 115, 116; made of cotton, 121, 159–60
Biological: anthropology, 26; heritages, 26, 161–62, 163, 166; classification, 26–27, 41–43; traits, 27, 169–70; pluralities, 163
Biologies, 26, 166
Bird-head pendants, 87, 88
Black-Caribs (Garifuna), 38, 161